Privacy & Personality

Privacy & Personality

J. Roland Pennock
John W. Chapman
editors

Routledge
Taylor & Francis Group
LONDON AND NEW YORK

First published 1971 by Transaction Publishers

Published 2017 by Routledge
2 Park Square, Milton Park, Abingdon, Oxon OX14 4RN
711 Third Avenue, New York, NY 10017, USA

First issued in hardback 2017

Routledge is an imprint of the Taylor & Francis Group, an informa business

Library of Congress Catalog Number: 2007018155

Library of Congress Cataloging-in-Publication Data

Privacy and personality / J. Roland Pennock and John W. Chapman, editors.
p. cm.
Includes bibliographical references.
ISBN 978-0-202-30979-8 (alk. paper)
1. Privacy. 2. Personality. 3. Social psychology. 4. Sociology. I. Pennock, J. Roland (James Roland), 1906- II. Chapman, John William, 1923-

BF637.P74P74 2007
155.9'2—dc22 2007018155

ISBN 13: 978-1-138-53076-8 (hbk)
ISBN 13: 978-0-202-30979-8 (pbk)

PREFACE

Among the wasting assets of modern society, privacy ranks high. The products of modern technology and some of the direct and indirect effects of mass society combine to enhance its scarcity value.[1] In an absolute sense it would appear that some people, but by no means all, place a greater value on privacy than was the norm a century ago, but this shift in attitudes seems to be more than counterbalanced by the other factors mentioned. As modern polities grow more congested, complicated, and powerful vis-à-vis their citizens, disputes multiply, both in morals and in law, about the proper location of the boundaries between the private and the public.

It was, then, a timely choice for the American Society for Political and Legal Philosophy to select privacy as the topic for its 1968 annual meetings, which were held in Washington, D.C.,

[1] The comparison is with earlier periods in the modern era of civilized society. Among many primitive peoples, today as in the past, privacy is in exceedingly short supply, and their conditions are often such that modern ideas about privacy would be completely unrealizable.

in December, in conjunction with the meetings of the Eastern Division of the American Philosophical Association. The program for the meetings of the Society was arranged by a committee under the chairmanship of Professor Martin Golding of the John Jay College of Criminal Justice of the City University of New York. The chapters in this volume by Professors Freund and Silber were two of the main papers delivered at those meetings, while Professors Beardsley and Simmel were commentators. For a variety of reasons, the other participants in the program were unfortunately unable to contribute to the book. As usual, however, the editors subsequently solicited further papers, with favorable results. The interdisciplinary aspect of the Society's policy has been well maintained. Anthropology, sociology, and psychiatry are each represented by a chapter, even though in the case of anthropology it took two men to do it! Law and philosophy are represented, two and three times, respectively, while political scientists account for the remaining four chapters. The editors attempted to find and pin down for this occasion more politically oriented philosophers and philosophically oriented lawmen than they succeeded in securing, but they are happy with what they received and are grateful to all the contributors.

Although it treats of privacy in general, the present volume makes no attempt to provide a comprehensive or even a balanced discussion of the subject. The legal aspects of privacy have come in for extensive treatment in many places, and perhaps to an even greater extent the same is true of the many modern technological developments that threaten privacy.[2] *Nomos XIII* pays relatively little attention to law and even less to technology. It leans heavily toward the analytical, the justificatory, and the

[2] From the immense bibliography on these topics, it will perhaps not be invidious to single out for special mention Alan F. Westin's *Privacy and Freedom* (New York: Atheneum, 1967). This volume grew out of an extensive research project initiated and sponsored by the Special Committee on Science and Law of the New York City Bar Association, of which Professor Westin was the director. It provides us with by far the most thorough and well-grounded study of the subject in existence. The work of Edward A. Shils, beginning with his *The Torment of Secrecy: The Background and Consequences of American Security Policies* (Glencoe, Ill.: The Free Press, 1956), also deserves special mention for its recognition of the roots and significance of privacy.

speculative. It deals more with general aspects of the subject than with the special problems created by modern technology.

The first five papers of the volume deal for the most part with questions about the nature of privacy, its relation to liberty and other values, and with the grounds for valuing it. Carl Friedrich provides the most distinctively political discussion. Both he and Herbert Spiro discuss privacy as a kind of secrecy. They also introduce comparative aspects, as does the paper by anthropologists John Roberts and Thomas Gregor, in even greater degree. Spiro relates the topic to the study of political development and finds that the development of individual privacy and of its governmental counterpart, secrecy, are not unilinear. He accounts for certain differences between polities at roughly the same stage of development partly in terms of their differing legal systems, differences that arose from extraneous circumstances. Roberts and Gregor extend the field of comparison to primitive tribes, discovering striking differences but also clear evidence of common developmental tendencies. Ernest van den Haag raises and comments provocatively upon issues of public policy. Legal aspects of the subject, as enlightened by conceptual analysis, are considered by Hyman Gross. Paul Freund, after tracing the development of the legal concept of privacy from the Warren and Brandeis article to the present, brings to bear upon the question of whether or in what way the law should rely upon a unified concept of privacy a consideration of the human interests that law may serve in this area. Finally, two chapters deal with the psychological and moral aspects of privacy. John Silber argues, among other things, that in a secular era we must place increasing reliance upon law to provide the optimum opportunities for both disclosure and privacy. John Chapman likewise finds that a realm of privacy is both psychologically and morally essential. The rebellion of many young people against privacy is an unhealthy symptom, perhaps born of the psychic insecurity of the atomic age. Yet he finds in human nature stabilizing forces that leave him not without hope for the future.

In conclusion, it may be remarked that, while critics may find this volume unbalanced (not to mention the inevitable "uneven"), it is the editors' belief that the emphases of this collection of essays will tend to supplement the extensive attention that has been given in much of the literature to the technology of surveillance and to specific legal problems, especially those growing out of recent technological advances. It is also their hope that readers will find in these pages some new and helpful insights into a complex set of problems that are certain to be increasingly with us as the strains produced by *e pluribus unum* give them ever new forms and possibly shift their center of gravity.

J. Roland Pennock
John W. Chapman

INTRODUCTION

What is privacy? Like many concepts, it has a commonly accepted core of meaning with an indefinite or variable periphery. Some would even wish to enlarge the core. It would be pointless to attempt to establish a definition by way of introduction to a series of essays that themselves accept no single definition.

Some of the authors represented in this volume might agree to Alan Westin's definition of privacy as "the claim of individuals, groups, or institutions to determine for themselves when, how, and to what extent information about them is communicated to others."[1] Others clearly would not. For Elizabeth Beardsley, for instance, Westin's definition states but one of two aspects of the concept. Equally if not more important in her eyes is personal autonomy, the power to determine for oneself whether he will perform a particular act or undergo a particular experience. Expressing part of the same idea, Ernest van den

[1] Alan F. Westin, *Privacy and Freedom* (New York: Atheneum, 1967), p. 7.

Haag asserts that one's privacy may be invaded by an unwanted noise or a noxious odor.

Although no definition will be attempted, a few observations about the concept are in order. Of course, privacy relates to individualism—in ways of which more will be said in a moment. It also relates to and overlaps with the concept of liberty. But although it contains elements of liberty it does not usually include all of liberty. For instance, most people would not speak of liberty of speech as an example of privacy. (I have hedged the last two sentences because it would appear that Mrs. Beardsley's definition *would* include liberty of speech, and indeed all liberties.) Also it comprises things other than liberty, as in the example of the pollution of my living space by unwelcome sounds and odors.

Privacy is at least a penultimate good; perhaps, in certain usages—such as autonomy—it is an ultimate good, desirable for its own sake and grounded on nothing more final. Of course, the right of privacy may be asserted to conceal illegal or immoral acts. Here it appears to be put to an instrumental use. But, it may be suggested, insofar as we *justify* such claims, it is not because they prevent the detection of immorality or violations of the law. Rather, at least in the case of illegal acts, it is because the means being challenged themselves violate privacy. "Bugging," for instance, is harmful to human values regardless of the fact that it may also contribute to a good end. The claim in this instance can not be absolute; its justification involves a weighing of values. This fact is recognized by the terms of the Fourth Amendment to the United States Constitution, which bans "unreasonable" searches and seizures. The difference between reasonable and unreasonable searches and seizures relates less to privacy than to the public interest that is being weighed against it.

With respect to immoral acts that are not illegal, the case is rather different. Here a stronger argument can be made for the justification of privacy, for morality depends at least in part upon an action taken by a free and good will. Thus, if the invasion of privacy will result in bringing some coercive force to bear, it tends to interfere with free and responsible action, which, according to most ethical theories, is the very essence of morality.

Most fundamentally, then, it would seem that privacy relates to individual autonomy, whether or not it includes the whole of it. It may be defined, as Elizabeth Beardsley and Hyman Gross define it, as extreme individualism; or, more commonly, it may be related to one aspect of individualism, the desire to control what is known (and by whom) regarding oneself and one's activities. This kind of control appears to be essential to the development of self-respect, dignity (Benn's "respect for persons"), and perhaps to Michael Weinstein's "authenticity." It is worthy of note that even Arnold Simmel, who, in common with a strong sociological tradition, argues that the individual is made by society, points out that at any given time the individual is in conflict with society, and, moreover, needs some opportunity to develop apart from society.

The individual control–human dignity foundation for privacy is closely related to two others: relief from tension and opportunity for the development of intimate relations with others. All of us have standards of behavior that are higher than we can maintain at all times, and these standards are widely shared in the society in which we live. If we don't observe them we are likely to be criticized, or we fear that we shall be, and we suffer also from loss of self-esteem (back to "dignity"). Hence the need for times and places when we can be unobserved.

It is true that in certain primitive societies the opportunities for escaping almost continuous surveillance are very limited, and in these circumstances men seem to adjust to the situation and not to be disturbed by it. Yet even here, as the account of the Mehinacu by Roberts and Gregor illustrates, a measure of privacy seems to be necessary, and these people have developed complicated institutions to secure it. And, of course, it is a well-known fact that people do learn to adjust to situations that are so far from ideal as to hamper their natural development.

Whether in some final sense the concept of privacy is culture bound is impossible to establish, in the absence of any known society in which no trace of it is to be found. Plato, it is true, envisaged an ideal society in which each individual was so much a part of an organic whole that all felt, thought, and reacted alike, as if their psyches were merged into one.[2] But even Plato was not contending that this ideal was more than a limit that man might approach but never reach. Even he recognized the fact of human ambivalence. Indeed, it appears to be true that, while some individuals and some cultures lean much farther to the public side than others, all wish at some point to draw a line, to pull the shades, and to turn inward. It would seem that everyone requires at least some opportunity to contemplate his own thoughts and feelings, to regroup his forces, and to put his mental house in order.

The unconventional may seek privacy to protect themselves from the censure of the conventional, while the conventional seek it as an aspect of individualism in the sense of dislike of society.[3] Thus, in a highly communal society, individuals may yet seek some surcease from intrusions and surveillance, and in an individualistic society, where (almost by definition) intrusions will be less frequent and less penetrating, a similar tension will exist nonetheless, because privacy is more highly prized. The line between public and private—as to both norm and practice—will of course be at a different location in the two societies. But it will be there, and it will mark an area of tension within the society and often within the individual as well. It is interesting to note that the modern antiauthoritarian youth who decry bourgeois individualism are also greatly concerned to be able to "do their own thing," and to be let alone while doing it. (It must be granted that they frequently seem to prefer to do it in public, but this may be interpreted as a tactic in their battle against the mores of the society they are seeking to change.)

The last point leads naturally to a consideration of the third foundation for privacy, the development of intimate relations with others, a subject on which Charles Fried has written most

[2] *The Laws,* in *The Dialogues of Plato,* trans. and ed. by Benjamin Jowett, 3d ed., 5 vols. (London: Oxford University Press, 1892), V, 739.

[3] The less unified the society, the more concern for privacy may partake of mutual dislike and fear. On France, see Nathan Leites, *The Rules of the Game in Paris,* trans. Derek Coltman (Chicago: University of Chicago Press, 1969), chap. 4.

perceptively.[4] It is here that we are furthest removed from the notion of privacy as a good in itself. Yet neither is it to be conceived, in this aspect, as strictly instrumental. Rather, privacy provides the "rational context" in which intimacy, friendship, trust, and love can arise. Here is where Plato went wrong. The kind of intimate community he sought can be most nearly approached in quite small groups and, incidentally, in groups in which the distinctive element of the political—ultimate reliance upon force—is entirely absent.

Reference to the political suggests a topic that is treated only in passing in this volume, but which I cannot allow to go unmentioned here—privacy and democracy. That these two are closely related is indicated by the fact of their mutual kinship to autonomy. Yet today the egalitarian element of the democratic ideal is in the ascendant, sometimes at the expense of the libertarian element. Spiro concludes that "postmodern" societies —an appellation he attaches both to the United States and the Soviet Union—are moving, presumably as they become more egalitarian, away from privacy. In the United States, at least, as he observes, this movement is in some measure checked by the Supreme Court's efforts to stem the tide. (Perhaps nowhere is the tension between privacy and equality more evident than in the case of certain kinds of discrimination, a subject discussed in this volume by both Stanley Benn and William Weinstein.)

Will democracy, especially if it assumes more communitarian and participatory forms, prove inimical to privacy? Personally, I can see such a tendency as no more than another exemplification of the tensions—e.g., between man's curiosity and need for excitement and his need to retreat within himself—that always surround the demand for privacy. As Simmel argues, it is healthy that in any society the lines that separate the private from the nonprivate should be continually questioned and revised. But, as long as men differ, as long as they cherish their individuality, as long as Plato's dream remains less than completely realized, so long will the need and demand for privacy remain. If privacy

[4] Charles Fried, *An Anatomy of Values: Problems of Personal and Social Choice* (Cambridge, Mass.: Harvard University Press, 1970), chap. 9.

fails to gain more effective protection through democratic forms than through some other form of government, it would appear that those forms have ceased to operate as they should. And if the spirit, as contrasted with the form, of democracy seems at a particular period to value community more than autonomy, I would anticipate that this development is only one more manifestation of the tide-like character of social change in general, rather than being indicative of a secular trend.

Finally, however, it should be made clear that privacy is not just a single commodity of which we may have either more or less. It takes many forms, has many dimensions. How much is known about me and my activities by other people may be less important to me than my ability to control what they do know about me. I would gladly tell you many things that I would be most unhappy for you to learn by eavesdropping or spying. And what things a person would gladly tell about himself may vary greatly from one culture to another.

Enough. Let the reader explore for himself.

J. ROLAND PENNOCK

CONTENTS

CONTRIBUTORS

ELIZABETH L. BEARDSLEY
Philosophy, Temple University

STANLEY I. BENN
Philosophy, The Australian National University

JOHN W. CHAPMAN
Political Science, University of Pittsburgh

PAUL A. FREUND
Law, Harvard University

CARL J. FRIEDRICH
Political Science, Harvard University

THOMAS GREGOR
Anthropology, Cornell University

HYMAN GROSS
Law, New York University

JOHN M. ROBERTS
Anthropology, Cornell University

JOHN R. SILBER
Philosophy, University of Texas

ARNOLD SIMMEL
Sociology, The City University of New York

HERBERT J. SPIRO
Political Science, University of Pennsylvania

ERNEST VAN DEN HAAG
Sociology, Psychology, Social Philosophy
New School for Social Research, New York University

MICHAEL A. WEINSTEIN
Political Science, Purdue University

W. L. WEINSTEIN
Politics, Balliol College, Oxford

1

PRIVACY, FREEDOM, AND RESPECT FOR PERSONS

STANLEY I. BENN

When your mind is set on mating
It is highly irritating
To see an ornithologist below:
Though it may be nature-study,
To a bird it's merely bloody
Awful manners. Can't he see that he's *de trop!**

INTRODUCTION

If two people retire to the privacy of the bushes, they go where they expect to be unobserved. What they do is done

I wish to acknowledge my indebtedness to my colleague Geoffrey Mortimore for his many helpful suggestions and no less for his trenchant criticism of this paper.

* From "Bird-watching—The Song of the Redstart," in A. N. L. Munby, *Lyra Catenata* (printed privately 1948). Quoted in John Buxton, *The Redstart* (London: Collins, 1950).

privately, or *in private,* if they are not actually seen doing it. Should they later advertise or publish what they were about, what *was* private would then become public knowledge. Or they may have been mistaken in thinking their retreat private—they may have been in full view of passersby all the time. One's *private affairs,* however, are private in a different sense. It is not that they are kept out of sight or from the knowledge of others that makes them private. Rather, they are matters that it would be inappropriate for others to try to find out about, much less report on, without one's consent; one complains if they are publicized precisely because they are private. Similarly, a private room remains private in spite of uninvited intruders, for, unlike the case of the couple in the bushes, falsifying the expectation that no one will intrude is not a logically sufficient ground for saying that something private in this sense is not private after all.

"Private" used in this second, immunity-claiming[1] way is both norm-dependent and norm-invoking. It is norm-dependent because *private affairs* and *private rooms* cannot be identified without some reference to norms. So any definition of the concept "private affairs" must presuppose the existence of *some* norms restricting unlicensed observation, reporting, or entry, even though no norm in particular is necessary to the concept. It is norm-invoking in that one need say no more than "This is a private matter" to claim that anyone not invited to concern himself with it ought to stay out of it. That is why the normative implications of "Private" on a letter or a notice board do not need to be spelled out.[2]

The norms invoked by the concept are not necessarily immunity-conferring, however; one can imagine cultures, for instance, in which they would be prohibitive, where to say that

[1] I do not use "immunity" in this paper in the technical Hohfeldian sense. Where it is not used in a simple descriptive sense, I intend that a person shall be understood to be immune from observation if he has grounds for complaint should anyone watch him; an activity is immune if it is not appropriate for unauthorized persons to watch it.

[2] Of course, though "Someone has been reading my private letters" is enough to state a protest, it need not be well founded; the letters may not really qualify as private, or even if they are, there may be other conditions overriding the implicit claim to immunity.

someone had done something in private would be to accuse him of acting inappropriately—perhaps cutting himself off from a collective experience and cheating others of their right to share in it. Or again, "privacy" might apply mandatorily; that is, anything private *ought* to be kept from the knowledge of others. This is rather the sense of the somewhat old-fashioned phrase "private parts," referring not to parts of the body that one might keep unseen if one chose, but to parts that one had a duty to keep out of sight. In our culture, sexual and excretory acts are private not merely in the sense that performers are immune from observation but also in the sense that some care ought to be taken that they are not generally observed. Thus, liberty to publicize, that is, to license scrutiny and publicity, whether generally or to a select public, is commonly but by no means necessarily associated with the right to immunity from observation.

The norms invoked by the concept of privacy are diverse, therefore, not only in substance but also in logical form; some grant immunities, some are prohibitive, some are mandatory. There may be cultures, indeed, with no norm-invoking concept of privacy at all, where *nothing* is thought properly immune from observation and anything may be generally displayed. It might still be possible, of course, to seek out private situations where one would not be observed, but it would never be a ground of grievance either that an action was or was not open for all to see or that someone was watching. But whatever the possible diversity, some privacy claims seem to rest on something a bit more solid than mere cultural contingency. The first objective of this paper is to explore the possibility that some minimal right to immunity from uninvited observation and reporting is required by certain basic features of our conception of a person.

THE GENERAL PRINCIPLE OF PRIVACY AND RESPECT FOR PERSONS

The umbrella "right to privacy" extends, no doubt, to other claims besides the claims not to be watched, listened to, or reported upon without leave, and not to have public attention focused upon one uninvited. It is these particular claims, however, that I have primarily in mind in this paper. It deals, therefore, with a cluster of immunities which, if acknowledged, curb the freedom of others to do things that are generally quite innocent if done to objects other than persons, and even to persons, if done with their permission. There is nothing intrinsically objectionable in observing the world, including its inhabitants, and in sharing one's discoveries with anyone who finds them interesting; and this is not on account of any special claims, for instance, for scientific curiosity, or for a public interest in the discovery of truth. For I take as a fundamental principle in morals a general liberty to do whatever one chooses unless someone else has good reasons for interfering to prevent it, reasons grounded either on the freedom of others or on some other moral principle such as justice or respect for persons or the avoidance of needless pain. The onus of justification, in brief, lies on the advocate of restraint, not on the person restrained. The present question, then, is whether any moral principle will provide a quite general ground for a prima facie claim that B should not observe and report on A unless A agrees to it. Is there a principle of privacy extending immunity to inquiry to all human activities, to be overridden only by special considerations, like those suggested? Or is it rather that there is a general freedom to inquire, observe, and report on human affairs as on other things, unless a special case can be made out for denying it with respect to certain activities that are *specifically* private?

My strategy, then, is to inquire, first, whether anyone is entitled, prima facie, to be private if he chooses, irrespective of what he is about: would the couple in the bushes have grounds for complaint if they discovered someone eavesdropping on their discussion of, say, relativity theory? Second, whether or not such grounds exist, can any rational account be given (that is, an account not wholly dependent on conventional norms) of "private affairs," the area in which uninvited intrusions are judged *particularly* inappropriate?

The former, more sweeping claim may appear at first sight extravagant, even as only a prima facie claim. Anyone who wants to remain unobserved and unidentified, it might be said, should stay at home or go out only in disguise. Yet there is a difference between happening to be seen and having someone closely observe, and perhaps record, what one is doing, even in a public place. Nor is the resentment that some people feel at being watched necessarily connected with fears of damaging disclosures in the Sunday papers or in a graduate thesis in social science. How reasonable is it, then, for a person to resent being treated much in the way that a birdwatcher might treat a redstart?

Putting the case initially at this rather trivial level has the advantage of excluding two complicating considerations. In the first place, I have postulated a kind of intrusion (if that is what it is) which does no obvious damage. It is not like publishing details of someone's sex life and ruining his career. Furthermore, what is resented is not being watched *tout court,* but being watched without leave. If observation as such were intrinsically or even consequentially damaging, it might be objectionable even if done with consent. In the present instance, consent removes all ground for objection. In the second place, by concentrating on simple unlicensed observation, I can leave aside the kind of interference with which Mill was mainly concerned in the essay *On Liberty,* namely, anything that prevents people doing, in their private lives, something they want to do, or that requires them to do what they do not want to do.[3] Threatening a man with penalties, or taking away his stick, are ways of preventing his beating his donkey; but if he stops simply because he is watched, the interference is of a different kind. He could continue if he chose; being observed affects his action only by changing his perception of it. The observer makes the act impossible only in the sense that the actor now sees it in a different light. The intrusion is not therefore obviously objectionable as an interference with freedom of action. It is true that there are special kinds of action—any that depend upon surprise, for example—that could be made objectively impossible merely by watching and reporting on them; but my present purpose is to ask whether a *general* case

[3] W. L. Weinstein's illuminating contribution to this volume, "The Private and the Free: A Conceptual Inquiry," is mainly concerned with Mill's questions; I shall touch on them only indirectly.

can be made out, not one that depends on special conditions of that kind.

Of course, there is always a danger that information may be used to harm a man in some way. The usual arguments against wiretapping, bugging, a National Data Center, and private investigators rest heavily on the contingent possibility that a tyrannical government or unscrupulous individuals might misuse them for blackmail or victimization. The more one knows about a person, the greater one's power to damage him. Now it may be that fears like this are the only reasonable ground for objecting *in general* to being watched. I might suspect a man who watches my house of "casing the joint." But if he can show me he intends no such thing, and if there is no possibility of his observations being used against me in any other way, it would seem to follow that I could have no further reasonable ground for objecting. Eliza Doolittle resents Professor Higgins's recording her speech in Covent Garden because she believes that a girl of her class subject to so close a scrutiny is in danger of police persecution: "You dunno what it means to me. Theyll take away my character and drive me on the streets for speaking to gentlemen."[4] But the resentment of the bystanders is excited by something else, something intrinsic in Higgins's performance, not merely some possible consequence of his ability to spot their origins by their accents: "See here: what call have you to know about people what never offered to meddle with you? . . . You take us for dirt under your feet, dont you? Catch you taking liberties with a gentleman!" What this man resents is surely that Higgins fails to show a proper respect for persons; he is treating people as objects or specimens—like "dirt"—and not as subjects with sensibilities, ends, and aspirations of their own, morally responsible for their own decisions, and capable, as mere specimens are not, of reciprocal relations with the observer. This failure is, of course, precisely what Eliza, in her later incarnation as Higgins's Galatea, complains of too. These resentments suggest a possible ground for a prima facie claim not to be watched, at any rate in the same manner as one watches a thing or an animal.

[4] G. B. Shaw, *Pygmalion,* Act I.

For this is "to take liberties," to act impudently, to show less than a proper regard for human dignity.

Finding oneself an object of scrutiny, as the focus of another's attention, brings one to a new consciousness of oneself, as something seen through another's eyes. According to Sartre, indeed, it is a necessary condition for knowing oneself *as* anything at all that one should conceive oneself as an object of scrutiny.[5] It is only through the regard of the other that the observed becomes aware of himself as an object, knowable, having a determinate character, in principle predictable. His consciousness of pure freedom as subject, as originator and chooser, is at once assailed by it; he is fixed *as something*—with limited probabilities rather than infinite, indeterminate possibilities. Sartre's account of human relations is of an obsessional need to master an unbearable alien freedom that undermines one's belief in one's own; for Ego is aware of Alter not only as a fact, an object in his world, but also as the subject of a quite independent world of Alter's own, wherein Ego himself is mere object. The relationship between the two is essentially hostile. Each, doubting his own freedom, is driven to assert the primacy of his own subjectivity. But the struggle for mastery, as Sartre readily admits, is a self-frustrating response; Alter's reassurance would be worthless to Ego unless it were freely given, yet the freedom to give it would at once refute it.

What Sartre conceived as a phenomenologically necessary dilemma, however, reappears in R. D. Laing's *The Divided Self*[6] as a characteristically schizoid perception of the world, the response of a personality denied free development, trying to preserve itself from domination by hiding away a "real self" where it cannot be absorbed or overwhelmed. The schizoid's problem arises because he cannot believe fully in his own existence as a person. He may *need* to be observed in order to be convinced that he exists, if only in the world of another; yet, resenting the necessity to be what the other perceives him as, he may try at the same time to hide. His predicament, like Sartre's, may seem to him to arise not from the *manner* of his being observed, but to be implicit in the very relation of observer and observed.

[5] See J.-P. Sartre: *L'être et le néant* (Paris, 1953), Part 3, "Le pour-autrui."
[6] Harmondsworth, England, 1965.

Sartre, however, does not show why the awareness of others as subjects must evoke so hostile a response. Even if it were true that my consciousness of my own infinite freedom is shaken by my being made aware that in the eyes of another I have only limited possibilities, still if I am not free, it is not his regard that confines me; it only draws my attention to what I was able formerly to disregard. And if I *am* free, then his regard makes no real difference. And if there is a dilemma here, may I not infer from it that the Other sees me too as a subject, and has the same problem? Could this not be a bond between us rather than a source of resentment, each according the other the same dignity as subject?

It is because the schizoid cannot believe in himself as a person, that he cannot form such a bond, or accept the respectful regard of another. So every look is a threat or an insult. Still, without question, there are ways of looking at a man that do diminish him, that provide cause for offense as real as any physical assault. But, of course, that cannot be a reason either for hiding or for going around with one's eyes shut. Yet it does suggest that if, like a doctor, one has occasion to make someone an object of scrutiny and study, or like a clinician the topic for a lecture, the patient will have grounds for resentment if the examiner appears insensible to the fact that it is a person he is examining, a subject to whom it makes a difference that he is observed, who will also have a view about what is discovered or demonstrated, and will put his own value upon it.

It would be a mistake to think that the only objection to such examination is that an incautious observer could cause damage to a sensitive person's mental state, for that could be avoided by watching him secretly. To treat a man without respect is not to injure him—at least, not in *that* sense; it is more like insulting him. Nor is it the fact of scrutiny as such that is offensive, but only unlicensed scrutiny, which may in fact do no damage at all, yet still be properly resented as an impertinence.

I am suggesting that a general principle of privacy might be grounded on the more general principle of respect for persons. By a *person* I understand a subject with a consciousness of himself as agent, one who is capable of having projects, and assessing his achievements in relation to them. To *conceive* someone as a person is to see him as actually or potentially a chooser, as one attempting to steer his own course through the world, adjusting his behavior as his apperception of the world changes, and correcting course as he perceives his errors. It is to understand that his life is for him a kind of enterprise like one's own, not merely a succession of more or less fortunate happenings, but a record of achievements and failures; and just as one cannot describe one's own life in these terms without claiming that what happens is important, so to see another's in the same light is to see that for him at least this must be important. Professor Higgins's offense was to be insensitive to this fact about other people. Of course, one may have a clinical interest in people as project-makers without oneself attaching any importance to their projects. Still, if one fails to see how their aims and activities could be important for them, one has not properly understood what they are about. Even so, it requires a further step to see that recognizing another as engaged on such an enterprise makes a claim on oneself. To *respect* someone as a person is to concede that one ought to take account of the way in which his enterprise might be affected by one's own decisions. By the principle of respect for persons, then, I mean the principle that every human being, insofar as he is qualified as a person, is entitled to this minimal degree of consideration.

I do not mean, of course, that someone's having some attitude toward *anything* I propose to do is alone sufficient for his wishes to be a relevant consideration, for he will certainly have attitudes and wishes about actions of mine that do not affect his enterprise at all. B's dislike of cruelty to animals is not in itself a reason why A should stop beating his donkey. It is not enough that B will be gratified if he can approve A's action, and disappointed if not; it is the conception of B as a chooser, as engaged in an active, creative enterprise, that lays an obligation of respect upon A, not the conception of him as *suffering* gratifications and disappointments. This can be a ground for sympathetic joy or pity, but not respect. B's attitudes are considerations relevant for A's decisions only if what A does will make a difference to the conditions under which B makes *his* choices, either denying him an otherwise available option (which would be to interfere with his freedom of action) or changing the significance or meaning for B of acts still open to him. B may disapprove of A's watching C or listening to his conversation with D, but B's own conditions of action—what I have called B's enterprise—remain unaffected. On the other hand, if C knows that A is listening, A's intrusion alters C's consciousness of himself, and his experienced relation to his world. Formerly self-forgetful, perhaps, he may now be conscious of his opinions as candidates for A's approval or contempt. But even without self-consciousness of this kind, his immediate enterprise—the conversation with D—may be changed for him merely by the fact of A's presence. I am not postulating a private conversation in the sense of one about personal matters; what is at issue is the change in the way C apprehends his own performance—the topic makes no difference to this argument. A's uninvited intrusion is an impertinence because he treats it as of no consequence that he may have effected an alteration in C's perception of himself and of the nature of his performance.[7] Of course, no *damage* may have been done; C may actually enjoy performing before an enlarged audience. But C's wishes in the matter must surely be a relevant consideration (as B's are not), and in the absence of some overriding reason to the contrary, if C were inclined to complain, he has legitimate grounds.

The underpinning of a claim not to be watched without leave will be more general if it can be grounded in this way on the principle of respect for persons than on a utilitarian duty to avoid inflicting suffering. That duty may, of course, reinforce the claim in particular instances. But respect for persons will sustain an objection even to secret watching, which may do no actual harm at all. Covert observation—spying—is objectionable because it deliberately deceives a person about his world, thwarting, for reasons that *cannot* be his reasons, his attempts to make a rational choice. One cannot be said to respect a man as engaged on an enterprise worthy of consideration if one knowingly and deliberately alters his conditions of action, concealing the

[7] Of course, there are situations, such as in university common rooms, where there is a kind of conventional general license to join an ongoing conversation. A railway compartment confers a similar license in Italy, but not in England. In such situations, if one does not wish to be listened to, one stays silent.

fact from him. The offense is different in this instance, of course, from A's open intrusion on C's conversation. In that case, A's attentions were liable to affect C's enterprise by changing C's perception of it; he may have felt differently about his conversation with D, even to the extent of not being able to see it as any longer the same activity, knowing that A was now listening. In the present instance, C is unaware of A. Nevertheless, he is wronged because the significance to him of his enterprise, assumed unobserved, is deliberately falsified by A. He may be in a fool's paradise or a fool's hell; either way, A is making a fool of him. Suppose that in a situation in which he might be observed, there is no reason why he should not choose to act privately (for instance, he is doing nothing wrong); then for anyone to watch without his knowledge is to show disrespect not only for the privacy that may have been his choice, but, by implication, for him, as a chooser. I can well imagine myself freely consenting to someone's watching me at work, but deeply resenting anyone's doing so without my knowledge—as though it didn't matter whether I liked it or not. So a policeman may treat suspected criminals like this only if there are good grounds for believing that there is an overriding need to frustrate what they are about, not because they have no rights as persons to privacy. Psychiatrists may be entitled to treat lunatics like this —but only to the extent that being incapable of rational choice, they are defective as persons. (Even so, their interests, if not their wishes, will be limiting considerations.)

The close connection between the general principle of privacy and respect for persons may account for much of the resentment evoked by the idea of a National Data Center, collating all that is known about an individual from his past contacts with government agencies. Much has been made, of course—and no doubt rightly—of the dangers of computerized data banks, governmental or otherwise. The information supplied to and by them may be false; or if true, may still put a man in a false light, by drawing attention, say, to delinquencies in his distant past that he has now lived down. And even the most conforming of citizens would have reason for dread if officials came to regard their computers as both omniscient and infallible. A good deal of legislative invention has been exercised, accordingly, in seeking safeguards against the abuse of information power. Yet for some objectors at least it altogether misses the point. It is not just a matter of a fear to be allayed by reassurances, but of a resentment that anyone—even a thoroughly trustworthy official—should be able at will to satisfy any curiosity, without the knowledge let alone the consent of the subject. For since what others know about him can radically affect a man's view of himself, to treat the collation of personal information about him as if it raised purely technical problems of safeguards against abuse is to disregard his claim to consideration and respect as a person.

I have argued so far as though the principle of respect for persons clearly indicated what a man might reasonably resent. This needs some qualification. If someone stares at my face, I cannot help seeing his gaze as focused on me. I am no less self-conscious if I catch him scrutinizing the clothes I am wearing. But would it be reasonable to resent scrutiny of a suit I am not wearing—one I have just given, perhaps, to an old folks' home? Or of my car outside my home? Or in the service station? Granted that I can reasonably claim immunity from the uninvited attentions of observers and reporters, what is to count for this purpose as *me?* As I suggested above, it cannot be sufficient that I do not *want* you to observe something; for the principle of respect to be relevant, it must be something about my own person that is in question, otherwise the principle would be so wide that a mere wish of mine would be a prima facie reason for everyone to refrain from observing and reporting on anything at all. I do not make something a part of me merely by having feelings about it. The principle of privacy proposed here is, rather, that any man who desires that he *himself* should not be an object of scrutiny has a reasonable prima facie claim to immunity. But the ground is not in the mere fact of his desiring, but in the relation between himself as an object of scrutiny and as a conscious and experiencing subject. And it is clearly not enough for a man to *say* that something pertains to him as a person and therefore shares his immunity; there must be reasons for saying so.

What could count as a reason? The very intimate connection between the concepts of *oneself* and *one's body* (about which philosophers have written at length) would seem to put that much beyond question (though some schizoids' perception of the world would suggest that dissociation even of these concepts is possible). Beyond that point, however, cultural norms cannot be ignored. In a possessive individualist culture, in which a man's property is seen as an extension of his personality, as an index to his social standing, a measure of his achievements, or an expression of his taste, to look critically on his clothes or his car is to look critically on him. In other cultures, the standards might well be different. The notion we have of our own extension, of the outer limits of our personalities—those events or situations in respect of which we feel pride or shame—is unquestionably culture-variant; consequently, the application even of a quite general principle of privacy will be affected by culturally variant norms—those regarding family, say, or property.

APPLYING THE GENERAL PRINCIPLE

Allow that the principle of respect for persons will underpin a general principle of privacy; even so, it would amount only to a prima facie ground for limiting the freedom of others to observe and report at will. It would place on them a burden of justification but it would not override any special justification. The principle might be thought quite inadequate, for instance, to sustain on its own a case for legal restraints; the protection of privacy is less important, perhaps, than the danger to political freedom from legal restrictions on reporting. It might be argued that in every case it is for the press to show what reasonable public interest publicity would serve. But so uncertain a criterion could result in an overtimorous press. The courts have been properly wary of recognizing rights that might discourage if not disable the press from publicizing what *ought* to be exposed.

General principles do not *determine* solutions to moral problems of this kind. They indicate what needs to be justified, where the onus of justification lies, and what can count as a justification. So to count as an overriding consideration, an argument must refer to some further principle. Consider the difficult case of the privacy of celebrities. According to a learned American judge, the law "recognizes a legitimate public curiosity about the personalities of celebrities, and about a great deal of otherwise private and personal information about them."[8] But is all curiosity equally legitimate, or must there be something about the kind of celebrity that legitimizes special kinds of curiosity? Is there no difference between, say, a serious historian's curiosity about what (and who) prompted President Johnson's decision not to run a second time and that to which the Sunday gossip columnists appeal? If a person is in the public eye for some performance that he intends to be public or that is in its nature public—like conducting an orchestra—this may, as a matter of fact, make "human interest stories" about him more entertaining and exciting than similar stories about an unknown. But the fact that many people enjoy that kind of entertainment is no reason at all for overriding the principle of privacy; for though there is a presumptive liberty to do whatever there is no reason for not doing, there is no general claim to have whatever one enjoys. To treat even an entertainer's life simply as material for entertainment is to pay no more regard to him as a person than to an animal in a menagerie. Of course, anyone who indiscriminately courts publicity, as some entertainers do, can hardly complain if they are understood to be offering a general license. But merely to be a celebrity—even a willing celebrity—does not disable someone from claiming the consideration due to a person. Admittedly, it opens up a range of special claims to information about him, to override his general claim to privacy. Candidates for appointment to the Supreme Court must expect some public concern with their business integrity. Or—a rather different case—because an eminent conductor participates in a public activity with a public tradition, anyone choosing conducting as a profession must expect that his musical experience, where he was trained, who has influenced his interpretations, will be matters of legitimate interest to others concerned as he is with music. But this is not a warrant for prying into other facts about him that have nothing to do with his music: his taste in wines, perhaps, or women. The principle of privacy would properly give way in one area, but it would stand

[8] See W. L. Prosser, "Privacy," *California Law Review,* 48 (1960), 416–417.

in any other to which the special overriding grounds were irrelevant. For the principle itself is not limited in its application; it constitutes a prima facie claim in respect to *anything* a man does.

"PRIVATE AFFAIRS" AND PERSONAL IDEALS

To claim immunity on the ground that an inquiry is an intrusion into one's *private affairs* is to make an argumentative move of a quite different kind. For this concept entrenches the privacy of certain special areas far more strongly than the mere presumptive immunity of the general principle. To justify such an intrusion, one has to have not merely a reason, but one strong enough to override special reasons for *not* intruding. So while the interests of phonetic science might justify Professor Higgins's impertinence in Covent Garden, they would not be good enough reasons for bugging Eliza's bedroom.

The activities and experiences commonly thought to fall within this special private area are diverse and largely culture-dependent. Some seem to have no rational grounds at all. For instance, why should the bodily functions that in our culture are appropriately performed in solitude include defecation but not eating? Of course, so long as certain acts are assigned to this category anyone who has internalized the social norms will experience a painful embarrassment if seen doing them; embarrassment, indeed, is the culturally appropriate response in a society with the concept of *pudenda,* and anyone not showing it may be censured as brazen or insensitive. But though this furnishes a kind of rational interest in privacy of this kind, its rationale depends on a conventional norm that may itself be wholly irrational.

Not all areas of privacy are like this, however; others are closely related to ideals of life and character which would be difficult, perhaps impossible, to achieve were privacy not safeguarded. The liberal individualist tradition has stressed, in particular, three personal ideals, to each of which corresponds a range of "private affairs." The first is the ideal of personal relations; the second, the Lockian ideal of the politically free man in a minimally regulated society; the third, the Kantian ideal of the morally autonomous man, acting on principles that he accepts as rational.

The Privacy of Personal Relations

By personal relations, I mean relations between persons that are considered valuable and important at least as much because of the quality of each person's attitude to another as for what each does to, or for, another.

All characteristically human relations—I mean relations of a kind that could not exist between stones or wombats—involve some element, however small, of role-expectancy. We structure our relations with others according to an understanding of *what* they are and what accordingly is due to them and from them. That may exhaust some relations: if the railway booking clerk gives me the correct ticket in exchange for my fare, he has fulfilled his function. Moreover, the point of the relationship calls for no more than this; the grating that separates us, with just space enough to push through a ticket or a coin, appropriately symbolizes it. One cannot be indifferent to his performance, but one need not attend to his personality.

The relation between father and son, or husband and wife, is necessarily more than this, or if in a given instance it is not, then that instance is defective. Here, too, there are role-expectancies, but each particular set of related persons will fulfill them in a different way. There is room for being a father in this or in that manner. Moreover, only a part of what it is to be a father has been met when the specified duties of the role have been fulfilled. Beyond that, the value of the relation depends on a personal understanding between the parties, and on whether, and how, they care about one another. Father and son might be meticulous in the performance of the formal duties of their roles, but if they are quite indifferent to each other, the relationship is missing its point. The relationship between friends or lovers is still less role-structured than family relations, though even here there are conventional patterns and rituals—gifts on ritual occasions, forms of wooing, etc. But they are primarily symbols: their main point is to communicate a feeling or an attitude, to reassure, perhaps, or make a proposal. And though they could be gone through even if the feeling did not really exist, such a performance would surely be a pretense or a deception, and therefore parasitic on the primary point.

Personal relations can of course be of public concern; children may need to be protected, for instance, from certain kinds of corrupting relations with adults. But while it may be possible and desirable to prevent such relations altogether, there is little that third parties can do to regulate or reshape them. By inducing the booking clerk to do his job more efficiently, or passengers to state their destinations more clearly, the railway staff controller can improve the relation between them. But this is because he can keep them up to the mark—they are all interested exclusively in role-performance, and each can have a clear notion of the standard that the other's performance should reach. But friends can be kept up to the mark only by one another. There is no "mark" that anyone outside could use to assess them, for friendship is not confined by role requirements.[9]

To intrude on personal relations of this kind may be very much worse than useless. Of course, people do take their troubles to others, to friends or marriage counselors for guidance and advice. But this is to invite the counselor to become, in a small way perhaps, a party to the relationship—or rather, to enter into a relationship with him, the success of which depends on his resolve to keep it a purely second-order relationship, demanding of him a sensitive and reticent understanding of the first. Personal relations are exploratory and creative; they survive and develop if they are given care and attention; they require continuous adjustment as the personalities of the parties are modified by experience, both of one another and of their external environment. Such relationships are, in their nature, private. They could not exist if it were not possible to create excluding conditions. One cannot have a personal relation with

[9] "According to the newspaper *Szabad Nép,* some members of the Communist Party in Hungary have not a single working man among their friends, and they are censured in a way that implies that they had better quickly make a friend of a worker or it will be the worse for them" (*The Times* [London], July 20, 1949, quoted by P. Halmos, *Solitude and Privacy* [London, 1952], p. 167).

all comers, nor carry on personal conversations under the same conditions as an open seminar.[10]

If we value personal relations, then, we must recognize these at least as specifically private areas. And since the family and the family home are the focal points of important and very generally significant personal relations, these must be immune from intrusion, at least beyond the point at which minimal public role requirements are satisfied. A father who regularly beats the children insensible cannot claim, of course, that intrusion could only spoil his personal relations. But while the public is properly concerned that there should be no cruelty, exploitation, or neglect, these are only the minimal conditions for personal relations. The rest are the private business of the parties.

Preoccupation with privacy—in particular with the privacy of family relations—has been criticized by some writers, however, as an unhealthy feature of post-Renaissance bourgeois society. Consider Edmund Leach's strictures:

> In the past, kinsfolk and neighbors gave the individual continuous moral support throughout his life. Today the domestic household is isolated. The family looks inward upon itself; there is an intensification of emotional stress between husband and wife, and parents and children. The strain is greater than most of us can bear. Far from being the basis of the good society, the family, with its narrow privacy and tawdry secrets, is the source of all our discontents.[11]

Paul Halmos, too, speaks of "a hypertrophied family devotion and family insularity," arising from the attempt by contemporary man "to transcend his solitude. . . ."

> [He] may finally negate his apartness in an obsessional

[10] Charles Fried has argued that privacy is logically prior to love and friendship, since a necessary feature of these concepts is a "sharing of information about one's actions, beliefs, or emotions which one does not share with all, and which one has the right not to share with anyone. By conferring this right, privacy creates the moral capital which we spend in friendship and love" ("Privacy," in G. Hughes, ed., *Law, Reason, and Justice* [New York, 1969], p. 56).

[11] E. Leach, *A Runaway World,* The 1967 Reith Lectures (London, 1968), p. 44.

> affirmation of family ties. . . . Friendship and companionship, when manifestly present in the marital couple, is regarded as an instance of great virtue even when it is equally manifestly absent in all other relationships. Furthermore, the nepotistic solidarity of the family is another symptom of the contemporary attitude according to which the world is hostile and dangerous and the family is the only solid rock which is to be protected against all comers.[12]

The insistence on the private area is, in this view, either a symptom or a contributory cause of a pathological condition. But to concede this diagnosis need not weaken the argument I am advancing for the right of exclusion, for it may imply only that in modern society we seek personal relations with too few people, the ones we succeed in forming being overtaxed in consequence by the emotional weight they are forced to bear.

Halmos concedes the value and importance of the personal relations between lovers and "the composed intimacy and companionship of man and wife," admitting these as properly and necessarily exclusive: "Such retreat and privacy may vary according to cultural standards but they are on the whole universal among mankind and not infrequent among animals."[13] It is not clear, however, how much value Halmos attaches to personal relations in general. It may be that men suffer least from neurotic maladjustments in communities like the kibbutz, where everyone feels the security and comfortable warmth of acceptance by a peer group, without the tensions of too-personalized individual attachments. But the children of the kibbutz have been found by some observers defective as persons, precisely because their emotional stability has been purchased at the cost of an incapacity to establish deep personal relations. Perhaps we have to choose between the sensitive, human understanding that we achieve only by the cultivation of our relations within a con-

[12] P. Halmos; *Solitude and Privacy* (London, 1952), pp. 121–122.

[13] Halmos, *Solitude and Privacy,* p. 121. The standpoint Halmos adopts may be inferred from the following passage: "While . . . the material needs of man . . . have been increasingly satisfied, since the Industrial Revolution, the bio-social needs have been more and more neglected. Culture, a fortuitous expression of the basic principia of life, rarely favoured man's pacific, creative gregariousness . . ." p. 51.

fined circle and the extrovert assurance and adjustment that a *Gemeinschaft* can confer. However this may be, to the extent that we value the former, we shall be committed to valuing the right of privacy.

Though personal relations need some freedom from interference, different kinds of interference would affect them differently. An extreme kind is to attempt to participate—to turn, for instance, a relation *à deux* into one *à trois*. It is not evident, however, that the attentions of the observer and reporter are necessarily so objectionable. A strong-minded couple might pursue their own course undisturbed under the eyes of a reasonably tactful and self-effacing paying guest. Of course, the uncommitted observer makes most of us self-conscious and inhibited —we do not find it as easy to express our feelings for one another spontaneously, to produce the same kind of mutually sensitive and responsive relations, in full view of a nonparticipant third party, as we do in private. I do not know, however, whether this is a psychologically necessary fact about human beings, or only a culturally conditioned one. Certainly, personal relations are not impossible in places where people live perforce on top of one another. But they call for a good deal of tact and goodwill from the bystanders; there is some evidence that in such conditions, people develop psychological avoidance arrangements—a capacity for not noticing, and a corresponding confidence in not being noticed—that substitute for physical seclusion.[14]

The importance of personal relations suggests a limit to what can be done by antidiscrimination laws. Whatever the justification for interfering with the freedom to discriminate in, say, hiring workers, there are some kinds of choice where a man's reasons for his preferences and antipathies are less important than that he has them. If the personal relations of a home are valued, its constituent members must be left free to decide who can be accepted into it, for example, as a lodger. Club membership might be different. True, we join clubs to cultivate personal relations, like friendships; but we do not expect to enter into such relations with every member. The mere presence in the clubroom of people whom one would not invite to join one's

[14] See A. F. Westin; *Privacy and Freedom* (New York, 1967), p. 18, for references to evidence of this point.

circle of intimates need not endanger the relations within that circle. Nevertheless, if the club's members are, in general, antipathetic to a particular group, to deny them the right of exclusion may create tensions defeating the end for which the club exists.

Of course, merely having prejudices gives no man a right to discriminate unfairly and irrationally in all his relations at whatever cost to the personal dignity of the outsider; insofar as the relations can be specified in terms of role-performances, it is reasonable to demand that discriminations be based only on relevant differences. But to the degree that the point of the relationship has built into it a quality of life depending on reciprocal caring, it qualifies as an area of privacy, and therefore as immune from regulation. (There may be overriding reasons, in times of racial tension and hostility, for discouraging the formation of exclusive clubs, whose rules can only appear inflammatory. But this is to adduce further special reasons against privacy, overriding reasons for it based on the value of personal relations.)

The Privacy of the Free Citizen

The second personal ideal to which privacy is closely related is that of the free man in a minimally regulated society, a way of life where, first, the average individual is subject only within reasonable and legally safeguarded limits to the power of others, and, second, where the requirements of his social roles still leave him considerable breadth of choice in the way he lives. The first of these considerations, the one that has received most attention in the polemical literature on privacy, I have referred to already. The dossier and the computer bank threaten us with victimization and persecution by unscrupulous, intolerant, or merely misunderstanding officials. But these misgivings might be set at rest, at least in principle, by institutional safeguards and assurances. More fundamental is the second consideration, which depends on a conceptual distinction between the private and the official.

The judge's pronouncements on the bench have public significance; though he may not be easily called to account, still there is an important sense in which he has a public responsibility. What he says in his home or in his club—even on matters of law—is another matter; it has no official standing and no official consequences. Of course, if he happens also to be club secretary, what he says about other members in *this* official capacity is not "his own private affair"; but conversely, the members might resist a police inquiry into its secretary's statements as an interference with the club's private affairs. What is official and what is private depends, therefore, on the frame of reference. But for there to be privacy of this kind at all the distinction between official and nonofficial must be intelligible. Admittedly, we may all have some public (that is, official) roles as voters, taxpayers, jurymen, and so on. But we distinguish what we do as family men, shopkeepers, and club treasurers from such public functions. A private citizen, unlike a public official, has no *special* official roles, just as a private member of parliament, not being a minister, has no special official function in Parliament.

This conception of privacy is closely bound up with the liberal ideal. The totalitarian claims that everything a man is and does has significance for society at large. He sees the state as the self-conscious organization of society for the well-being of society; the social significance of our actions and relations overrides any other. Consequently, the public or political universe is all inclusive, *all* roles are public, and every function, whether political, economic, or artistic, can be interpreted as involving a public responsibility.

The liberal, on the other hand, claims not merely a private capacity—an area of action in which he is not responsible to the state for what he does so long as he respects certain minimal rights of others; he claims further that this is the residual category, that the onus is on anyone who claims he is accountable. How he does his job may affect the gross national product, and not only his own slice of it. But he will grant that this is socially significant only in the same way that a drought is, for that too can have serious economic consequences. He may consent to public manipulation of the environment of private choices, by subsidies or customs duties, for instance, as he may agree to cloud-seeding to break a drought, but he resists the suggestion that every citizen should be held publicly responsible for his economic choices as though he were a public servant or the governor of the central bank.

This ideal of the private citizen provides no very precise criteria for distinguishing the private realm; it is rather that no citizen other than actual employees of the administration can be held culpable—even morally culpable—for any action as a failure in public duty unless special grounds can be shown why this is a matter in which he may not merely please himself. Of course, there will be duties associated with roles he has voluntarily assumed—as husband, employee, and so on—but such responsibilities are of his own choosing, not thrust upon him, like his public roles of juror, or taxpayer.

Just as the privacy of personal relations may be invoked to rationalize an obsessive preoccupation with the restricted family, to the exclusion of all other human concern, so the privacy of the free citizen may be invoked to rationalize a selfish economic individualism. One critic, H. W. Arndt, has written that

> The cult of privacy seems specifically designed as a defence mechanism for the protection of anti-social behaviour. . . . The cult of privacy rests on an individualist conception of society, not merely in the innocent and beneficial sense of a society in which the welfare of individuals is conceived as the end of all social organisation, but in the more sepecific sense of "each for himself and the devil take the hindmost." . . . An individualist of this sort sees "the Government" where we might see "the public interest," and this Government will appear to him often as no more than one antagonist in the battle of wits which is life—or business.[15]

There is room for a good deal of disagreement about the extent to which considerations like those of general economic well-being, social equality, or national security justify pressing back the frontiers of the private, to hold men responsible for the way they conduct their daily business. For the liberal, however, every step he is forced to take in that direction counts as a retreat from

[15] H. W. Arndt, "The Cult of Privacy," *Australian Quarterly,* XXI: 3 (September 1949), 69, 70–71.

an otherwise desirable state of affairs, in which because men may please themselves what they are about is no one's business but their own.

Privacy and Personal Autonomy

The third personal ideal is that of the independently minded individual, whose actions are governed by principles that are his own. This does not mean, of course, that he has concocted them out of nothing, but that he subjects his principles to critical review, rather than taking them over unexamined from his social environment. He is the man who resists social pressures to conform if he has grounds for uneasiness in doing the conformist thing.

Much has been made of the need for privacy, as a safeguard against conformism. Hubert Humphrey has written:

> We act differently if we believe we are being observed. If we can never be sure whether or not we are being watched and listened to, all our actions will be altered and our very character will change.[16]

Senator Edward V. Long deplores the decline in spontaneity attendant on a situation where "because of this diligent accumulation of facts about each of us, it is difficult to speak or act today without wondering if the words or actions will reappear 'on the record.' "[17]

It is not only the authorities we fear. We are all under strong pressure from our friends and neighbors to live up to the roles in which they cast us. If we disappoint them, we risk their disapproval, and what may be worse, their ridicule. For many of us, we are free to be ourselves only within that area from which observers can legitimately be excluded. We need a sanctuary or retreat, in which we can drop the mask, desist for a while from projecting on the world the image we want to be accepted as ourselves, an image that may reflect the values of our peers

[16] Foreword to Edward V. Long, *The Intruders* (New York, 1967), p. viii.
[17] *Ibid.*, p. 55.

rather than the realities of our natures. To remain sane, we need a closed environment, open only to those we trust, with whom we have an unspoken understanding that whatever is revealed goes no farther.

Put in this way, however, the case for privacy begins to look like a claim to the conditions of life necessary only for second-grade men in a second-grade society. For the man who is truly independent—the autonomous man—is the one who has the strength of mind to resist the pressure to believe with the rest, and has the courage to act on his convictions. He is the man who despises bad faith, and refuses to be anything or to pretend to be anything merely because the world casts him for the part. He is the man who does not hesitate to stand and be counted. That sort of man can be greatly inconvenienced by the world's clamor—but he *does* what lesser men claim that they are not free to do. "There is no reason," writes Senator Long, "why conformity must be made an inescapable part of the American dream. Excessive pressures can and must be prevented: there must be preserved in each individual a sphere of privacy that will allow his personality to bloom and thrive."[18] One wonders, however, whether the Senator has drawn the right moral. Excessive pressures can be prevented not merely by allowing an individual to hide, but by tolerating the heresy he is not afraid to publish. Socrates did not ask to be allowed to teach philosophy in private. Senator Long quotes a speech of Judge Learned Hand, with apparent approval: "I believe that community is already in process of dissolution . . . when faith in the eventual supremacy of reason has become so timid that we dare not enter our convictions in the open lists to win or lose."[19] But the moral of that sentiment is that preoccupation with the need for a private retreat is a symptom of social sickness.

Of course, there are not many like Socrates in any society; not many have the knowledge of what they are, the virtue to be content with what they know, and the courage to pretend to be nothing else. For the rest of us, the freedom we need is the freedom to be something else—to be ourselves, to do what we

[18] *Ibid.*, p. 62.
[19] *Ibid.*, p. 63.

think best, in a small, protected sea, where the winds of opinion cannot blow us off course. We cannot learn to be autonomous save by practicing independent judgment. It is important for the moral education of children that at a certain stage they should find the rules porous—that sometimes they should be left to decide what is best to do. Not many of us perhaps have gone so far along the road to moral maturity that we can bear unrelenting exposure to criticism without flinching.

This last stage of my argument brings me back to the grounds for the general principle of privacy, to which I devoted the first half of this paper. I argued that respect for someone as a person, as a chooser, implied respect for him as one engaged on a kind of self-creative enterprise, which could be disrupted, distorted, or frustrated even by so limited an intrusion as watching. A man's view of what he does may be radically altered by having to see it, as it were, through another man's eyes. Now a man has attained a measure of success in his enterprise to the degree that he has achieved autonomy. To the same degree, the importance to him of protection from eavesdropping and Peeping Toms diminishes as he becomes less vulnerable to the judgments of others, more reliant on his own (though he will still need privacy for personal relations, and protection from the grosser kinds of persecution).

This does not weaken the ground for the general principle, however, for this was not a consequentialist ground. It was not that allowing men privacy would give them a better chance to be autonomous. It was rather that a person—anyone potentially autonomous—was worthy of respect on that account; and that if such a person wanted to pursue his enterprise unobserved, he was entitled, unless there were overriding reasons against it, to do as he wished. The argument there was in terms of respect for the enterprise as such, irrespective of the chances of success or failure in any particular instance. In this last section, I have suggested a further, reinforcing argument for privacy as a condition necessary, though to a progressively diminishing degree, if that enterprise is to succeed.

2

THE PRIVATE AND THE FREE: A CONCEPTUAL INQUIRY

W. L. WEINSTEIN

Without assuming there is a definitive answer, let alone a simple one, I pose the question: What may be the main presuppositions of a belief in a private sphere of action or human relations?

Granted that the line dividing the private and the public can be shifting and uncertain, different in different times and places, as well as subject to both reconcilable and intractable disagreements, my immediate concern is not with a recipe for drawing the line in a particular way, important as this can be, but with an issue which is at least implied in any such line-drawing enterprise, namely: What must I believe (or correspondingly reject) if I assert (or deny) that there is a private sphere? I hope here to present a brief exposé of some of the essentials at stake in arguments in the private versus public territory, for example, factors on which shifts in the dividing line may depend. But the fundamental issues here, involving nothing less than our ways, often messy and ill-defined, of conceiving of human actions and their social contexts, are so complex that in the end I may succeed in showing no more than that general accounts, such as mine, of the nature of controversies in this territory are themselves as subject to controversy as particular ways of distinguishing between the private and the public. In fact the two types of controversy may well be closely connected.

The importance of the questions posed above may be explained in at least two preliminary ways. First, our thinking that there ought to be a sphere of private actions and relations is a necessary, though not sufficient, condition of the existence of such a sphere, that is, something constituted by recognition and observance in actual social behavior.[1] Thus spheres of the private exist when they do as parts of the community's ways of thought—its recognized ways of claiming to be immune from intrusion or control. In this sense part of social reality itself, for example, the reality of counting on being protected against interference or intrusion by others in what is seen by the agents as a private concern, is constituted by the beliefs of the agents who are involved; that is, by individuals in sufficient number or of sufficient importance, or some combination of the two, claiming and respecting claims to a certain sphere roughly marked, "Not your business: keep out." By the same token a sphere of the private, such as may exist at a given time, may be extinguished by not respecting the rules required to preserve it; it may of course be sufficient to police it out of existence even when there are beliefs hostile to such repression, and easier still never to constitute it by not developing the beliefs that are essential to its existence. However, to see spheres of the private as typically depending on generally accepted beliefs in a community is not to see all the possibilities. It is equally important to understand the sense in which individuals who systematically opt out of the roles, relations, and activities their

[1] Taken without qualification this statement would best apply to societies like our own, in which recognition of the private in several specific forms is explicit and there are highly articulated general conceptions of the private and the public. In some societies the relevant distinctions may be made, if at all, only implicitly, and it may be difficult for an anthropologist or historian to decide whether, for instance, a given limit on authority counts as recognition of the claims of the private.

community makes available to them, or imposes on them, may thereby create a private sphere for themselves in opposition to prevailing conceptions of the private (certain Stoics, for example).

Second, an answer to "What belongs in the private sphere?" admitting of several overlapping answers, and perhaps some different or even mutually opposed ones, can be much affected by the presuppositions that underlie claims to such a sphere. That is, what I claim to be properly a private matter—whom I befriend or love or marry, or what religion (if any) I profess—may be determined by why I claim it as such. Thus a relation can be so conceived that its point is to give effect to my likes, or a conviction can be held whose very nature is seen as a matter for the individual freely to accept or reject.

I

There is in our own culture alone an extensive range of diverse views, which may not even share a common moral footing, about what matters are properly private; from this range a few examples may be selected in outlining some familiar views. No doubt these examples are historically determinate ones. For example, it may well be true, as Arendt among others has argued, that the importance ascribed to "intimacy" is distinctively modern; and that modern liberals' ways of marking off some forms of private life (including those extending beyond personal and family relations) as freedoms of the individual stand in contrast to the ancient Greeks' equations of freedom with participation in public activities, and of privacy (in the household, the realm of women, children, and slaves) with deprivation of the highest human status.[2]

One might best begin with ways in which we often think of privacy as intimacy. Where there is recognition of intimate aspects of life on one's own or in relation to others, there are conventions, of morality or etiquette, specifying the circum-

[2] Hannah Arendt, *The Human Condition* (Chicago: University of Chicago Press, 1958), chaps. 4–9; Isaiah Berlin, *Four Essays on Liberty* (London: Oxford University Press, 1969), pp. xl–xlii; Benjamin Constant, *De l'esprit de Conquête* (1814), Part II, chap. 6 (excerpt translated by John Plamenatz, ed., *Readings from Liberal Writers* [London: George Allen & Unwin, 1965], pp. 60–62).

stances in which persons should not be observed, counseled, talked about, or physically intruded upon. For example, a stranger's tendering uncalled-for advice to parents about how their children should be reared may count as an invasion of a sphere that is of intimate concern to them. Such an intrusion may cause offense or embarrassment, or be merely a distraction; it is therefore a nuisance, though not an interference with the parents' freedom. For the giving of advice, even if unwanted or without entitlement, does not make the choice of an action less available to the agent who is intruded upon.[3] To insist on one's privacy in these circumstances is not to stake a claim to freedom.

Similarly, observing people when they are off-guard or unaware, as in voyeurism, counts as an intrusion upon privacy, but not as an interference with the freedom of the observed agent so long as his behavior remains uninhibited (because of his being unaware). If the agent knew he was being observed and did not care, one might be inclined to say that, for him at any rate, privacy was not violated, although it might still be thought that observing him was improper and that he should care. Again, prying into a person's innermost feelings and thoughts, even when he is a willing subject (such as a volunteer for psychological testing), may be felt to be an invasion of privacy, especially if his everyday defenses and inhibitions are overcome. Furthermore, many of us feel embarrassed or disturbed by others eagerly baring their souls, though reactions to certain kinds of personal revelation do vary with individuals, groups, and nationalities, some taking them as steps toward honesty in social relationships, others as improper attempts to impose one's private life on other people's private lives.

It is hardly possible here to analyze the very complex beliefs that may account for the feeling that revelations of the intimate, whether extracted from or willingly provided by the agent, are somehow wrong or unpleasant, at any rate in certain circumstances. Perhaps a particular range of such taboos, against physical and, as it were, psychological, nudity, is connected with beliefs about the maintenance of a certain personal identity or integrity in social relations, or about treating people as agents

[3] This point is argued more fully in S. I. Benn and W. L. Weinstein, "Being Free to Act, and Being a Free Man," to be published in *Mind*.

rather than as objects, or possibly about the risk of changing profoundly important human phenomena into trivial or vulgar ones through overexposure. The nature of these and other relevant types of belief is far from clear. Moreover, nowadays one has to reckon with conflicting theories, some of which call for the preservation of the intimate in the name of a civilized way of life as well as freedom, whereas others see human liberation and happiness in some therapeutic process that involves stripping away at least some privacy conventions which have hitherto counted as the bases of correctly restrained social behavior. There are important variations in how the bounds of the intimate aspects of personality and behavior are drawn, and correspondingly, in opinions about who, and in what circumstances, may legitimately acquire what sort of knowledge or experience of which other people. For example, Mumford remarks on a shift in attitudes toward nudity and sexual intercourse in the presence of others even when they occur between spouses.[4]

The two examples mentioned so far, unsolicited advice-giving and voyeurism, seem not to raise doubts about the freedom of the agent whose privacy is held to be invaded; in fact, successful voyeurism, unlike advice-giving, does not even imply an intention to change the agent's behavior.[5] But such doubts may begin to arise in other cases: gate-crashing a wedding reception, disturbing a widow in her grief to find out more about it, or persisting in talking to people on airplanes who want to get on with their sleep or reading. It is arguable that the agents intruded upon remain free to continue what they had been doing, or experiencing, before, and that at least in the first two examples in this trio it might be supposed that the intruder does not intend to affect the mood or action of those he intrudes upon. Yet there is perhaps a real enough sense in which they are disturbed directly, and possibly seriously, by what is done to them. They may reasonably, if not convincingly to all, claim that they are not free to do, or experience, what they had been

[4] Lewis Mumford, *The Culture of Cities* (London: Secker & Warburg, 1940), p. 41.

[5] However, this is not to suggest that intentionality is always a necessary condition for counting an interference as an interference with freedom. The impersonal operation of social forces, once seen as in principle subject to human control, may be identified as a source of unfreedom.

doing, or experiencing, before the intrusion occurred, though the strength of their claim may depend on the particular description, among the several that could be available, of what they claim is interfered with, as well as the importance ascribed to it.

However, cases on the borderline of intrusions upon privacy that either do or do not count as interferences with freedom fall outside the scope of this paper, which may be more clearly defined with the aid of further distinctions. First, the claims of privacy as intimacy may be at odds with other claims, such as those made on behalf of what is held to be the interests of other persons or the wider community, of some worthwhile activity or the very person whose private life is intruded upon. Such counterclaims may extend to knowledge only, or beyond to advice-giving or open discussion, or further to interference.[6] I shall be concerned with privacy as intimacy only to the extent that claims for and against it touch on its freedom, and even more so with those claims to privacy which identify it as intrinsically free in a sense which will be explained in due course.

Second, privacy as intimacy refers to certain aspects of the single person or his relations with only one other or a few. Privacy in this sense is what is of intimate concern to me or us; how strongly or extensively others are excluded varies with the

[6] The intimate is not always thought to be improperly revealed or investigated; and even when unspecified individuals belonging to the public at large have no title to go beyond a particular conventional boundary, the state or some other agency may justifiably claim it. Thus, the police or a coroner may properly disturb a widow in her grief; a private party may properly be the subject of a public inquiry; a judge in a divorce case may have to go into intimate details. Probing the intimate may be justified in the interests of knowledge and general human welfare; one notes the controversy over the use of a sex laboratory divulged in W. H. Masters and V. E. Johnson, *Human Sexual Response* (Boston: Little, Brown, 1964). Revelations in psychiatric treatment or the confessional, though equally the strict observance of confidentiality, may be held to be for the good of the person; furthermore, outsiders' attempts to break an intimate relation between persons, one of whom is dominant and the other submissive, may arguably promote the latter's autonomy. Treating certain forms of sexual behavior as inherently sinful may go with unreadiness to vouchsafe to them protective conventions of secrecy and freedom, which may surround other forms of such behavior on grounds of their intimate nature: to turn a blind eye to the works of the Devil is not easily condoned by those who are determined to fight him.

example. On the other hand, there is a wide range of instances where to speak of something as private is not to imply intimacy. Individuals not intimately related may nevertheless assert that their relation or activity is a private one in the sense that it is not the proper concern of the community or some institution, such as the state, a church, or a business firm; and a church or firm may in turn claim that it is itself private vis-à-vis the wider community or the state.[7] This second range of uses occurs in, for example, private enterprise, private medical care, and private school. What goes on in a private meeting, or an institution placing itself in a private sphere, may be widely known within it, but attempts by outsiders to obtain information or exert control may be resisted. Indeed, private enterprise or private property, when allied with ideals of free competition, implies that the state may not do what competitors may attempt against each other: to drive the other out of business.

As this analysis proceeds we shall see that examples of the two types of the private distinguished here may count as freedoms, for the individual, and where appropriate for a group or an institution, when the involvement, whether it is friendship or philosophical inquiry, is seen as crucially requiring freedom. However, all this begins to suggest that there are multiple applications of the notion of "public" as well, and therefore perhaps immediate hazards in its use. But once it is assumed that "public" and "private" are contrast-concepts jointly exhausting the full range of *social* phenomena and that they typically have a normative basis and function in moral and political discourse, it is possible to make good use of their variability. If by "public" one loosely means what counts as being of proper concern to some community which is identified as the *wider* social context of an action or relation, then it is possible to see why it is no more helpful to restrict "private" to a formula such as "the atomic individual," or "the person when unrelated to others," or "being alone" than it is strictly to conceive of "public" as "the widest possible relevant community," for example, the

[7] In principle, though not normally in choice of words, a state's claim to manage its internal affairs without outside interference, or even help, involves a similar claim to a private sphere.

state.[8] For my purposes the two notions are probably best seen as layers of onion skin, any given layer potentially counting as private in relation to one or more outer layers, that is, various publics. This would help to explain why the solitary individual is not necessarily implied when we refer to private enterprise, but why on the other hand within a firm so characterized we may identify both officially required types of privacy (confidentiality, for example) and informal, discretionary types (friendship); and equally, how forms of group life (religious organizations or much less institutional units such as neighbors on a street) may sensibly be seen as part of a wider community or more inclusive group, and thus be counted as private for at least certain purposes.

In what is to follow I shall examine forms of the private, some of them seen as having aspects of intimacy and others not, in human involvements which tend to be assimilated to the concept of freedom typically developed within a liberal perspective, though similar views have found a place in other perspectives. Briefly, freedom in this perspective is understood in terms of the range of options available to an agent who is seen, at least potentially, as a chooser.[9] Furthermore, the focus will be on that area of private actions, relations, and beliefs marked off because the element of freedom in them is often thought to carry a special value, either instrumentally or, more interestingly, noninstrumentally. What is at stake in this narrowed area of inquiry is the possibility of seeing some human involvements as opportunities to exercise choices and not (or not merely) in terms of the individual's sensibility and the need to respect, that is, not intrude upon, what is considered his

[8] This is not to imply rejection of such formulae. Privacy as intimacy includes, among other things, individual solitude as well as certain innermost thoughts and feelings; and it may be morally relevant to know the location of an action, for example, whether nudity or the loud crinkling of a popcorn wrapper occurs in seclusion or in a classroom. The special sense of "public" cited above, as "an indefinite number of nonassignable individuals," familiar to readers of Bentham, has a special range of uses: see Brian Barry, *Political Argument* (London: Routledge & Kegan Paul, 1965), pp. 190–192. (For several points in this analysis I am indebted to my colleague, Alan Montefiore.)

[9] An interpretation explained in Benn and Weinstein, "Being Free to Act, and Being a Free Man."

intimate feelings and relations.[10] This distinction, often difficult and sometimes impossible to apply, may be illustrated as follows. Members of a small group practicing free love may see themselves as exercising their freedom of choice in sexual relations in ways not made available by the strict observance of "bourgeois" morality, but consistently with this could complain of a concomitant lack of sheer privacy—not having enough moments of solitude, for example, or for easily cooking and eating occasionally apart from others.

II

Beliefs in the private sphere as a sphere of freedom seem to require at least two types of presupposition. First, freedom is a principle. Interferences with it require justification, though they may be justifiable; and it is in place to ask for a justification for restrictions if we can suppose that things could be otherwise than they are.[11] Second, there ought to be an area of human involvements which is not the normal province of a wider community, of public policy, though not of course in the sense that the freedom of such involvements should not be publicly endorsed and protected.

However, more than this is required. Although the first presupposition explains why certain intrusions upon the private may be condemned as more than an uncivilized nuisance or disrespectful behavior, there can be important variations in belief as to the value of freedom—that is, why it is claimed in given cases. And why it is claimed is relevant when assessing the relative strength of attempts to justify interferences with freedom. This consideration applies equally to the second presupposition, which requires content, namely, accounts of particular human involvements.

Two main types of belief in the value of freedom, instrumental and noninstrumental, will be compared briefly, and the

[10] But this is not to exclude the possibility that freedom may be seen as necessary to the creation and fulfillment of an intimate relation. (Many issues not focused upon in this paper are, however, clarified in Mr. Benn's contribution, "Privacy, Freedom, and Respect for Persons.")

[11] The complex arguments needed to defend this view are developed in Benn and Weinstein, "Being Free to Act, and Being a Free Man."

latter will provide the peg on which the rest of this paper will hang.

First, it has been believed that interference with the choices of individuals is not required in certain circumstances to achieve a particular result, for example, when interference would be inefficient or too easily evaded, or if effective nevertheless too costly. Thus there could be left to the individual some area of choice, allowing him to achieve the good, typically his own, that may be involved. A kind of Hobbesian residue of freedom may exist by virtue of the absence of legal and social restrictions. But it is not more than a residue, its extent depending on the existing, and possibly changing, distribution of the relevant knowledge and resources as between individual agents on the one hand and the authorities, even if beneficently disposed, on the other. This defense of freedom from a purely instrumental, or, more narrowly utilitarian, point of view[12] has troubled liberals at least since Bentham's rejection of natural rights theory, in spite of the possibility of taking utilitarianism as a blank check for the pursuit of any possible object of human desire, so long as it increases the agent's happiness. How, then, might the special preserve of "private" freedoms be explained in more positive terms, creating a stronger presumption in its favor?

One answer had been sought by some utilitarians themselves by postulating that each individual is more likely than anyone else to know what would promote his interests, adding that even if he made mistakes on particular occasions it is more likely that he would learn from such experience if he were left free.[13] The difficulties in this view have been pointed out too often to call for repetition here,[14] though it is not one which is unworthy of further salvage efforts; nor has it ceased to be argued with political success.

[12] Exemplified by Bentham, *Introduction to the Principles of Morals and Legislation,* chap. 17.

[13] This was usually held to be valid for sane adults. See J. S. Mill, *On Liberty,* chap. 4, para. 4; chap. 5, paras. 18, 19 (women were pointedly included in this category in some of Mill's other writings); Henry Sidgwick, *Elements of Politics,* 3rd ed. (London: MacMillan, 1908), chaps. 4, 6, 9.

[14] See John Plamenatz, *The English Utilitarians* (Oxford: Basil Blackwell, 1958), chap. 8.

There is, however, a second type of claim to freedom not so directly (though it may nevertheless be) limited by considerations of efficiency and the distribution of knowledge in reaching some good, such as happiness or welfare. This claim consists in the belief that the individual has a right to exercise a choice as to whether, and possibly how or on what terms, he shall become involved in certain activities and relations because *their nature* is such that other people's or the state's legitimate concern with them, if they have any at all, has a definite limit.

This belief does not imply that all claims to freedom are necessarily claims to "private" freedom in the special sense intended here, which would normally exclude, for example, voting rights. Nor is its hard-core sense derived strictly from the notion of negative freedom, of being left alone by others, though perhaps that phrase has been used to express it.[15] It is more than this; it is the notion that certain human involvements are defective, lose all or much of their value or special quality, when the agent concerned is not free to act on his own preferences or in his own way.[16]

For example, when I claim that I am not answerable, not obliged to give reasons, to anyone for the making up of my invitations list for a dinner in my home, and still less that anyone has a right to interfere, I may be implying that this is the sort of thing in which to be deprived of the choice of my own guests would defeat the enterprise, involving, as it may be seen to do, the choice of my friends, or more widely, of company I expect to be congenial. Seen in these terms, my preferences for certain people may be accepted as sufficient reasons for inviting

[15] See Isaiah Berlin, *Two Concepts of Liberty* (Inaugural Lecture, Oxford: The Clarendon Press, 1958), pp. 7–16, reprinted in Berlin, *Four Essays on Liberty,* pp. 122–131; but see H. J. McCloskey, "A Critique of the Ideals of Liberty," *Mind,* LXXIV (Oct. 1965), especially pp. 486–494.

[16] No doubt this thesis contains possibilities for divergent interpretations, not least about what is to count as a person's preference or the conditions in which his preference is properly his own (and not, say, vicarious or determined by antecedent social or psychological factors); and such divergencies may have important political implications. But, holding these issues in reserve, my immediate aim is to make clear how a noninstrumental view of freedom's value may be presupposed when a special domain of freedom is marked off as private, as I take Mill to have attempted in *On Liberty.*

them. It is preeminently in such a sphere that one finds apposite Hart's claim that if one believes that an agent's disapproval or disgust may override another agent's preference, one can hardly begin to regard oneself as a believer in freedom.[17]

It is worth adding at once that actions and relations conceived in such terms may nevertheless affect others: Jones's hope of receiving an invitation may be disappointed, as may Smith's of avoiding the embarrassment of refusing one. The essence of the claim that choice is integral to the value of a certain range of social relations is not that the exercise of choice has no effect on others or is of no interest to them.[18] Nor does it amount to, or strictly depend on, the view (which may well be complementary) that there are some aspects of social relations which could *safely* be left to individual choice when no harm would be caused to others. It is rather that, even when others may be

[17] H. L. A. Hart, *Law, Liberty and Morality* (London: Oxford University Press, 1963), pp. 46–47. See also J. R. Lucas, "Against Equality," *Philosophy,* XL: 154 (October 1965), 307.

[18] As J. C. Rees rightly argued when attempting to tidy up Mill's distinction between "self-regarding" and "other-regarding" actions, in "A Re-reading of Mill on Liberty," *Political Studies,* VIII:2 (June 1960), 113–129. Rees usefully moves the argument one stage further, to a consideration of interests that might be prejudicially affected, but only one stage.

However, many liberals of a later day, such as Hobhouse, have argued against Mill that *in principle* there is nothing done by the individual which may not be the proper concern of the community. It seems reasonable to interpret this, not as support for a kind of totalitarianism, but as a readiness to appreciate that there may be, but are not always, public causes sufficiently weighty to justify interferences with what may be counted as a private freedom, and that claims for the latter, often implying inalienability, exist instead in a continuously changing balance against rival claims. Nevertheless, it is one thing to criticize Mill for assuming a priori that there are certain private freedoms which could not justifiably be interfered with by the community, but quite another to reject the thesis that choices are integral to a certain range of relations, activities, and beliefs. Perhaps Mill's liberal critics have also been tempted to reject his thesis that all choosing as such is good, because it is argued with very little awareness of the difficulties. On the other hand, I doubt whether they could have rejected a more limited thesis, depending on certain characterizations of selected human involvements, which is sketched in this paper. See L. T. Hobhouse, *Liberalism* (London: Oxford University Press, 1911), pp. 120, 142; A. D. Lindsay, Introduction to *J. S. Mill, Utilitarianism, Liberty, & Representative Government* (New York: E. P. Dutton, 1951), p. xxvii; Isaiah Berlin, *Two Concepts of Liberty,* p. 40; *Four Essays on Liberty,* p. 155.

affected prejudicially or in ways they merely dislike,[19] the agent's choice is a necessary value in the involvement in some specified activity or relation. The value is conceived noninstrumentally, though endorsement of choices on particular occasions may be qualified or withdrawn because of the agent's ignorance or imprudence, his illusions or malevolent motives, and the like.[20] Nevertheless, in this view, even assuming choices of certain types and in certain circumstances to be genuine and untainted, there may be justifications for interfering with them, based on considerations of, say, justice or the prevention of harm to others; and, as will be explained more fully below, the introduction of such principles may involve reclassifying as "public" what had been understood as something "private."

How there may be ways of picking out a private freedom may be explained through a more detailed example. The mutual exercise of choice of marriage partners in one type of society, given the importance ascribed to mutual love in the making of a match, counts as an item in the modern catalog of private freedom.[21] Were a computer employing a science of compat-

[19] "Merely dislike": added to cover cases where others have no legitimate counterclaim, for example, I have no duty to invite Jones to dinner or to marry one person rather than another, although one might freely create such obligations.

[20] But this is no easy line of argument to sustain while continuing to adhere to the general value of choice-making. Mill says that we abdicate our freedom when we, presumably, choose slavery (*On Liberty*, chap. 5, para. 11). If this were the only case where it was arguable that the agent's freedom could be interfered with for the sake of preserving or improving his capacity as a chooser, the liberal's position would be much easier than it is in fact. See McCloskey, "A Critique of the Ideals of Liberty," pp. 498–503; S. I. Benn, "Freedom and Persuasion," *Australasian Journal of Philosophy*, 45 (1967), 259–275; Benn and Weinstein, "Being Free to Act, and Being a Free Man." The thesis that choices have a special value, *when* made by men with the capacity to choose, remains, however, something worth defending.

[21] For the sake of simplicity only the choices of whether to marry and, if so, whom, are picked out here. There are, however, many other relevant points of potentially large implications. For instance, taking into account subjective factors that may affect the formation of the marriage partners' choice of spouse, were the choices they made really free? If only monogamous marriage makes available certain kinds of satisfaction in a society, in what sense is the choice between marrying and not marrying effectively free? Or again, if the marriage role itself is seen as severely circumscribed by pressures to conform to a social pattern, what importance in the catalog of private freedoms

ibility profiles able to arrange marriages with a given aim, durable happiness, say, in the view under analysis here, even if people were prepared to acknowledge the computer's superiority and that mutual love at the outset is no guarantee of lasting happiness, they would justifiably prefer it as an adviser, like a confidant or premarriage guidance counselor, whose advice need not be sought at all, or if sought not taken, rather than as an agent to whom one's choice may be derogated. What can be properly resisted, then, is pressure to accept the computer's advice, even if it is good advice.[22]

From this perspective one may see how in another society a similar human involvement may be classified as public in some sense that it is not in our own, though it remains private vis-à-vis many other institutions in that society, with the possible consequence that the role or relation into which people enter may not be seen by them as crucially requiring an element of individual choice. The institution of marriage, even when implying some form of consent by the parties concerned, can operate in a community in which marriages are arranged by relations, the purpose being to maintain the social position, the traditions, and reputation of the family or kin-group. Within their perspective such interests may not be seen as hostile to the desires or preferences of marriageable individuals, who are seen as representatives acting in the family's interest, which is their interest. The practice of interdynastic marriages in a monarchy-ridden Europe was on a similar footing, marked, however, by a close conjunction of family and state interests.

---

could then be attached to the freedom to choose or reject a partner? In general, classical liberalism tended to focus on the option to *enter* certain roles and relations (freedom of contract, the career open to talents) and commitments (religious belief or disbelief), making certain assumptions about the conditions and consequences of choices, social and psychological, which, for example, Marxism and Freudian analysis called into question. Some implications of these remarks are briefly followed up at the end of Section IV.

[22] Nowadays there are more commonly corresponding ways of conceiving the nature and value of the whole sphere of sexual relations such as to bring it under the banner of private freedom. In the terms thus far used here, these represent, at least in part, attempts to reject, or possibly to expand, the type of private relations hitherto officially (or at any rate in some social groups, conventionally) reserved to only male and female in the role of marriage partner.

Although such marriages, once contracted (possibly under duress), might carry a bonus of conjugal affection and devotion, and possibly on that account a crumb of comfort to the critical liberal by providing a ground for arguing that the same couple might have wished to marry had they both had freedom of choice and sufficient knowledge of the future, plainly the main point was not to give effect to the preferences of the individuals —preferences conceived, of course, in abstraction from their family responsibilities and in terms of what the liberal takes to be the centrally relevant reason for marrying.

The liberal critic may be prepared to concede, should the facts justify it, that the intimacy which, at least in part, makes marriage informally what it is, could well be respected as properly private even in a community which gave people no choice as to whom they married. But he would hardly endorse the thesis that the legitimacy of choice depends on a kind of knowledge of the future of a marriage that could not reasonably be expected of the normal person, though he assumes some minimum of experienced judgment and prudence when he draws the line at minors' right to marry. On the other hand, his defense of individual choice is understood to include cases of people who, without dictation, might dutifully marry for *raison d'état* or *raison de la famille;* although such cases, like some others, may provoke doubts, perhaps founded on evidence as to how choices may be determined by some process of socialization, about whether individuals have chosen "for themselves" or as autonomous agents. Furthermore, resisting the implication of "illusory choices" that one might try to extract from a strong correlation between choice of marriage partner and similarity of social background in the liberal's own society, which he tends to see as one of individually mobile people freed from the yoke of the kin group, the liberal would emphasize that within such socially determined limits there remains a vital element of non-assignability of potential spouses in a marriage free market: this, for him, gives sufficient reality to the choices that are made.[23]

[23] Another dimension to the claim to private freedom in this sphere is that, by an analogy with free economic competition limited by the criminal law and duties arising from the law of tort and specific contracts between individuals, the orthodox liberal associates mutual love as the centrally

It is evident through the thick and thin of these complexities that the liberal sees the invasion of freedom stemming from the way in which the marrying individual is deprived of a choice; instead, his family, or some authority within it, makes the choice. The area of private freedom in relation to some wider community is seen as coextensive with the family unit, and though it is not natural for us to do so, one may speak of the choice of spouse by the family as a decision on a "public" level vis-à-vis the individual. If he had his own preference, based on love, the onus of justifying his claim to choose would be on him in such circumstances. Just how a liberal may characterize marriage, as well as some other relations, activities, and beliefs, as specially relevant to individual fulfillment, conceived in particular ways, and how he sees the making of choices as deeply imbedded in such phenomena, are points on which further comments will be made in Section IV.

III

It is now appropriate to consider examples in our own type of society of conflict between the claims of private freedom, its value conceived noninstrumentally, and those of public policy, such as the promotion of justice, or welfare, or social solidarity.

Suppose that I will not invite black men into my home, but that in the wider community the choice of employees by employers, of house-buyers by house-vendors, of pupils by schools, is restricted for the sake of preventing deprivation to blacks of options normally available to whites. In other words, these latter types of choice are seen as partly belonging to the public (and in one of our usual senses, political) sphere. Furthermore, assuming there are no calls, à la Sorel, for the preservation of the life style and group solidarity of blacks, but on the contrary there are demands in the name of fraternity for fuller social

relevant reason for marrying with open competition, at any rate among as yet unmarried individuals, the hazards of which may be balanced against the benefit of noninterference by family, church, and state.

integration, my preference may then become exposed to criticism and possibly demands for interference.

It would still make sense, however, to hold that whom I choose to invite into my home is not a matter with which the community could properly be concerned.[24] It is not "political" because no evidence suggests that such choices are systematically connected with ways in which blacks are deprived economically and politically. Yet such a view, while implying that it is groundless to complain that I, as a white, am depriving blacks of an intimate relationship with me, also implies that I would have to change my mind should the weight of evidence be balanced differently. Nor might I be content to argue, even if I thought it true, that any attempt to enforce fraternity on this level would in fact fail or be too costly. What might seem the strongest argument is that the very notion of issuing an invitation incorporates a right, which in turn implies choice. But lest this argument should appear to depend directly on property rights (especially the right to exclude others), which would in their turn require justification, I may fall back on another rationale. This would consist in the claim that in this sphere of human relations what is paramount is the kind of satisfaction that depends crucially on personal preference and inclination. To attempt to enforce fraternity, or more strongly, friendship, is to mistake its essential nature. True, invitations may be issued for many different purposes; they may be instrumentally useful, as when I call in the plumber to mend a broken pipe or invite the boss to dinner with the hope of promotion, but they are not useful merely in this way when it comes to friendship or similar personal relations, which are in part constituted by the disposition to issue invitations. In other words, the disposition normally counts, in our society at any rate, as part of what is friendship. Whether or not friendship is valuable intrinsically (or functionally, as part of, though not literally a means to, the individual's health or well-being), in this view not to see the decisive importance of the exercise of personal preference and the scope for choice this

[24] Assuming of course that no criminal actions are committed or plotted in my home, and that what is done there is not a serious nuisance or an injury to my neighbors.

normally implies is not to have a grasp of this human relationship. It would follow that I am not obliged to give reasons for my choice of invitees for friendship's sake; indeed my likes are sufficient reasons.[25]

I have in effect been restating part of the classic liberal distinction between society and the state, by noting the way in which political arguments for classifying something as public may be resisted by the claim that it is, by its nature, essentially private and free. Of course, governments have been known to move the line dividing public and private, though not often for the sake of fraternity; notoriously the South African government, for instance, seeks to prevent racially mixed company and sexual relations.[26] There is, however, another important dimension to arguments about the politicization of the private which has been no more than implied thus far. It may be picked out more clearly by transposing the example of invitations to a slightly more institutional level.

A golf club, all white, may insist that its own affairs are private vis-à-vis the rest of the community, regarding its main purpose, besides golf itself, as extending relations of friendship and sociability that at the same time depend on a network controlled by individual choices. These choices, by whites of whites for membership, may be seen as political in character; and equally, club members, rebutting such a view, may see outside (or, if they exist, inside) agitators as "bringing politics into" a situation normally seen from the inside as nonpolitical. Yet the agitators may reasonably deny that they are arbitrarily introducing a political ingredient into the situation, for it is already there: the social reality they describe is one seen as created not by their agitation but by the club's policy. Each side, one may say, has a theory of social life, which, because it determines the way in

[25] It is a further issue, arguably relevant in this context, whether I must have reasons for liking and disliking people, and on what criteria certain reasons are actually irrelevant or bad. Thus, the blackness of a man's skin may be held to be no more relevant to liking or disliking him as a person than for treating him differently from whites on issues of equality and justice. This issue is not faced by Lucas, who claims that liberty implies unfairness when the exercise of a personal preference is legitimate, as in love, friendship, and the like ("Against Equality").

[26] Immorality Act, 1950.

which reality is depicted, can lead to a conflict as to how human actions and their contexts should be classified. In one view the club rests on a rationale of sport and friendship; in the other, it is seen as a microcosm of a larger community which in other spheres similarly deprives blacks of opportunities. However, the conflict need not be total. The agitators need not be blind to the special points of golf or friendship, but only prepared to override them in this case for the sake of some greater good in their view, and not prepared to accept as a sufficient defense the argument that black men as such are not excluded but merely that, as the criteria of choice are golfing ability and sociability, they are contingently ineligible. Nevertheless, the way in which men on opposite sides, the club members and the agitators, may hold their opponents responsible for creating "the situation," itself given a different account within their own respective terms, suggests that there can be a wider range of normative implications to such accounts of social reality. Such implications may be extracted in the following way.

Although I have tried to be objective and detached in describing this conflict, it may be a real question as to whether it is possible for me or others to remain neutral observers. For even if I saw no interest of mine prejudiced or promoted by the victory of one side or the other, it may well appear that I am taking sides if I suppose that the golf club, all things considered, is essentially private. If I then hedge about this, I may be seen by club members and their supporters as giving theoretical aid and comfort to the other side. Although it may then be argued that my neutrality is based precisely on my becoming caught in the middle—exposed to hostility from each side to the degree that I adopt the account used by one side or the other—this may only presuppose that neutrality consists in being thought by each side to be unfavorable to itself. Yet, even accepting this (for how, logically, could both sides be right?), the possibilities of my remaining uninvolved with both sides may be distinctly limited. If, for example, I were to retreat into a "private" position of indifference, the views held by either side may nevertheless imply, somewhat paradoxically perhaps but sensibly, that such a retreat was itself a political act; and thus a third corner of the argument over the public and the private may develop.

Indeed, in such circumstances, even if it were possible to dispel all reasonable doubt as to whether a neutral position as among all relevant perspectives its attainable, it would still be possible to ask whether it is desirable.[27]

These questions open very large and difficult areas of philosophical inquiry lying beyond the scope of this paper, though not in principle that of its subject. However, the foregoing discussion may have been sufficient to suggest that positions taken in disputes (and even when there are no disputes) about what is public and private depend on the terms for explaining social phenomena, including the nature of the individual, for example, his characteristic involvements and their associated satisfactions or achievements, as well as their wider social context. Since there is not, or at any rate seems not to be, a definitive way of settling the terms (a view which, like its contrary, requires philosophical argument), no analysis of the nature, scope, or importance of private freedom can expect to be definitive: no more than, and for the same reasons as, corresponding accounts of the proper ends and scope of politics.

With these remarks in mind I shall now examine more fully the terms in which liberals have understood some human involvements, by covering a wider range of phenomena that have been characterized in terms implying their necessary independence and therefore their status as private freedoms. Some problems raised by such characterizations will also be identified. In consequence the functions in political discourse of such concepts as the private and the public may emerge more clearly.

[27] Cf. W. H. Morris Jones, "In Defense of Apathy," *Political Studies,* II: 2 (1954), 25–37, where it is argued that citizens have a right to opt out of politics, such a private freedom standing against the politicization tendencies of a totalitarian regime, in which anyone seen as failing in his duty to contribute to a 100-percent voters' turnout counts as a political enemy. It is true that modern democratic theories normally imply a right not to become involved politically, but by legitimating conflicts, at any rate within certain limits, over the public and the private, such theories in principle underwrite attempts by groups that are in conflict to involve a wider public on one side or the other. Although groups in conflict are given no right to compel others to take sides, there can nevertheless be strong politicization tendencies in democratic theories, potentially putting them at odds with liberal theories.

IV

We have seen how a certain rationale of a human involvement, such as marriage or friendship, explains the anti-interference, and specifically antipoliticization, position of liberalism. Stated more generally, this position requires us to see human fulfillment not in terms of one achievement (such as man qua citizen in a perfect community) but of diverse achievements appropriate to man's different powers. He is seen as capable of achievements and satisfactions in a variety of directions. Such involvements may also be seen, as they were by Mill, as constituting some, or several different types of, harmonious whole.[28] But it is by giving an account of the special point of each involvement, each according a satisfaction or achievement not necessarily afforded by any or some others, that the liberal seeks to explain the plurality of values in his perspective.[29] However, it is also important to consider just how the special point

[28] Mill, *On Liberty,* chap. 3, paras. 2, 4, 5, 9.

[29] It will be obvious by now that the ideas here ascribed to liberals, for the sake of bringing out presuppositions and problems in their theories, have had wide currency and a long history. They exist in some minimal form in any society with a division of functions and a system of beliefs which has both instrumental and noninstrumental justifications of activities. Marx, in the *German Ideology,* depicts a "communist society, where no one has one exclusive sphere of activity but each can become accomplished in any branch he wishes." Hegel, in the *Philosophy of Right,* Part III, depicts a community containing diverse values in a diversity of involvements, bringing out the separate value of family life on the one hand, and philosophy, religion, and art on the other. Hegel's importance as a critic of classical liberalism partly consists in his systematic attempt to extract the moral implications of seeing human involvements from a "public" point of view, arguing that such involvements collectively constitute a community's way of life, and that men's understanding of the value of any one involvement, because connected conceptually and in practice with the value of others, is revisable and subject to increasing complexity. In Hegel's view such an understanding requires a fully consistent and coherent philosophy of politics. But this understanding, like social harmony, he seems to argue, is unattainable unless men learn by experience to modify the radical claims made on behalf of the ideals they attach to each of their involvements; they learn this as they see their ideals given institutional or practical form in an actual community. My later remarks on "internal" and "external" characterizations of human involvements bear some resemblance to this Hegelian view of the interplay between the ideal and the real.

of an involvement is characterized. To see it as an essentially free and private thing in a particular social milieu requires an account whose features may be illustrated, if not exhaustively summarized, by the following types of example.

The pursuit of knowledge, the creation or appreciation of works of art, and religious belief are, it is often claimed, understood as containing considerations intrinsic to each. Similar claims have, by extension, been made for loosely formed groups or highly formal organizations, such as universities and churches, which may be seen as promoting their respective values, even if not exclusively by themselves or successfully. The rationale of each is immanent within the structure of thinking and acting which characterizes it. Knowledge, art, and religion are not to be seen as good or bad in terms of phenomena that, *ex hypothesi*, lie outside them, for they are to be appraised by standards immanent in them.[30] To seek the value of art in its political or economic utility is thus to subvert its autonomy,[31] just as to see the family as only a unit for the making of good citizens, or to abolish it for failing in this respect (as Plato advocated), is to destroy a distinctive form of fulfillment and private freedom.[32] On the contrary, to grasp the independent identity of these things implies a readiness to demand control over social conditions or limitations on authorities which threaten their autonomy or internal qualities.[33]

However, the task of explaining the special character and status of each form of human activity and relationship involves making distinctions which may have to cover (or by implication would cover) the full range of human phenomena. It also in-

[30] See R. S. Peters, *Ethics and Education* (London: George Allen & Unwin, 1966), pp. 154-155.

[31] See Stuart Hampshire, "The Conflict between Art and Politics," *The Listener* (October 13, 1960), 629.

[32] As the earlier analysis of "public" implies, the "political" is only one level of public contrasted by liberals to the private. Thus to disavow Plato is not fully to establish the family as a sphere of private freedom in modern terms. At any rate historically in Europe the family's close control by the Church suggests that a secular characterization of the internal nature of family life, no doubt derived from the Church's own teachings, was required before the family could be seen in such terms.

[33] Thus claims made on behalf of certain human involvements to be free of political control may in certain contexts lead proponents into active politics; to limit the jurisdiction of "politics" is a moral-political decision.

volves seeing how given activities and relations answer, instrumentally or expressively, to given needs, or how the needs imply the activities and relations; and marking off spheres of excellence and achievement implies corresponding accounts of what is understood as the essential human capacities, their limits and potentialities. For example, to grasp the intrinsic worth of the pursuit of knowledge requires understanding how and with what difficulties it is acquired, which is connected with theses as to what properly counts as knowledge. In this way political theories depend on theories of human nature, which in their turn presuppose philosophies of mind and knowledge.

In fact it is just in such philosophies that certain possibilities of choice are often defined, and at times the nature of some human involvements has been explained in terms that call for choice. For example, the nature of religious belief or experience may be explained as the acceptance of a body of true knowledge, expounded by God's chosen intermediaries. But if, while upholding the truth of a doctrine, what is seen as inherent in such beliefs is that they must be those of the believer, that it is for him to come to terms with God as best he can, then the way is opened to diversity of conviction, even though commitment is still required. It is to invite men to interpret the truth as each of them sees it. Furthermore, to be allowed (or by virtue of some theory of knowledge to demand) to challenge the whole body of belief as untrue, or as neither true nor false, is to open further possibilities for the individual: either to believe in his own way or not to believe at all.[34]

Similarly, to see artistic creation as essentially the outpouring of the active individual's imagination, of his capacity to conjure up what is novel and striking, and as a necessary way of com-

[34] The suspicion may be well founded that this is a potted version of transitions from Catholicism to Lutheranism to the rationalism of the eighteenth and nineteenth centuries, seen through liberal- or Hegelian-tinted spectacles. Be that as it may, it is only an account of how religious beliefs, and perhaps associated moral and political ones, may come to be seen as matters of private freedom vis-à-vis religious (and allied secular) authorities. Long before Luther and on many occasions since, churches have claimed special immunity against political authority; their claim to be treated as a private enterprise has depended on a particular view of their internal character, namely, their other worldly concerns or their constitution as a community of Christian brothers seeking salvation.

plementing his life as a creature of reason by bringing forth his gifts as a sensuous being, is to imply that dictation is at odds with its nature as an essentially individually fulfilling involvement. In this sense such experience is conceived as "private," in potential opposition to claims made on behalf of some relevant wider community (possibly by virtue of a different view of art, such as Socialist Realism), but not as something occurring in absolute isolation, any more than mathematics would be in an account of its special nature.[35]

Thus accounts of the intrinsic nature of some involvements have far-reaching implications for the manner in which they are classified as either essentially free and private in relation to some wider community or as public. The foregoing analysis has suggested the kind of theory which forms the basis for the belief in areas of private freedom—a belief which functions in political discourse to deflect "public" claims, or to make claims on the wider community, in the name of intrinsically fulfilling involvements requiring scope for individual choice. Of course identifying the "essential" nature of any such phenomenon is a moral activity itself; and to claim that some involvement is "essentially free" is often to make the point that it ought to be free when in fact it is not, while conversely involvements not so classified may

[35] See Hampshire, "The Conflict between Art and Politics." However, these are only examples, as were friendship and marriage earlier in this paper. Although men have at times sought to understand a particular human involvement in terms modeled on some other, my argument implies that one reasonable way of proceeding is to take each phenomenon in turn, explaining how a given way of characterizing its distinctive properties may imply that it is inherently valuable or fulfilling, and that it requires certain choices, such as initially to opt in or out, or subsequently in the course of the involvement itself. Nevertheless, how one characterization is presented may have logical implications for others. Yet not all human involvements have always been described in terms suggestive of their intrinsic value (contracts, for example), though perhaps aspects of them may have been. Typically we tend not to see involvements in trade and industry in such terms (though ways have been tried), but instrumentally. Of course labor in production has its defining characteristics; it has its rules, standards of performance, and appropriate objects. But beyond this labor may be seen, as Marx saw it, as an activity fundamentally marked by its noninstrumental importance. To see it as a species of art, and thus as potentially fulfilling in the way that the creation of works of art can be, is to see it also as inherently "free activity." To deprive men of choices in their labor is thus to deny them both freedom and fulfillment. In this context, see Arendt, *The Human Condition.*

in fact be free. Philosophies create the possibility of not taking a certain human phenomenon on its own terms, as these may be commonly represented at a given time, but of seeing it, as Marx, for example, saw religion, as a social activity without independent validity, the need for which would some day disappear (or would, as in the Soviet Union, be helped to disappear), or of seeing another, as Marx saw labor, as understood and treated merely instrumentally by a society that inescapably does violence to its intrinsic nature as a free, creative activity.

However, in addition to the possibility of conflict over the internal nature of a human involvement and whether it is essentially free in the sense explained above, there are important problems that arise from representing it in such terms. How these problems are contended with may affect, or be affected by, the ways in which agents identify and value the particular freedoms of choice associated with a private freedom. The problems that arise do so because the involvement is not an isolated phenomenon in any actual social world.

Activities, relations, and beliefs, as well as theories about them, exist in social contexts. The pursuit of knowledge, for example, has a history of its own development which cannot be separated from the history of other social phenomena. In general the connections between social phenomena in the same historical context are often so close, even without conscious efforts to bring them still closer,[36] that the liberal pluralist may have real difficulties in preserving the distinctions necessary to his arguments for the independent identity and value of a range of involvements; or the validity of such arguments may be questioned because of the position of such involvements in an actual society. When such involvements are seen in institutions and practices, and therefore as having certain necessary relations with other items in a social structure, it may be difficult to distinguish be-

[36] On an individual level we are often aware of the fact that behavior in one sphere may be relevant to performance in another, and this could become a source of tension. If I drink for fun it may affect my competence as a teacher. Moreover new standards set in one sphere may require instrumental interpretations of what occurs in another; the efficient running of business firms may change the internal qualities of family life for the sake of the breadwinner's career (see Margaret L. Helfrich, *The Social Role of the Executive's Wife* [Athens, Ohio: Ohio State University Press, 1965]).

tween a given phenomenon's "internal," that is, "essential," nature (for example, labor as a species of art, or a university as a community of scholars) and its "external" relations, that is, how its own nature is in fact affected by such other items, and what effects it has on them (labor as assembly-line production, or universities as parts of the job market). At the very least, when such distinctions are made, there remains the problem of deciding whether "internal" or "external" considerations are to carry more weight in a given policy argument.

Adherence to such "internal" descriptions in the face of supplementary or rival "external" descriptions, or acceptance of the validity of the latter (with or without continuing allegiance to some version of the former), has important moral and political implications.[37] Policies and tactics may depend on whether an institution is seen as corrupted, according to a standard determined by its "internal" nature. To assert its status as essentially free and private may involve internal reform or rejection of the institution; or it may involve political, public action, such as rejection of controls exerted by, or disengagement from commitments to, the wider community. And that community, or the state, instead of responding to demands for changes in its own structure designed to meet the needs of the institution, may claim that it is in the public interest to maintain the existing internal identity and social position of the institution.

Thus, for example, a university may claim academic freedom vis-à-vis the wider community by virtue of ideals of objective, politically uninvolved scholarship and free inquiry. There may, however, be disputes as to how far it has fulfilled itself and which factors in the wider social context are compatible with or hostile to its "internal" nature. Such choices as it had made in the past may be seen to have undermined its pretensions to, or possibilities for, academic freedom. Furthermore, the types of option effectively available in a given situation may be in dispute. Some may hold that the situation is such that no relevant option represents an escape from political involvement, others that no real options exist. The differences between Paris and Prague in 1968 over the role of universities in the wider com-

[37] As the example of the golf club began to show.

munity suggest that in different circumstances, as well as within each set of circumstances, there can be different assessments of "internal" and "external" identities, their relations and relative priority, and of the possibilities and significance of choice. The tensions between accounts of social phenomena in terms of their "internal," independent (ideal and abstract) nature on the one hand and, on the other, their positions, achievements, and possibilities in a given social context provide some of the stuff of ideological conflict.

The liberal pluralist may face similar difficulties in distinguishing between what properly counts as the individual (conceived in terms of essential needs and purposes) and what is the social context which makes him what he is and his involvements what they are. Here, too, there are tensions between the ideal value set on something seen as essentially private and free and what is understood to be its actual nature in social reality.

Societies may be seen as both making a range of choices available and limiting them by rules, the types of its activities and relations, and the structure of its prevailing beliefs. Thus, for example, as part of a general picture, liberal in inspiration, of a society affording diverse opportunities for individuals to enter relations at their option (and often with scope to negotiate at entry, or to interpret subsequently), to choose a spouse without dictation may count as one kind of private freedom. That freedom may also be seen as partially extending to the scope for development of an intimate relation in marriage.

However, it is possible to see that the relation, once entered, involves duties and other restrictions that form part of a common social pattern to which couples are expected, and become disposed, to conform. It may become a real issue as to how much an individual can modify the role, which he did not create, or on what conditions he can withdraw from it. Furthermore, the sense in which individuals in a system of marriage by free contract may be effectively choosing (either whether to marry, or if so, whom), may be questioned by analysis of the social and subjective conditions of choice. For example, if preferences are seen as decisively shaped by a socialization process, it may be argued that the freedom of choice commonly assumed to exist is in fact illusory.

By such arguments as these, existing provisions for a human involvement, commonly represented as private and free, may have their value called into question. The involvement may be held to require types and conditions of choice which an existing community excludes or diminishes the chance of having. Hence the contrast between "bourgeois" marriage and ideals of free love as a perfect (if not in some versions of free love a wholly obligation-free) expression of a private freedom. Against the background of such ideals, even if modified, it is possible to see more clearly that justifications of freedom of choice on entering "bourgeois" marriage presuppose that, all things considered, there is sufficient scope for choice and for fulfillment of its general rationale. Recognition of its inadequacies may give rise to reformist demands to modify "external" factors working against fulfillment in it, or to grant individuals greater freedom of choice, or to a plea for acceptance of those seeking the same fulfillment without marriage or to radical rejection of the arrangement itself.

It is worth noticing, however, that up to this last point most examples have represented a conflict between some claim that might be made by a wider community and that which might be made on behalf of a private freedom, presumably to expand or protect its domain. Another possibility is suggested by the clash between ideal characterizations of an involvement and what is taken to be its identity in reality. If we see society as providing unfulfilling or illusory options, and conceive of fulfilling and authentic alternatives, we may be led to reject what is available, as Marx rejected wage labor. To see himself properly as free, in one view of freedom, man must be capable of choosing and therefore rejecting the forms of private freedom made available to him, and of seeing other forms as more faithful to his appreciation of his necessary involvements.

At this point to speak of private freedom may well imply not what is generally meant in a given society, nor even action to establish a new boundary line around a private freedom, but in fact opting out of society. Indeed, at times men may see themselves as having a choice between a quietist withdrawal and radical political action to change society. Although Marx drew very different conclusions from those of Hegel, we may let Hegel, who saw more deeply into many issues reviewed in this paper than any other modern theorist, have the last word on this last point:

> When the existing world of freedom has become faithless to the will of better men, that will fails to find itself in the duties there recognized and must try to find in the ideal world of the inner life alone the harmony which actuality has lost. . . . It is only in times when the world of actuality is hollow, spiritless, and unstable, that an individual may be allowed to take refuge from actuality in his inner life.[38]

[38] *Philosophy of Right* (Oxford: The Clarendon Press, 1942), translated by T. M. Knox, pp. 92, 255. Of course, the particular words quoted, from Part II, were hardly his last on this subject.

3

PRIVACY: AUTONOMY AND SELECTIVE DISCLOSURE

ELIZABETH L. BEARDSLEY

The most dependable clue to the content of the norm of privacy in any given society is found in the nature of conduct held to violate privacy. Alleged violations seem to fall into two major categories: conduct by which one person Y restricts the power of another person X to determine for himself whether or not he will perform an act A or undergo an experience E, and conduct by which one person Y acquires or discloses information about X which X does not wish to have known or disclosed. I shall say that conduct of the first sort is a "violation of autonomy," and of the second sort, a "violation of the right to selective disclosure." Autonomy and selective disclosure will be referred to at times as "moral norms," but occasionally as "facets" of the more complex norm of privacy, though whether the two are indeed best construed as "facets" or "aspects" of a single more complex norm will have to be considered later. I shall discuss autonomy and selective disclosure as *moral* norms, raising some questions about the content and moral rationale of each, as well as questions about their relationship. In these reflections, I shall address myself very nearly exclusively to the *moral* nature and status of the norms under consideration, leaving questions of legal and political theory to those who are qualified to deal with them.

I should add that data concerning cultural and individual variations in attitudes concerning autonomy and selective disclosure will be largely, though not wholly, discounted in what follows.

AUTONOMY

It may seem useful to regard X's "power to determine whether or not he will perform A or experience E" as including two elements: (a) X's power to choose A or E and (b) X's power to bring about what has been chosen. This distinction may or may not be useful in the present context; it will be best to look at it again in connection with a concrete example. In any case, philosophers of mind have shown us how deep the conceptual waters here are, but for my present purposes I shall not need to plumb their depths very far.

It will be convenient at times to represent the two norms of privacy as embodied in moral rules (of prima facie obligation). Thus I shall speak of Rule I—"Do not restict X's ability to determine for himself whether or not he will perform an act A or undergo an experience E"—and Rule II—"Do not seek or disseminate information about X which he does not wish to have known or disseminated." And I shall at times speak of Rule I as the "rule of autonomy" and of Rule II as the "rule of selective disclosure."

Some acts and practices which have long been held to be violations of privacy, and also some for which this charge is currently being introduced, appear to be morally objectionable principally as violations of autonomy. An interesting case to consider in this connection is that of unwanted noise, and the problem of protecting the individual from offensive sound. The claim has been made by some civil libertarians that unwanted noise intrudes on privacy. It "interferes with the individual's right to be let alone."[1] There is something more appealing than clarifying in the phrase "the right to be let alone." The moral rationale for "letting X alone" seems to be our (prima facie) obligation not to restrict X's power to determine for himself whether he will do A, or undergo E, or not. Noise removes his power to choose effectively between sound and silence, or between one sound and another, as features of his immediate experience. Of course noises which (like thunder) are not produced by the intentional acts of human beings, or which (like subway clatter) could reasonably have been predicted by X to be part of an environment into which X has chosen to enter, or which (like the roar of compressed air drills and *perhaps* like some recorded music) have a redeeming social utility, have come to be accepted; questions about "violations of privacy" are often not so much as thought of, as far as most of the din of modern life is concerned.

When we consider unwanted noise as a violation of autonomy, we see that our tentative distinction between (a) reducing X's power to choose whether to perform a certain act A or to experience a certain experience E and (b) reducing his power to perform A or experience E once chosen is not very helpful. The infliction of unwanted noise on X may be regarded equally well as a restriction on X's power to choose (his available options having been narrowed) or as a restriction on his power to bring about what he has chosen (the preferred act or experience being beyond his control). It appears that violations of autonomy need not be subdivided along the lines of our tentatively proposed distinction.

The entire subject of acts of commission or omission that cause or permit deterioration of the environment has been represented on occasion as a violation of privacy.

> In recent years, there has been increasing discussion of the theory that the Constitution protects one's right to privacy of the person. . . . In numerous ways the abuse or misuse of the environment, as sanctioned or encouraged by government, intrudes upon the individual's zone of privacy.

[1] Minutes of American Civil Liberties Union Committee on Privacy, October 8, 1969.

> Obvious examples are noise and air pollution. The use of pesticides is similarly obtrusive. Insofar as government is responsible for these unwarranted intrusions, the individual's privacy has been infringed.[2]

When we are examining the *moral* status of norms of privacy, rather than their legal or political status, we can concentrate on asking why it is wrong to produce or permit certain deteriorations in X's environment, rather than on asking why we should not allow the government to do either of these things. What connection is there, if any, between producing (or permitting) environmental abuse and our norms of privacy? As in the example of noise, it seems clear to me that the operative norm here is autonomy: to abuse X's environment restricts his power to determine for himself whether he will drink pure or polluted water, breathe clean or polluted air, etc. (The fact that drinking and breathing have interesting dissimilarities when considered as "acts" need not detain us here.) Of course it can be argued that the harm or risk of harm done to X and others is moral reason enough to prohibit abusing the environment; but our question is whether we can find a plausible moral rationale in terms of any distinctive norm of privacy. I shall return to this question later in this section.

The injunction against violations of autonomy is so broad and so basic that it can appropriately occupy a place at or near the foundations of any set of moral principles; yet it remains a prima facie rule, and many of the interesting problems involve decisions about when it may be justifiably overridden.

The general sorts of claim that might with some initial plausibility be advanced as justifications for overriding Rule I have become familiar in ethical theory. I cannot do more here than list some of the major sorts, and indicate, somewhat summarily, my own view of the moral force of each. It might be contended that we are justified in overriding Rule I when any one of the following claims can validly be made:

[2] ACLU working paper, "Civil Liberties and the Environment," prepared by the staff for the Due Process Committee. The position set forth in this working paper has not been officially adopted by ACLU.

1. that to violate X's autonomy in situation S will maximize general utility;
2. that to violate X's autonomy in S will maximize X's own well-being;
3. that X *desires* to have his autonomy violated in S;
4. that X belongs to a class of human beings to whom Rule I does not apply;
5. that X, because of some intentional act of his own, does not deserve to have his autonomy respected in S;
6. that a more stringent moral obligation requires the violation of Rule I for X in S.

I believe, though I shall not here defend my belief, that claim 2 may, when and only when certain very special circumstances are present, have a moral force sufficient to justify violating X's autonomy. It must be the case that there is a "clear and present danger" of substantial *harm* to X if his autonomy is not violated.[3] The possibility, or probability, that a violation will *benefit* X, even substantially, does not seem to me to warrant an infraction of Rule I. And violating X's autonomy to avert harm to him is of course much more acceptable, morally, if there are good reasons for judging that X himself does not know of the risk of harm. Claim 1 also may have moral force sufficient to justify violating X's autonomy, but again only under special conditions: here it must be the case that there is a very considerable discrepancy in social utility between respecting and violating the autonomy of X in S. It takes more, that is, to justify overriding some prima facie rules of moral obligation than others, and the burden of justification for violating Rule I is very great. Claim 5 in itself, when unsupported by claim 1 or 2, seems to me to have only limited moral force: considerations of X's deserts may serve as necessary conditions for treating him in certain autonomy-violating ways, but they cannot serve as sufficient conditions.[4] Claim 4 is, in the formulation given

[3] Mill's defense of this point deserves mention, but is too familiar to call for citation.

[4] For a different view of the moral relevance of deserts to questions of this general sort, see the discussion of punishment by D. D. Raphael, *Moral Judgement* (London: George Allen & Unwin, 1955), chap. 5.

above, ambiguous in a certain crucial respect. If to say that there is any class of human beings to whom Rule I "does not apply" means that there is a group whose autonomy as agents we have no prima facie moral obligation to respect, then it seems to me that this is false; hence claim 4 can never be validly made and is morally vacuous. Such characteristics as extreme youth, extreme age, physical or mental disability, lack of certain sorts of experience, etc., which have been called upon in this connection, simply cannot do the job at all, when unsupported by any of the other claims. This is not to deny that the possession of X of a certain characteristic can legitimately serve as a reason for violating his autonomy in S. Still, it must be understood that a genuine prima facie obligation to the possessors of that characteristic is being overridden. Doubtless the least problematic instances concern the treatment of very young children; and even here we may well be grateful for the sensitivity of those few specialists in child development who have cautioned against encroachments on the privacy of children. It is probable that such cautionary remarks are addressed primarily to violations of Rule II rather than violations of Rule I, yet Rule I "applies to" young children along with the rest of the human race.[5]

It is useful to think of X, in this kind of case, an exercising a "second-order autonomy." X's power to determine for himself whether or not he will do A or undergo B may be considered to belong to his first-order autonomy. His power to determine for himself which options, as to acts and experiences, he will keep open belongs to his second-order autonomy. It is conceptually possible for X to elect not to keep certain options open; in such a case, he has violated his own first-order autonomy, but has, in so doing, exercised his own second-order autonomy. What is the moral obligation, in such a case, of Y toward X? This sort of question is not unfamiliar in legal and political theory. In general, it would seem to me that Y need

[5] "Nobody denies," wrote the philosopher who most perceptively discerned violations of autonomy, "that people should be so taught and trained in youth as to know and benefit by the ascertained results of human experience" (Mill, *On Liberty* [Chicago: Gateway, n.d.], p. 72). Such an "undeniable" assertion is likely to arouse a faint uneasiness in today's civil libertarians.

not respect X's autonomy in an area, during a period, or for a class of options in which X himself has explicitly disavowed interest. Thus certain conduct widely regarded as violating Rule I may in a given case not do so; but the burden of justifying a violation of X's first-order autonomy is heavy, particularly with respect to conduct that most people (though possibly not X) would regard as autonomy-violating. Any violation in this kind of case remains prima facie wrong, of course, but the act in question may actually be morally permissible.

It is important to note that claim 3 justifies a violation of first-order autonomy in the name of second-order autonomy. It does *not* permit us to argue that Y is justified in violating X's autonomy on the ground that, although an option for X has been restricted, this does not matter, since the alternative retained, or chosen for X, is the one X himself prefers. To be given what one wants is very different from choosing what one wants, and the norm of autonomy owes little, if any, of its moral force to the claim that autonomous choices are most likely to secure the agent's desires. The autonomy-violating act by which Y gives X what he wants remains actually wrong, as well as prima facie wrong; but a belief on Y's part that he *is* giving X what he wants, and a desire on Y's part to do just this, are relevant to the question of Y's moral culpability for his violation of Rule I.

We must now raise, for brief and rather superficial consideration, the question whether some claim of a sort not represented among our claims 1–5 might also serve as adequate moral justification for violating Rule I. We should scarcely be justified in running through a "complete" list of such possible rules, but one or two general observations may be made. For example, suppose that Y has promised Z that he will do something that would violate X's autonomy: it will not be seriously contended that the moral obligation to respect X's autonomy is superseded by the moral obligation to keep a promise. Indeed, the obligation to respect autonomy appears to me to be an easy victor in almost any conflict of duties I can think of. Certain conflicts with more moral bite to them arise with respect to the norm of selective disclosure and will be mentioned in the next section.

Although I have alluded indirectly to the circumstances in a particular situation in which it is proposed to violate the autonomy of X, I have not yet commented on their role in any general way. Are there kinds of situation in which it is *never* justifiable to violate X's autonomy, so that questions about the moral weight of claims 1–5 do not arise at all? Perhaps there are areas in which autonomy should, for moral reasons, *always* be respected, or in which our prima facie obligation to respect it is particularly difficult to override. Here I think one must conclude that, although the notion of a "zone of privacy" for individuals is valuable in legal and political contexts, its status as a *moral* norm is more debatable. Given that X sets a particularly high value on autonomy in one sphere, and Y on autonomy in another, it does not seem that there is any independent morally relevant consideration based on the nature of the "spheres" by which we can support a judgment that the obligation to respect X's autonomy in S_1 is more stringent than the obligation to respect Y's autonomy in S_2. By "independent consideration" here I mean a consideration not deriving from or supported by one of the claims 1–5 already noted. Of course if we have reason to think that all or most human beings cherish autonomy in certain kinds of situation with a special fervor, then moral rules of thumb are justified. And we have many such, for example, "Don't enter X's home without his consent." But if X places no value on determining for himself whether he is alone in his home or not, then we do not violate his autonomy as a moral offense by entering his home uninvited. If X has no preference for A over not-A, or for E over not-E, then we do not "restrict his options" in any morally objectionable way of arranging matters so that one of these alternatives is unavailable to him: we have here a "technical" but not a "moral" offense. And thus it may be misleading to speak of such a "restriction" as "violating X's autonomy," if X's second-order autonomy has been preserved. Of course we must recognize that X may *develop* a preference in an area in which he has hitherto been indifferent, and thus a way of treating X may be morally objectionable as a potential violation of X's autonomy.

What has just been said is, however, too simple in at least two respects. First let us note that it is not enough to claim that X *is* indifferent to keeping a certain option open: X must himself announce his indifference, so that a violation of his first-order autonomy in the name of his second-order autonomy has been duly authorized by X himself. Plainly for moral rather than legal purposes such authorization procedures may be informal, but it must be established beyond doubt that X wants to restrict his own options in a certain sphere at a certain time. Y's belief about options to which X is indifferent, however correct, cannot serve as a moral warrant for violating X's first-order autonomy; but plainly such a belief *is* relevant to assessing whether, and to what degree, Y is morally culpable for violating Rule I vis-à-vis X.

A second way in which X's own attitudes with respect to violations of his own autonomy are of moral significance concerns the question whether there is any restriction of first-order autonomy that X himself has a moral obligation to avoid. Principles of autonomy are obviously very close to Kant's injunction to treat human beings (oneself included) as ends, never as means only. Can X, in authorizing certain restrictions of his own first-order autonomy, do something morally objectionable? Those philosophers who find that the concept of moral obligation to oneself has no application will answer this question without hesitation, of course. I am inclined to think that it is sometimes preferable, and this for moral reasons, for X not to carry restrictions on his own autonomy beyond a certain point; but this skeletal assertion cannot be fleshed out here. In any case, to turn to something much less controversial, it would probably be agreed that though one person Y can often in good moral conscience abide by another's restrictions of his own first-order autonomy, Y may also in some situations permissibly take steps to change X's attitudes in the matter, and may even have an obligation to try to do so. For example, a parent who recognizes that a small child is growing up without any desire for solitude, might well feel (and have) an obligation to give the child some appreciation for this state, with a view to fostering a maximal development of the child's potentialities of various sorts. To take as final X's *present* interest in keeping certain of his own options open and not others is, in short, not always morally warranted.

It seems to me that the norm of autonomy as embodied in Rule I is so fundamental as to be an ultimate principle of normative ethics. It does not appear possible to give it a utilitarian justification, even in terms of a sensitive and sophisticated rule-utilitarian theory. The discovery that violations of autonomy for certain individuals or groups would maximize utility would leave the moral norm of autonomy quite unshaken.[6]

SELECTIVE DISCLOSURE

The norm of the right to selective disclosure, or, more briefly, the norm of selective disclosure, has been formulated above as a moral rule (of prima facie obligation): "Do not seek or disseminate information about X which X does not wish to have known or disseminated." The first question to consider is whether this principle is anything more than a special case of the principle of autonomy. Are violations of selective disclosure with respect to X morally offensive strictly qua violations of X's autonomy with respect to his determining for himself whether or not he will have known or disseminated a certain fact about himself in situation S? They are indeed morally objectionable for this reason; the question is whether any *other* considerations are morally relevant. Even if the autonomy-violating character of violations of (the rights to) selective disclosure is the whole story here, morally speaking, it is worth noting that autonomy in this area deals with a very special sort of human interest or concern. Restrictions on X's ability to determine for himself what is known or divulged about him do not interfere with his own activity or felt experience, at least in any direct way. We are in the presence of a very special form of interest on the part of X and his species. Considerable emphasis has recently been placed on the continuity between human beings and other animals with respect to the need for control of a certain "territory," the need for the presence, at an optimal saturation, of other members of the same species (neither too many nor too few), and other factors which can perhaps be

[6] Mill's celebrated statement that "mankind are greater gainers by suffering each other to live as seems good to themselves, than by compelling each to live as seems good to the rest" (*On Liberty*, p. 16) is flawed beyond a ready emendation; whatever is at the moral heart of this matter, it is not any form of "gain."

understood in terms of some facet of the concept of privacy. But man, so we may very plausibly claim, is the only animal with a "need" for selective disclosure of facts concerning himself. However, while such a line of thought (for me a purely speculative one) may be useful in dramatizing the distinctive nature of a concern for selective disclosure, it scarcely answers questions about the moral rationale for respecting privacy in this dimension.

Instead of tackling directly the question whether to violate X's right to selective disclosure of facts about himself is morally objectionable *only* as a violation of X's autonomy, it may be useful to inquire into conditions that would justify the overriding of Rule II, with the thought that such an inquiry may uncover dissimilarities between autonomy in general and selective disclosure in particular as moral norms. For this inquiry, the list of claims 1–5 can be used; I shall, again summarily, indicate my view of the moral force of each with respect to the norm of selective disclosure as embodied in Rule II. The comments made earlier regarding claims 1 and 2 in relation to Rule I seem to me to apply to Rule II. We may note that violations of X's (right to) selective disclosure are less likely to cause harm to X or to others than violations of Rule I are, so that the burden of justifying a violation here in terms of *results* (for society or for X himself) may in typical situations be somewhat different. But this consideration does not in itself change the moral status of claims 1 or 2. In any case, harm is where we find it; and since some individuals fervently cherish the right to selective disclosure, any calculations of the results of violating this norm for X in S must be based on an accurate assessment of the relevant attitudes of *this* individual and others affected. Statements made earlier regarding claims 4 and 5 in relation to Rule I also seem to hold good, mutatis mutandis, where Rule II is concerned.

Claim 3, as before, calls for more extended comment. Here the questions concern the moral relevance of X's own attitudes. The moral relevance and force of this consideration seem to be essentially the same for Rules I and II. Of course, that there are enormous individual and cultural and subcultural variations in attitudes toward selective disclosure need scarcely be stressed.

Even a single individual may hold within the suspension of his inner life a mixture of greatly varying attitudes toward the disclosure of different sorts of fact about himself.

Public figures are usually held to differ markedly from the rest of us with respect to their attitudes to disclosure; yet that public figures may also differ markedly from each other has become clear. My morning newspaper quotes an associate of one American president as saying that the latter, in a certain vacation retreat, "doesn't have to worry that every time he scratches himself someone will take a picture"[7]—a remark doubtless calculated to bring to mind the very different attitude on disclosure widely attributed to another American president of another party. That it is psychologically possible for X to wish to restrict his autonomy with respect to selective disclosure in situation S, while Y and Z stand aghast at his willingness to do so, is a fact of life in our society. This imposes a special obligation on Y and Z to ascertain what X's desires in the matter of self-disclosure really are. Projective interpretation of the desires of another on the basis of one's own will not take us very far in this delicate and complex area. Let us note in this connection the words of Professor Alan Westin: "Neither law nor public pressure should force anyone to have privacy if that person, assuming he is an adult of sound mind, wants to give up his privacy for psychological, commercial, or humanitarian reasons."[8]

I believe that this statement can be extended to cover any privacy-related treatment of one person X by another Y—not merely what might be done through law or public pressure. I believe also that the nature of X's reasons for wishing to "give up his privacy" is not morally relevant to Y's obligations in this connection.

Forcing X to have privacy when he does not want it is a violation of X's second-order autonomy. But X's *right* to privacy is another matter. Can *this* be waived? It might seem that a legal obligation on the part of Y, if not a moral one, can indeed be set aside in this way, and this is doubtless true in some spheres. But in the same context as the statement cited

[7] *The New York Times,* Jan. 17, 1970, p. 29.
[8] *Privacy and Freedom* (New York: Atheneum, 1967), p. 374.

above, Westin goes on to add this: "in certain areas of special importance, American law does not allow individuals to consent to waive their rights when there is inequality in the bargaining position, as with statutes outlawing 'yellow dog' contracts. . . ."[9] Thus a *legal* obligation of Y in this sphere may be less affected by considerations about X's own second-order autonomy than Y's *moral* obligation is. The crucial point, of course, is the need for us to assure ourselves, whether we are governmental agents or private citizens, that X, in exercising his second-order autonomy to determine which options he will keep open, "knows what he is doing." This is the importance of the stipulation in the first statement quoted from Westin that X be "an adult of sound mind."

An interesting application of the principle that we must know what X "really" wants concerns the giving of permission to publish data concerning oneself which has been collected in social research. Colvard discusses whether persons who are the subjects of social research should be allowed to look again at material in its final form, to allow for the possibility that permissions given in advance might later be withdrawn.[10]

In general, violations of Rules I and II seem to be justified in the same ways, and to the same extent, so that the inference that selective disclosure derives its moral authority from the more fundamental norm of autonomy has not been challenged. This does not mean that violations of Rule II are always experienced as treatment that jeopardizes one's autonomy in other spheres. Indeed, it seems evident that some individuals find unauthorized disclosure of facts about themselves inherently

[9] *Ibid.*, p. 375.

[10] Richard Colvard, "Interaction and Identification in Reporting Field Research: A Critical Reconsideration of Protective Procedures," in Gideon Sjoberg, ed., *Ethics, Politics, and Social Research* (Cambridge, Mass.: Schenkman, 1967). Colvard's essay also includes an extremely interesting discussion of the moral dilemma posed by the possibility that anonymity-protecting procedures in reporting social research may risk significant distortions of the behavior reported. This is one of the genuine moral conflicts posed by the norm of selective disclosure. See also H. Pilpel, "The Challenge of Privacy," in Alan Reitman, ed., *The Price of Liberty* (New York: Norton, 1968); and Edward A. Shils, "Social Inquiry and the Autonomy of the Individual," in Daniel Lerner, ed., *The Human Meaning of the Social Sciences* (New York: Meridian, 1959).

objectionable. The belief that facts about themselves are learned or disseminated in a way which they have not authorized is to some persons intensely objectionable, even though they might at the same time feel convinced that no harmful or autonomy-violating consequences to themselves would follow.

It has been maintained that it is the possibility that unauthorized information might lead to a low assessment of themselves that appears threatening to individuals who cherish the norm of selective disclosure. Certainly this aspect of the matter cannot be discounted, but it can scarcely be the whole story. I have known persons who object to the unauthorized acquisition or dissemination of information about themselves (for example, by someone who has read their mail) even when they believe that the information places them in a highly favorable light.

The psychological and phenomenological study of attitudes on selective disclosure deserves more attention. Here, however, our concern is with the status of this concept as a moral norm. Perhaps the most interesting question in this area is this: is there any intermediate-level principle that can be adduced as a moral rationale for respecting this norm of privacy? A suggestion worth examining, though it is made in a legal context rather than an explicitly moral one, has been made by Westin. Arguing that the right to privacy rests on the First Amendment, Westin writes:

> . . . the constitutional right to privacy from unreasonable surveillance would seem to rest most securely and properly on the First Amendment. It is time for the Court to recover the precepts of "freedom of communion" and "liberty of silence" that Francis Lieber and Justice Story declared to be what the First Amendment meant to the men who wrote it and to their contemporaries. Freedom of communion means, clearly and unquestionably, freedom to speak, debate, and write in privacy, to share confidences with intimates and confidants, and to prepare positions in groups and institutions for presentation to the public at a later point. The right to speak, to publish, to worship, and to associate cannot survive in the modern age of scientific penetration of house, auto, office, and meeting room unless the courts and public mores install a curtain of law and

> practice to replace the walls and doors that have been swept away by the new instruments of surveillance.[11]

Eloquent as these words are, I do not find them persuasive. The right to communicate freely may conceivably include the right to autonomy in determining under what conditions one will communicate, but surely it does not include the right to determine under what conditions one will be communicated *about,* much less to determine what will be *known* about one. I see no alternative to justifying the norm of selective disclosure directly in terms of the norm of autonomy, and to recognizing the latter as an ultimate moral principle, standing on its own feet. It is reassuring to reflect that Kant understood this even though the author of *On Liberty* did not. One of these great moral philosophers knew what violates autonomy, and the other knew why we should respect it.

In conclusion, it seems reasonable to say that, although some contemporary usage brands as "violations of privacy" acts and practices which violate only the more general norm of respect for autonomy, clarity of thought would be promoted if we restricted the concept of privacy-violating conduct to violations of the right of selective disclosure. The norm of autonomy is, I have argued, what gives our obligation to respect another's right of selective disclosure its moral rationale. But selective disclosure constitutes the conceptual core of the norm of privacy. A manageable distinction can be drawn between those violations of autonomy which violate X's right to selective disclosure and those which do not. One who construes violations of privacy more broadly is likely to use as his operative criterion a line between those violations of the first-order autonomy of X which X himself holds to be violations of his second-order autonomy as well, and those which X does not hold to violate his second-order autonomy. The advantages of a distinction in terms of selective disclosure seem evident.

[11] *Privacy and Freedom,* p. 398.

4

PRIVACY IS NOT AN ISOLATED FREEDOM

ARNOLD SIMMEL

Respect for another's privacy is a legitimate expectation in all social relationships. As a value privacy does not exist in isolation, but is part and parcel of the system of values that regulates action in society. Whenever anyone has anything to do with another person, it may happen that he butts into something which is not his business, or that he improperly touches upon something personal, or that he intrudes upon a private sphere. But the mere ubiquity of a touchy concern for privacy is no proof that privacy is an essential part of a value system. Mutual attractiveness is a value that plays a role in all human relationships. Clearly, standards of attractiveness can change vastly without affecting other values. Privacy has a much more ramified and intimate relationship to the whole structure of human interaction and values, and to the nature of individual personality. If privacy prospers, much else will prosper. If privacy is extinguished, much else that we care about will be snuffed out. If privacy changes, much else will change. That is the point of this paper.

We live in a continual competition with society over the ownership of our selves. Society continues to lay claim to them. Society makes demands upon us, invoking our obligations as good citizens. But we maintain that each of us has the right to be his own man.

In the course of this competition, a territory gets to be staked out that is peculiarly our own. Its boundaries may be crossed by others only when we expressly invite them. Within these boundaries our own interests are sovereign, all initiative is ours, we are free to do our thing, insulated against outside influence and observation. This condition of insulation is what we call privacy.

The competition between ourselves and society takes many forms. The territory that we claim as our private sphere varies with the adversary we face. It is quite a different thing, depending on whether "society" manifests itself as government, or community, school, or employer, neighbor, friend, or spouse. Yet all these situations have something in common. Every assertion of our right to personal privacy is an assertion that anyone crossing a particular privacy boundary is transgressing against some portion of our self. Privacy boundaries, accordingly, are self-boundaries. The self may be an abstract psychological concept or a metaphysical one, but our concern is not with any definition of an abstract concept, but with the social processes that delimit the space of free movement of the individual, and thus define in the course of social interaction a socially agreed-upon concept of the individual, which is reflected in the individual's own definition of his self. Conversely, those individual definitions of self collectively become part of the social definition of the individual. This is important because the individual occupies a central position in our value system. It is different in a culture in which the individual counts for little, where the individual is thought to exist *for* the institutions and not vice versa, be they state, church, family, or whatever. In such a society the self will be different, as will the notion of individual liberty and privacy, if it exists at all.

We get to be what we are by progressively differentiating ourselves from others. At birth we are lot like everyone else, on biological grounds if on no others. Very quickly we let it be known that we are different. Soon we discover that asserting our distinctness is often rewarded with criticism and rejection, while being like others gains us their approval. We return, therefore, every now and then to the comforts of being like others.

But if a man's sole aim is integration, continuity with others, the comfort of being part of his social surroundings, he should never have allowed himself to be brought into the world. "Yanked out of his hyperexclusively ultravoluptuous superpalazzo" (in e. e. cummings' phrase), he is born and weaned and suffers whatever other separations life continues to rain upon him. Without these separations, he could not develop as an individual, neither as a physically distinct organism nor as a psychologically and socially distinct person.

We need to be part of others, of intimate circles, families, communities, nations, part of humanity, and we need to be so recognized by others, to be supported by their approval for our affiliation and our likeness to them. But we need also to confirm our distinctness from others, to assert our individuality, and to proclaim our capacity to enjoy, or even suffer, the conflicts that result from such assertions of individuality. Just as we experienced the separations in early childhood as rejections, so the world tends to experience our demands for individuality as rejections. We can always hope that the world will not react with quite the same anger as an infant, but it's nothing to rely on. This is the price we pay for individuality. The charismatic self —what we perceive in ourselves as different, freedom-demanding, *ausser-alltaeglich,* unquestionable, and worthy of complete loyalty—makes no pretense that the world is a Garden of Eden, but says, like another charismatic figure, "I bring not peace, but the sword."

Privacy, it may be thought, is valued precisely because it helps avoid much of this conflict. Indeed, we retreat to privacy when our expressions of individuality might be too much for our fellow citizens. But that is not the only use we have for privacy. In privacy we can develop, over time, a firmer, better constructed, and more integrated position in opposition to the dominant social pressures. And this is surely one of its central contributions to the development of individuality, of distinct and independent selves. But conflict is an inevitable part of that contribution.

The development of the self through the life cycle consists of an alternation of conflict and consensus with society. Gouldner and Peterson have distinguished between *self-esteem,* based on compliance and the resulting social approval, and *self-regard,* derived from a sense of potency which can manifest itself in indifference or even in opposition to one's social group. The sense of self is said to gain confirmation in consensual validation, which adds to self-esteem and in conflictual validation, which supports self-regard. "It is in part because the self needs periodic consensual validation from others that its sense of separateness from them is painful and it must lower its boundaries occasionally. On the other hand, it is because there can be no self without some boundaries, no self without some differences from . . . others, that the self sometimes seeks out and sharpens tensions with others. . . . The maintenance of the highly developed self entails an endemic rift between self and society."[1]

Erikson[2] sees the life cycle as a series of stages which may be described, at least partially, in terms of developments at the boundary of the self. Thus the first stage of life is said to have as its primary task the development of "basic trust," so that the infant can face the world with confidence and allow himself to be open to experience. If the child does not learn the pleasure of contact, it may establish a self-boundary so removed from the concrete pressures of the external world that the self lacks a realistic basis for healthy development. An extreme disorder that matches this description is autism, a disease that begins to manifest itself in the first year of life by a peculiar lack of relationship between mother and child, the child having retreated from the boundary where interaction between mother

[1] Alvin W. Gouldner and Richard A. Peterson, *Notes on Technology and the Moral Order* (Indianapolis: Bobbs-Merrill, 1962), pp. 44–47.

[2] Erik H. Erikson, *Childhood and Society* (New York: Norton, 1950), 219–231. See also Erik H. Erikson, "Identity and the Life Cycle" in George S. Klein, ed., *Psychological Issues* (New York: International University Press, 1959), 55–100.

and infant usually takes place to an inner region where he is relatively insulated against influence and communication from without. We have here an example of "privatization," the development of "privacy" of a sort that has little to do with any right to privacy. It is a form of isolation, but one which has negative connotations of withdrawal, of insufficient contact with the world to promote integration of the personality or to generate and maintain the regularities within the personality which are necessary for integration and further adaption.

The second psychosocial stage, according to Erikson, has as its central problem the development of autonomy. This is not a mere capacity to operate in relative isolation—though that is part of its meaning—but refers to the self-regulation of action within socially approved limits with pride in the achievement rather than shame or doubt. Erikson suggests that this development in the child will be fostered by the parents' "sense of rightful dignity and lawful independence," which, in turn, depends on their relationships to each other, to employers, to government. It is implied that if parents have a decent, self-respecting sense of self, they can support the development of autonomy in their offspring. A child's failure in this respect is in extreme cases a causal factor in "symbiotic psychoses,"[3] severe mental illnesses associated with the failure to separate emotionally from the mother and to develop clear self-boundaries.

From the third of Erikson's stages, in which initiative is the principal achievement, one particular aspect, intrusiveness, is relevant to our discussion. The child is now capable of intruding into the physical environment; for example, he has not only learned to walk, but can do so freely and automatically. He intrudes into other people by aggressive talking and noise-making. He intrudes with eyes and shovels and other tools into whatever he can. These are experiences which provide much opportunity for learning limits and transgressions, for the feelings of competition, rivalry, and guilt. Here the distinctions between self and other are experienced poignantly.

Of course, the child's age mates reciprocate with intrusion,

[3] See, for example, Jane W. Kessler, *Psychopathology of Childhood* (Englewood Cliffs, N.J.: Prentice-Hall, 1966).

and it becomes necessary to learn to reject intrusion. At this "Oedipal" stage the child also experiences a new sense of privacy in its attempt to reject others' intrusions upon its partly real, partly fantasied relationship to the parent of the opposite sex.

During the next stages, the latency period, one essential task is learning, emphasized by the child's first venture into an extra-familial institution, the school. This experience brings with it not only a sense of competence and self-satisfaction, but also invidiousness and feelings of relative superiority and inferiority. Besides, the child encounters here most explicitly the difference between his own family and other families, between the family and the school, between "us" and the rest of the world. As adolescence approaches, and increasingly during adolescence, affiliation with groups which compete with the family becomes more and more important, both as a possibility and as a reality. At the same time, the competition of one's interests with those of various peer groups becomes periodically explicit. Thus new boundaries of the self are being forged, and new types of boundary become important: the boundaries of the family against other families and the community, the boundaries of the peer group against all comers. This is an important development because now the parent-child relationship is not any more a safely insulated private matter, but subject to competition from the outside. This has implications for far more than meets the eye.

Families have different kinds of privacy boundaries. It is not entirely their doing; it depends in considerable part on what kind of society surrounds them. Consider two contrasting idealized cases. Let us call an *open* family one which is easily accessible to the surrounding community. Without locks on the doors, people pass freely into one anothers' houses, they have relatively few secrets from one another, they mind one anothers' business, and children are supervised and chastised by the neighbors just as often as by their own parents. Clearly the open family is likely only in situations where there is a high degree of homogeneity in the population, where parents do not worry about their children being exposed to influences much at variance with their own values, where, in fact, the activities people engage in are rather similar from family to family. If this were not so, and the families maintained their openness, we would expect greater homogeneity to develop very rapidly. The central ingredient of the process of developing compliance is visibility,[4] and where visibility is high, actions will quickly converge toward a norm. Openness is almost inevitably linked to homogeneity. If families in the community have similar values, this has the further consequence that parents are somewhat relieved of the responsibility to make their children learn the norms of the community and to act in accordance with them. The social pressures impinging upon members of open families from sources outside the family are just the same as the social pressures exerted upon them within the family. In the closed family this is much less likely.

A *closed* family is one which, like our city family, does not admit anyone into the house without special invitation; it certainly does not give children free rein to roam through others' houses. Conversely, it does not permit others to chastise the children.

If the closed family is not different from its surroundings in the first place, by virtue of its relative isolation it is likely to develop some norms of its own. If it does, it will surely take some pride in its particular views and habits. And from this follows an interest in maintaining its individuality. To maintain a difference, a degree of isolation against the outside is necessary, thus reinforcing what boundaries exist against external influence. But children are so peculiarly subject to influence. If they are to maintain and represent their parents' values even when they are out of the immediate control of their parents, these values must be made part of their personalities. This is much less important if the children, whether at home or in the community, are always under the external control of others who think just like their parents. Sociologists talk about two principal processes which keep actions largely in conformity

[4] See, for example, Hans L. Zetterberg, "Compliant Actions," *Acta Sociologica,* 2 (1957), 179–210, which beautifully develops a social-psychological theory of compliance, in which, however, visibility appears as a precondition rather than as a variable. See also the sociological consideration of the matter by Robert K. Merton, in *Social Theory and Social Structure,* 2nd ed. (New York: The Free Press, 1957), pp. 336–337, 374–377.

with the norms of society: *social control,* the exercise of sanctions by others, and *socialization,* the development of conforming self-regulation. In a society, therefore, in which families tend to be closed, we would expect the development of internal controls to play a much larger role in the growing up process than in the more homogeneous society with the open family. Granting that this contrast between the open and the closed family is an oversimplification, it does illustrate an interdependence between boundaries at different system levels. The nature of boundaries between families, or between family and society, has an effect on the boundaries of the personalities that develop as members of these families.

But if it is true, in a rough and general way, that the social system with the open family depends on social control, while the closed family relies much more heavily on socialization, that is, on the internalization of social norms and values, we may anticipate a further difference. Where controls come primarily from the environment, the growing individual must develop a thick skin, since it is on his skin that he is likely to feel the social pressures aimed to enforce his compliance. In contrast, the family that is trying to develop its norms in the personalities of its children requires an open sensitivity, a thin skin, that permits the parents and particularly the parental norms to "get under the skin" of the children. In a sense, the child whose parents try to influence it by external means has greater privacy, the boundaries of its self are closer to the surface; while parents who demand of their child a character structure and a particular character resembling their own, exercise a type of psychological manipulation which reaches into the child's personality far more deeply, granting it less privacy at least during some stages of its development.[5]

There is a remarkable regularity in the pattern we are describing—bearing in mind that we are describing a model of human relationships, which in real life is never so neat, never so clear-cut, and never exists in such splendid isolation from other factors that confuse the situation. The *closed* family demands a

[5] See Arnold W. Green, "The Middle Class Male Child and Neurosis," *American Sociological Review,* 2 (Feb. 1946), 34–41.

degree of *openness* on the part of its members, while the *open* family seems likely to develop a certain *closedness* in its members. Looking outward, the two types of family are likely to prosper in different social contexts. The open family can afford to be open insofar as it lives in a small homogeneous community —a community which, we may assume, will be quite closed to strangers. On the other hand, the city in which small, isolated families have their existence is a relatively open place: anyone can come and go, but, of course, he may not be let into any closed subgroup.

It is easy to find examples of open systems which contain closed subsystems, and of closed systems which contain open subsystems. An open society permits the development and existence of a great many organizations within it. A closed society cannot tolerate any subgroups, since any subgroup appears conspiratorial. Note that while the words "open" and "closed" are being used with somewhat shifting meanings, these meanings have maintained common elements. The open society is one which is open not only to its members but is relatively unafraid of outsiders and open to contact and communication with them. The closed society is likely to perceive itself surrounded by enemies, and thus maintains its borders as an impenetrable barrier. The example of Nazi Germany comes to mind; she declared herself surrounded by enemies and attempted to eradicate all independent suborganizations. They were either forbidden entirely, or incorporated into the state apparatus. This extended to the family, whose boundaries were breached by the demand that party members should spy on members of their families; in particular, children were encouraged to tattle on their parents' conduct.

Other examples of closed groups demanding openness of their subunits are secret societies, which insist on knowing in all detail what their members have been up to, be it by "self-criticism" in the communist cell surrounded by anti-communists, or public confession in a fundamentalist sect, surrounded by the godless. Notice a parallel in the professions: two of the identifying marks of a profession are the insistence on setting the standards for admission and on autonomy of control: no one but a physician is to judge another physician's medical acts.

What control there is of the professional, what open inspection there may be, takes place within the guild. The case of malpractice suits supports rather than contradicts this point. First, they are highly exceptional, and second, there is extreme reluctance on the part of physicians to testify against their peers. But how is it that professionals who perform many vital functions in society are so relatively immune to supervision? Why are they granted so much privacy in the realm of work?

Two mechanisms were mentioned earlier that maintain order in society: social control and socialization. Within some limits these two are functional substitutes for each other: where there is more of one, there can be less of the other. One of the essential aspects of professional training is that *responsibility* must be developed in the candidate; he must learn to function according to professional norms without external supervision or control. In other words, professional socialization must be long and deep enough to ensure the *internalization* of professional norms. This brings us back to our discussion of psychosocial development.

The question of responsibility, while it comes up quite early in childhood, begins to become crucial as children gain a serious measure of independence from their families, as they have relatively much free movement without supervision, and as they begin to have opportunities to dispose of a serious part of the resources of the family—when, for example, they start driving the family car. Clearly adolescence is such a period of accelerating growth of independence. At this stage one needs privacy to engage in the educational conspiracies for adventurous exploration, for opposing the adult conspiracies, and for more intimate voyages of discovery. A particular kind of privacy is necessary when the learning of responsibility is at stake. Not only must there be opportunities for activity which may result in increasingly serious mistakes, there must be a degree of tolerance for idiosyncratic forms of behavior quite at variance with the norms of the older generation.

Tolerance may be seen in certain situations as a functional substitute for privacy. Sometimes it may be greatly to everyone's advantage to be tolerant rather than by intolerant attitudes to terrify people into withdrawal. Tolerance may make it possible to maintain contact and communication with rule-breakers, thus contributing to their rehabilitation; while the retreat into privacy may result in confirmation of the rule-breaking behavior. However, the conditions under which a contact-maintaining tolerance is preferable to the isolating privacy are not clear. If parents feel guilty when their children do not confide every thought and experience to them, the parents may easily become so intrusive that no really independent action, and therefore no sense of responsibility for their own actions, can develop in the child. "Children must be allowed to make their own mistakes."

Of course, it is not true, not even of adolescents, that people want their privacy only in order to break rules with impunity. There is much that we want to do that someone might criticize or ridicule, in spite of the fact that there are absolutely no rules against it. Simply to avoid embarrassment or any other feeling that might interfere with a purely idiosyncratic pleasure is a common motive for privacy. The pleasures of sociability, intimacy, sexual passion tend to be exclusive. Where two is company, three is a crowd. And it goes farther than that: company *à deux* is not merely pleasant—it is a precondition for that part of identity development that Erikson describes as "losing and finding oneself in another." We become what we are not only by establishing boundaries around ourselves but also by a periodic opening of these boundaries to nourishment, to learning, and to intimacy. But the opening of a boundary of the self may require a boundary farther out, a boundary around the group to which we are opening ourselves. Those to whom we open ourselves in greatest intimacy also have the most intense influence on us, and it is independence from them as well as intimacy with them that may be needed to establish our individuality. Even in that most intimate of relationships, marriage, boundaries do not vanish: "Though in wedlock he and she go, each maintains a separate ego."

We have pursued Erikson's scheme of identity development to this point because it calls attention to the recurring phenomenon of opening and closing boundaries of the self. This does not cease at any point of the life cycle, but rather than continuing this sequence of illustrations we now turn to social factors more external to the personality that structure the relationship between the values of individuality and privacy to other social values.

The aspects of privacy that have been mentioned are not given much protection by the law. True, the boundaries between the state and organizations are, to a degree, so protected. Our homes have some legal protection against the state and all other outsiders. Indeed, much of what we commonly describe as "privacy" is protected under the laws of trespass, nuisance, property, etc. But note that the privacy of the marital couple had no explicit legal standing until the 1965 "Connecticut birth control" case (*Griswold et al. v. Connecticut*), which contested, and finally invalidated, a Connecticut statute that prohibited the use of contraceptives to everyone including married couples. For lack of any explicit constitutional protection or any precedent, the Supreme Court Opinion written by Justice Douglas had to rely upon "a right of privacy older than the Bill of Rights—older than our political parties, older than our school system," and this claim was opposed by the dissenting minority on the grounds that there is "no such general right of privacy in the Bill of Rights, in any other part of the Constitution, or in any case ever before decided by this Court." Thus we have lived for a long time with little legal protection of the most intimate forms of privacy, though very general social norms about the rights of the personality and legal protection against violations of the rights of the individual have formed a protective barrier of some efficacy. Much of the essential need for privacy in the development of the self seems quite unprotectable by law. We have seen that the type of privacy granted the child is not independent of the boundaries of the family, and these in turn are not independent of the nature of the surrounding society. Indeed, there is a large range of forms of social control between impulsive interpersonal coercion and the majesty of the law. These intermediate mechanisms are the cement between individual desires to be let alone and the social structures that may, in various ways and forms, protect this interest.

At the beginning of this paper it was asserted that privacy is a territory that gets to be "our own" in an uneasy truce between our selves and society. We shall assert this again as our conclusion. But if the same is said at beginning and end, something should intervene to give this conclusion some meaning or practical usefulness that was not there in the beginning.

It is not true that the competition between ourselves and society is entirely an affair of "every man for himself," though each of us knows times, situations, and moods in which this is by no means an unrealistic assessment of our relationship to the world. If it were in all ways true, we would indeed have the Hobbesian "Warre where every man is Enemy to every man . . . wherein men live without other security, than what their strength, and their own invention shall furnish them withall," and in which we would find life "solitary, poore, nasty, brutish and short." The regularities that social life imposes on itself and on individual life extend beyond the statistical regularities of individual activity that might result merely from self-protective behavior in a hostile environment. Neither parents nor society could stand the development of any individuality in children if individual interests and desires did not, to a degree, grow out of the interests of society, and if individual satisfactions did not become attached to socially valued actions. In other words, the internalization of social norms and values in the personalities of individuals is essential to order in society. This was mentioned earlier in connection with individual development, particularly the growth of responsibility. We must now focus on the part that society supplies, the norms and values that are to be internalized.

The boundaries between men may be truce lines, but they are not continually shifting, not entirely up to accidents of individual behavior or the fortuitous victories or defeats in interpersonal conflict. Nor are these boundaries determined to a large degree by our biological nature. True, our skins are a natural boundary, but the variety of social boundaries, to be seen not only in comparing what is typical in different cultures but also what is typical in different social situations within our culture, not to mention the idiosyncrasies of small social units, all attest to the fact that social systems create these boundaries and define themselves by means of them. Most of these boundaries are not mere physical barriers; indeed, most physical barriers are boundaries only by virtue of socially shared prescriptions not to cross lines which are obstacles more by definition than because they offer any genuine physical resistance.

Just as social norms, by internalization, become internal regulators of individual action, so individual actions, visible to others and calling forth reactions from them, tend to become external forces upon the individual, social facts, as Durkheim would call them, exterior and constraining, and objects of social norms. We can deduce, then, a social as well as an individual interest in privacy: activities that are valuable in their diversity must be protected from too much publicity if they are to be left unencumbered by social restrictions and protected against the ossification that is engendered by too many rules. Social norms may be necessary to assure a measure of agreement about how people should behave, at least as a preventive against the war of all against all, yet every norm is a restriction. "Every law," wrote Bentham, "is an infraction of liberty." How do we manage, then, to keep the potential oppressiveness of social norms from becoming an unbearable reality? It may be said that in important ways we do not succeed in this endeavor, nor will it be argued here that this is a matter for complacency. The question is, how are people restrained from interfering with the liberties of others, and how are the restraining mechanisms prevented from themselves becoming our oppressors?

We have to look for the answer to this question in the structure of society, the patterns of interaction, the web of norms and values. Our protection is not in the good will of individuals, nor in isolated norms, nor in any single institution. Law, an apparently all-encompassing institution, can provide a measure of safety. But as was pointed out earlier, there are realms of action where law is not likely to be effective. Respect for persons cannot be legislated. In families and school respect for individual rights may be generated, or supported, or undermined, or extinguished. But such respect is not exclusively determined by personalities. It will manifest itself in very different ways in different social contexts. How do different forms of the major institutions—community, economy, polity—affect respect for the individual? What are the boundaries recognized in each of these institutional realms? How much conformity is required, and how much visibility? How large a space of free movement does the individual have and what restrictions are imposed?

Fundamental ideas about justice are involved here; for example, the notion of equality, which puts bounds on individual self-expression. What are the dominant values—to maximize the freedom, opportunity, power, and wealth of the leading citizens, or to minimize unfreedom, oppression, and poverty of those who suffer most? The greatest good for some, the best possible average for all, or the least suffering for the most disadvantaged? Whatever choice a society makes will determine many aspects of individual and social action. Whichever of these principles of justice one espouses, one may honestly claim that the individual is a central value, at the root of this choice. Nonetheless, each alternative emphasizes a different set of individual rights as having primary importance.

Consider only the attitudes behind welfare legislation, and their bearing on such invasions of privacy as midnight visits to check that welfare recipients are not living with someone who might provide financial support. If a subsistence income is a matter of right, the question of the "worthiness" of the poor becomes irrelevant.

Consider the balance of rights granted employer and employee in situations in which employees are subjected to various kinds of surveillance and psychological investigation.

Where do the rights of the school and the rights of parents have their appropriate boundary? Are psychological tests appropriate for use by schools, and are parents entitled to know their results? What invasions of privacy occur in the name of mental health, and what controls are lacking to limit the powers of hospitals, clinics, and public health services over the individual?

How are our values about individuality and the self violated by the confusion of moral responsibility and mental health?

Such questions are invariably related to the aims, explicit or implicit, of the organizations that play a role in structuring action, setting standards, making demands, and giving rewards. Do schools exist primarily for the education of individuals, for *their* maximum advantage, or are they primarily acting as personnel agencies for the dominant powers in society? Are mental health services available to maximize the freedom and development of individual personalities, or to minimize public disturbance and bother?

Do the government's needs for security really justify the far-flung investigations into the past of employees? And where are the proper lines of privacy for governmental organizations against congressional committees and the public at large?

Does large-scale organization require the bureaucratic format as we are used to it, or may not a degree of autonomy of small suborganizations provide a measure of power to their members which they are entirely deprived of when they face the large-scale bureaucracy as isolated individuals? Are they willing to trade their anonymity for a sense of community, their privacy for political effectiveness?

If the privacy of the individual is a good thing, so may be the insulation of his group against some influences from the larger organization. But where the privacy of the individual may mean the maximum of freedom for him, the privacy of the group may imply precisely the opposite for the individual. Federal legislation and adjudication has been a great liberator against local oppression, yet small associations are our protection against the tyranny of big government. Are there no criteria that would provide a permanent basis for establishing boundaries between citizens, government, and intermediate organization? Clearly, what is needed for the protection of privacy is a universal agreement on the proper boundaries of the self, the family, and any other social organization; and having found this solution, to embody it in law. Then the degrees of freedom in every realm of action would be plainly spelled out. Our rights to be free from interference, and others' rights to interfere would be clear. And privacy would cease to be a matter of contention.

Not so. Whenever a matter of freedom ceases to be a matter of contention, freedom is in danger. There may have been historical periods in which this assertion would have been less true. But any modern large-scale society that allows any freedom at all contains sufficient contradictions to keep questions of freedom and of the competing rights and obligations of individuals, groups, and the society as a whole unsettled and in a state of debate. Given the size, density, and internal differentiation of population aggregates that we can assume to make up humanity in the foreseeable future, it would be fatuous indeed to think that so great a homogeneity, mutuality, and complementarity of interests would develop among men, that agreement would be universal on how men should behave toward one another, and that all interests would be so finely attuned to all other interests that no conflicts would ever arise. It would be fatuous, moreover, to think that there are final solutions to the conflicts over the rights of the individual. Tastes change, people change, new generations arrive on the scene, technology offers new possibilities of action, new organizational forms emerge. The competition for the territory that is our own will continue; indeed the territory without the competition can never exist for long. We think of privacy as a situation of calm and security from strife. But it exists only by virtue of a temporary settlement of a conflict. This is by no means a pessimistic view. Opposition to freedom raises the issue of freedom. If there were no opposition to freedom, it would have to be invented. It is only in the conflict over the boundaries of the self that individuality develops, that the self gets its definition. But this conflict is not without rules or limits. These rules derive their force from the system of norms and values of which they are an integral part. As is much in evidence, no such system is entirely sacrosanct. A vital society continues to question it, and to keep it in flux. But without it, there would not be a society, no basis for any claims, no freedom, no privacy, no boundaries, no individuals—but only the war of each against all.

5

THE USES OF PRIVACY IN THE GOOD LIFE

MICHAEL A. WEINSTEIN

Privacy, like alienation, loneliness, ostracism, and isolation, is a condition of being-apart-from-others. However, alienation is suffered, loneliness is dreaded, ostracism and isolation are borne with resignation or panic, while privacy is sought after. Frieda Fromm-Reichmann has written of the descriptive interpretations of loneliness that "various different experiences which are descriptive and dynamically as different from one another as culturally determined loneliness, self-imposed aloneness, compulsory solitude, isolation, and real loneliness are all thrown into the one terminological basket of 'loneliness.'"[1] The same criticism can be made of the various phenomenological accounts of privacy which may equate this condition with hysteric neurosis, anonymity, unbridled individualism, or alienation and loneliness. In each case the fact that privacy is highly regarded by the conscious person seeking it is either ignored

[1] Frieda Fromm-Reichmann, "Loneliness," *Psychiatry*, 22 (February 1959), 1.

or introduced as evidence of false consciousness and rationalization. The case for reducing privacy to some other less desired or actually averted condition is apt to be especially compelling in a social order which grounds self-definition in human relationships and interactions. In such a society the quest for privacy is likely to be distrusted and the way from distrust to abhorrence is quickly traversed. In general, the critics of privacy argue that a careful analysis of this condition reveals that it has no redeeming qualities because privacy represents a severance of social relationships, albeit a temporary detachment. Are there good reasons for defending this position or are different phenomena being confused?

Typical of the scholars who reduce privacy to some other condition is Edmund Leach, who argues that ". . . most of us are so deeply committed to being alone in a crowded world that we turn the whole problem back to front: we worry about privacy rather than loneliness."[2] Anthropologists who do field work in a "primitive society" complain about their lack of privacy, but this is a case of false consciousness. Privacy is "the source of fear and violence" and is defined as the creation of "artificial boundaries between men who are like us and men who are not like us."[3] Once the human universe has been sundered by the arbitrary institution of in-groups and out-groups, selves and others, fear of the other appears and the person is ". . . isolated, lonely and afraid because [his] neighbor is [his] enemy."[4] Privacy, on analysis, is really the condition of unwanted isolation accompanied by the emotion of fear and the latent desire for communion. As a phenomenological description this argument is weak. First of all, Leach presumes that privacy appears as an invidious and conventional distinction that a conscious person draws in order to separate himself from the natural condition of communion. The operation is carried out for no apparent reason and it inevitably ends in unhappiness supervening on consciousness. Further, when the distinction is made the person believes that he is proceeding toward a good. Why self-defeating

[2] Edmund Leach, *A Runaway World?* (New York: Oxford University Press, 1968), p. 46.
[3] *Ibid.*
[4] *Ibid.*

activity of this sort is such a prevalent phenomenon is left unexplained. Perhaps being-in-the-world involves an interplay between the poles of communion and separation rather than a dichotomy. If this is the case, privacy may be a condition of ambiguity and productivity instead of a fall from the perfection of tribal wholeness.

Bruno Bettelheim takes a similar approach, maintaining that privacy arises socially through the demands of a propertied elite for separation from others. As the ideology of bourgeois individualism becomes predominant, people begin to perform their bodily functions in seclusion and experience shame about their bodies. Shame breeds alienation from one's body, which results in discomfort in the presence of others. Even more privacy is desired as a futile palliative for the ills of alienation. In the end, bourgeois society leaves people with two selves: a private self with interests that cannot be pursued in public and a social mask for the conduct of human relations. When the conflict between covert and overt demands becomes too sharp, neurosis and hysteria appear.[5] While false consciousness in Leach referred to a departure from the healthy condition of communion, in Bettelheim this phenomenon is connected with a split between mind and body. Instead of fear, shame accompanies privacy and the latent desire is for a reunion of mind and body. Again the argument depends upon the claim that there is a primal experience of fullness which is not available in contemporary society. From a phenomenological point of view this position is difficult, because any demand for privacy will be interpreted as a self-defeating defense mechanism which can only cause more shame. The motives of the conscious person seeking privacy have no standing. However, both Leach and Bettelheim do propose tests in experience. Fear or shame should accompany the condition of privacy. That either of these emotions necessarily supervenes on the condition of privacy is doubtful.

Another attempt to reduce privacy to some other condition is made by Margaret Mead, who asserts that privacy and anonymity are frequently confused. At present many demands for privacy

[5] Bruno Bettelheim, "The Right to Privacy Is a Myth," *Saturday Evening Post* (July 27, 1968), 9.

are rationalizations for a refusal to fulfill one's responsibilities to his fellow man. People do not call the police or give aid and comfort when they see a fellow human being under attack by a criminal. They prefer to remain anonymous in such cases, demonstrating by their behavior that they are immature and too incompletely socialized to accept the duties of urban life. Privacy is sacrificed in favor of social control and solidarity in rural societies, and this normal condition should also prevail in urban societies.[6] Mead, then, equates the condition of privacy with the condition of being uninvolved in the concerns of one's neighbors. Since the natural and healthy life is one of relatedness and solidarity, the demand for privacy is an example of false consciousness about the human situation. While privacy should be accompanied by the feeling of guilt for one's parasitic tendencies, it appears in consciousness as associated with self-righteousness. Unlike Leach and Bettelheim, Mead does not posit a latent desire functioning beneath the wish for privacy. It is not that man must return to an original perfection, but that he must be socialized into acceptance of his proper estate. Thus, false consciousness for Mead is defined in terms of a sociological standard instead of a norm which supposedly operates in the state of nature. In view of this distinction she cannot be criticized for explaining away every demand for privacy as an example of self-defeating activity. It is in the interest of the individualist to shirk his social responsibilities, but what is comfort for the man in the short run is chaos for the society over the long term. Perhaps the most effective response to Mead's argument is the claim that often privacy is sought as a means for deepening one's involvement with others. If being-in-the-world involves polarity between withdrawal and participation, a life of unbroken solidarity with others is as partial as an existence of irresponsible autonomy.

The same critique applies to the arguments of Granville Hicks, who maintains that "complete privacy means complete irresponsibility, which in turn can mean extinction of the personality."[7] Hicks makes the useful point that limitations on privacy are

[6] Margaret Mead, "Our Right to Privacy," *Redbook,* 124 (April 1965), 16.

[7] Granville Hicks, "The Limits of Privacy," *American Scholar,* 28 (Spring 1959), 192.

probably less resented in tightly knit communities than they are in urban settings because restrictions on privacy in urban societies are enforced impersonally: ". . . intimate details of your life are fed into a business machine; the investigator who may get you fired hasn't the slightest interest in you as an individual; the photographer who infuriates you with his persistence is merely doing a job."[8] Simply, the necessity for limitations on privacy is easier to understand in a *Gemeinschaft* setting than it is in the context of a *Gesellschaft,* even though restrictions are equally needed in both situations. It would be foolish to argue that when people perceive that their social relations are constituted in such a way that they minimize personal concern, they will not tend to diminish their involvement in public responsibilities. Hicks at least provides a reason why the conscious person may seek anonymity. However, all demands for privacy are not demands for anonymity in disguise. The activities that occur while the person is in the condition of privacy are at least as important as the bare fact of being-apart-from-others.

The case for reducing privacy to some other condition has been argued along two lines. First, privacy may be interpreted as a fall from the primal condition of social communion or personal wholeness. If the argument proceeds in this way, privacy is itself evil and the demand for privacy is an expression of false consciousness. The claim is advanced that the condition of privacy is accompanied by such unpleasant feelings as alienation, loneliness, shame, and unhappiness. Phenomenologically, this approach is weak because conscious persons actively seek privacy and report satisfaction while in the condition. Second, privacy may be interpreted as an anonymity which allows a person to escape from his social responsibilities. Again privacy is evil and its pursuit as a good a rationalization. There is no claim, however, that privacy is unpleasant; it is immoral. The weakness of this argument lies in its neglect of the full range of reasons why conscious persons seek privacy.

The most striking aspect of the two arguments for depreciating privacy is the fact that they conceal theoretical interpre-

[8] *Ibid.*

tations of human nature. In short, Leach and Bettelheim argue from the position of a moral idealism usually associated with liberalism and radicalism, while Mead and Hicks proceed from a standpoint of moral realism that frequently accompanies conservatism. For Leach and Bettelheim there is a human essence, which is good, and its attainment has been thwarted by social contrivances. Privacy is the unfortunate result of ethnocentrism or class exploitation that breed alienation from self and alienation from others. The condition of privacy is essentially unnatural and would disappear with the discontinuance of ethnic or class distinctions. At best privacy is a flight from exploitation, conflict, and censure, in which the person trades suffering for loneliness. It may sometimes be the lesser of two evils. The human essence, which is defined as either communion or personal wholeness, perhaps has a reference point in a golden age. However, it is certainly not realized in the modern age and awaits fulfillment in the next stage of social development. Both Leach and Bettelheim look favorably upon a younger generation which seems to be less interested in privacy than its predecessors. On the contrary, Mead and Hicks are wary of privacy because they distrust human nature. Man is not so much deprived as he is depraved. In the absence of efficient socialization he will follow his narrow self-interest to the point at which public life becomes chaotic. To allow him satisfaction in his search for privacy means to grant him the right to behave in a socially irresponsible manner. Since the human essence is to be selfish, social policy demands that men be civilized to the degree that they do not destroy the means to life and health. Privacy, therefore, must be restricted, if not abolished.

It is not surprising that moral idealists and moral realists should agree in concluding that privacy should be reduced to some other condition. The one strives for the realization of a human essence which is not yet of this world and regards with suspicion the satisfactions which people claim to attain at the moment, while the other views with distrust the notion that a person may fulfill part of his moral being on his own. More significant is the fact that the claims of both moral idealists and moral realists are contrary to the position of existential phenomenologists because they involve affixing a determinate essence to the human being. If the human being is defined neither as a good soul corrupted by perverted institutions nor a depraved soul who must be kept in line, there may be no reason to scorn privacy in all cases.

Shorn of theoretical interpretation, privacy appears in consciousness as a condition of voluntary limitation of communication to or from certain others, in a situation, with respect to specified information, for the purpose of conducting an activity in pursuit of a perceived good. The variables of choice, limited communication, relevant others, a situational context, activity, and a good to be attained must all be present in the full construction of privacy. Any addition or subtraction of variables will define another phenomenon. For example, if the condition is entered involuntarily, it is isolation when a matter of circumstance and ostracism when a result of the choice of others. Either isolation or ostracism may become loneliness when accompanied by a desire for communication. In the condition of privacy there is no such unsatisfied longing for communication. Since privacy is a condition of being-apart-from-others, limitation of communication is required. However, when communication is restricted because the person believes that the other will misunderstand him because they do not hold common symbols, meanings, or values, there is a condition of alienation from other. While isolation, ostracism, and loneliness may be clearly distinguished from privacy, alienation is closely related to it. Often people seek privacy to perfect their communication with others, to understand why communication has failed. When such efforts to resolve misunderstandings are consistently ineffective, privacy fades into alienation. Privacy demands that there are relevant others with whom communication is possible. If there are no relevant others and communication is limited voluntarily, the condition is one of hermitic isolation. If limitation is involuntary, the condition is one of simple isolation. Privacy must be a function of certain defined situations rather than a condition which persists over all situations. Communication in some situations must be anticipated and even desired or else the condition of withdrawal appears. If no particular activity is contemplated in the condition of privacy, there is a state of mere seclusion. If no good is sought in or as a result of the condition of privacy, there is a state of irresponsible anonymity when an evil is contemplated and simple anonymity when neither good nor evil is contemplated. On the other hand, that type of privacy in which communication to certain others is limited may be called secrecy, while the kind of privacy in which communication is limited from certain others may be called solitude. The situation in which a group of people limits communication to others may be called by the old word "privity."

By no means is this a full phenomenological description of the different kinds of being-apart-from-others. Such a description would include the feelings which accompany each condition and the desires expressed in each condition. However, enough distinctions have been made to proceed with a discussion of the uses of privacy and a defense of this condition as a necessary aspect of the good life. It should be clear that privacy must not be confused with isolation, ostracism, loneliness, alienation, withdrawal, seclusion, or anonymity. It is a phenomenon with its own peculiar structure.

The essential structure of privacy described above is generally consistent with other treatments in the literature. The phenomenological description rendered by Alan P. Bates defines privacy as a structure of a "psychological region"; "Privacy . . . is a structured portion of a person's total phenomenological field. It is differentiated from the total field by the fact that the self is in some degree involved in excluding in some (or possibly all) circumstances, some (or possibly all) other persons from knowledge in the person's possession."[9] While this description really identifies secrecy and does not fully account for solitude, it does distinguish privacy from alienation and loneliness. However, the definition allows for hermitic isolation and withdrawal to be classed as types of privacy. This diminishes the precision of privacy as a condition of temporary and contextual being-apart-from-others. The significant aspect of privacy as a limitation of communication which is also voluntary is maintained,

[9] Alan P. Bates, "Privacy—A Useful Concept?" *Social Forces,* 42 (May 1964), 430.

although even here privacy may be confused with anonymity and seclusion because Bates does not discuss the purposes of private states.

Edward Shils also proposes a similar definition: "We may say that privacy exists where the persons whose actions engender or become the objects of information retain possession of that information, and any flow outward of that information from the persons to whom it refers (and who share it where more than one person is involved) occurs on the initiative of its possessors."[10] Again, solitude is not recognized and the uses of privacy are slighted. However, the situational character of privacy is accounted for.

Once privacy has been phenomenologically described, it remains to identify the activities and purposes which render this condition valuable in the realization of the good life. Just as was the case for commentators who depreciated privacy, there are at least two major kinds of argument present in the essays of writers who think privacy is desirable. On the one hand, privacy may be considered as essential for the maintenance of personality systems and social systems, while on the other this condition may be considered necessary for their improvement. Proponents of the first approach usually find some weakness which they claim is inherent in social relations and then argue that only personal privacy can prevent the dissolution of these relations. For example, Anthony West contends that human beings have both a social self and an actual self. The social self is constituted by activity and attitudes which are consonant with social norms, while the actual self is constituted by personal activities and inclinations. Although the two selves may overlap, it is impossible for the human being consistently to fulfill the social standards because they are too demanding and perhaps inconsistent. People recognize this situation and grant privacy to one another so that each can pretend he is better than he is. Social relations are, thus, maintained and the individual has a sphere of being-for-himself. Such pretense is functional for the maintenance of the social system because it gives people an in-

[10] Edward Shils, "Privacy: Its Constitution and Vicissitudes," *Law and Contemporary Problems,* 31 (Spring 1966), 282.

centive to realize social norms which would not be present if they were continuously confronted with the weak actual selves of their fellows.[11]

Similar to West's treatment is that of Bates, who argues that human beings need privacy for protection against the disclosure of damaging mistakes, for restoring self-esteem after "bruising" social contact, for evaluating strategies in the conduct of social relations, and for rationalizing disapproved conduct and inclinations.[12]

Barry Schwartz has presented the most complete exposition of the position that privacy is a necessary means to system maintenance. He remarks: "The very act of placing a barrier between oneself and others is self-defining, for withdrawal entails a separation from a role and, tacitly, from an identity imposed upon oneself by others via that role."[13] This type of separation between social self and actual self is functional because the person can invisibly transgress social norms and thereby keep up appearances in his social relations, undertake consumption which is disapproved, enact unorthodox postures, and, most important, relax after encounters with unbearable people with whom relations are necessary. In fact, excessive contact with anyone is dysfunctional to the relationship because it is ". . . the condition under which Freud's principle of ambivalence most clearly exercises itself, when intimacy is most likely to produce open hostility as well as affection."[14]

In brief, to the functionalist writers the condition of privacy is valuable because it is a means to lessening the personal tensions which are built into the conduct of social relations. Is the functionalist case phenomenologically sound?

Functionalism can be considered conservatism brought up-to-date. While being-apart-from-others is no longer described as base self-seeking, it is defined as inferior to states of relatedness. The condition of privacy is merely a palliative to relieve the

[11] Anthony West, "Secrets: Why You Need Them," *Vogue* (August 15, 1967), 127.

[12] Alan P. Bates, "Privacy—A Useful Concept?" pp. 432–433.

[13] Barry Schwartz, "The Social Psychology of Privacy," *American Journal of Sociology*, 73 (May 1968), 747.

[14] *Ibid.*, p. 741.

strains associated with social relations. Human existence is an interplay between the poles of publicity and privacy, both of which are unsatisfactory. As social self, the human being shows his best and is yet unsatisfied with it, while as actual self he enacts his weaknesses and must inevitably feel guilty for it. That is, he must feel guilty unless he adopts false consciousness by declaring that the condition of being-apart-from-others is somehow superior to being-with-others. In other words, the condition of privacy serves the latent functions of pattern maintenance and tension management and is justified by the manifest function of providing the individual with a sphere of being-for-himself. The functionalist position, then, describes human existence as tragic. The person must strive to fulfill social norms which are inconsistent and severe. Inevitable failure must be rationalized. The other person is hell because he is known only as role and knows me only as role. However, to know him in any other way would be to know his inferior actual self. Existence, thus, becomes a game of pretending that the actual self is really better than the social self, while everyone recognizes that the condition of privacy is at best a state of rest and relaxation and at worst a stage for the enactment of shameful deeds.

While it is true that in states of despondency and despair this view frequently appears, it is not a compelling description of the uses of privacy. First, the functionalists are ambiguous about the nature of pretense. Does the person really deceive himself that the condition of privacy is superior to states of relatedness? Does he falsify his weak actual self and contrive yet a new ideology or self-image which attributes to him desirable qualities? Is the extreme form of daydreaming in which the person loses consciousness that he is elaborating a fiction the main use of privacy? If all this is so, then the person actually will find privacy preferable to publicity and he will attempt to be rid of social relationships whenever possible. In this case, the condition of privacy would no longer be a means to pattern maintenance and tension management. Instead, it would be disruptive of social solidarity. On the other hand, if the person recognizes the disparity between social self and weak actual self, and perceives that justifications of privacy are merely excuses for letting oneself go, he will resent both the social norms and his own self. He will have consciousness of the absurd and lose commitment to irrational social relations. Again the latent functions will not be performed. In short, the fact that people often do seek privacy as a condition of rest, relaxation, and escape from social norms does not imply that these are the major uses of privacy and certainly does not imply that they are the only uses.

The functionalist approach can be questioned in the same way in which the arguments from moral idealism and moral realism were criticized. An essence is still attributed to the human being. In this case he is a soul divided between natural desires and social norms which restrict these desires. The social norms provide the conditions under which any life at all is possible, so the person must be tricked into fulfilling them. Since he cannot fulfill them consistently, he is granted a sphere of being-apart-from-others in which he can enact socially undesirable behavior without destroying the relational pattern. Of course, the wisdcm of the social norms is never questioned. They are the invariant rules under which the tragedy is played out. As in Mead and Hicks, the human being is an individualist who must be tamed. However, he is tamed here by granting him well-defined states of privacy. Discretion is the better part of valor. Functionalism, then, contains a theoretical interpretation which is phenomenologically inadmissible. The conscious person seeking privacy cannot be seen as a tool of latent social functions. To look at him that way is, in the end, to claim that he would seek privacy in all contexts (if he turns pretense into belief) or that he would never seek privacy (if he perceives existence as pretense).

While the functionalist writers develop a defense of privacy in terms of an essentially conservative interpretation of the human being and an organic theory of society, humanist and religious commentators who look favorably upon privacy carry forward the notion of communion. Essentially, they argue that the highest goods in human relations can only be attained if individuals are granted privacy. One group contends that privacy is essential for realizing the creation of worthwhile cultural objects—aesthetic, scientific, and utilitarian. Thus, Frieda Fromm-Reichmann speaks of states of "creative loneliness" which are "self-induced, and may be voluntarily and alternately sought out and rejected."[15] Such conditions of privacy are prerequisites for the conception of "nearly all works of creative originality," and "only the creative person who is not afraid of this constructive aloneness will have free command over his creativity."[16] Another point of view is held by Georg Simmel, who argues that privacy is necessary for devising plans to alter social relations: ". . . secrecy procures enormous extension of life, because with publicity many sorts of purposes could never arrive at realization. Secrecy secures, so to speak, the possibility of a second world alongside of the obvious world, and the latter is most strenuously affected by the former."[17] A third use of privacy is suggested by Howard B. White, who asserts that privacy is a requirement for the perfection of political understanding: "The greatest and most difficult duty of the private life must be to undermine the assumptions of civil society, provided that they are merely assumptions, that they are undermined in the interest of something better than assumptions, and that the undermining is done in such a way as to appeal only to reasonable men."[18] Finally, it can be argued that the condition of privacy provides an opportunity for experiences which are goods in themselves rather than means to the realization of social goods. Sidney Jourard speaks of "consciousness-expansion" which "illumines a man's being-for-himself, changes his being-for-others, and potentiates desirable growth of his personality."[19] Such development, borne of reflection and experimentation, can only occur in the condition of privacy. From a religious standpoint, privacy may be considered a necessary condition for spiritual growth and experience, both of which demand "a spirit of recollection and contemplation."[20] In either the secular or the religious argument

[15] Frieda Fromm-Reichmann, "Loneliness," pp. 22, 2.

[16] *Ibid.*

[17] Georg Simmel, "The Sociology of Secrecy and of Secret Societies," *American Journal of Sociology*, 11 (January 1906), 462.

[18] Howard B. White, "The Right to Privacy," *Social Research*, 18 (June 1951), 202.

[19] Sidney M. Jourard, "Some Psychological Aspects of Privacy," *Law and Contemporary Problems*, 31 (Spring 1966), 312.

[20] "Technology and Contemplation," *America*, 100 (November 15, 1958), 189.

an "interior man" who must be granted "concentric corridors of protective privacy" is identified.[21]

In all, the writers who defend the condition of privacy as essential to the realization of goods may define desirable private activities as the creation of valuable cultural objects, the contrivance of plans for better forms of social relations, the perfection of political understanding, and the experiencing of significant modes of consciousness. Two questions arise from this discussion. Do these activities have anything in common, and why is the condition of privacy necessary if the goods in which they are supposed to issue may be realized?

All of the activities cited by the commentators who defend privacy are, in Justus Buchler's terms, kinds of query. Query appears when human contrivance "assumes more purposive and elaborate proportions, when the qualitative aspect of the potential product grows in importance. . . ."[22] The consequences of concern with definite purpose and quality are a larger role for contrivance within "the total economy of effort," greater risk that activities will fail to realize objectives, an increased importance for human resourcefulness, more alternatives within the process of contrivance, and greater "rigor of selection and choice."[23] In short, query is the improvement of human judgment, through which life becomes art. As maker is succeeded by artist, "the process of making becomes crucial": "The materials of nature are no longer ready at hand but need as it were to be quarried. The greater the project of contrivance, the less adequate is the surface of nature."[24]

There are several types of query, each of which corresponds to a mode of human judgment. Assertive query aims at compelling assent, through evidence, to judgments of true and false; exhibitive query has as its purpose the creation of "a qualitative whole which needs no alteration"; and active query takes its object as a tenable social relationship.[25] Each of the activities which have privacy as one of their conditions exemplifies a type of

[21] "Let Me Alone!" *Christian Century,* 83 (September 21, 1966), 135.

[22] Justus Buchler, *Nature and Judgment* (New York: Columbia University Press, 1955), p. 60.

[23] *Ibid.*

[24] *Ibid.*

[25] *Ibid.,* p. 80.

query. Frieda Fromm-Reichmann's condition of creative loneliness is essentially a prerequisite for certain kinds of exhibitive query which issue in objects of the fine arts. Howard B. White defends privacy as necessary for the elaboration of assertive judgments concerning politics. Georg Simmel contends that secrecy is essential for the active query which devises new patterns of social relations. Finally, Sidney Jourard and the religious theorists hold that privacy is a necessary condition for query into the modes of human judgment themselves—the most comprehensive sort of philosophical or theological query, which Buchler does not discuss, but which is implied in his analysis of the other modes of judgment.

Thus, it is the category of query which unites the proposed uses of privacy. Most generally, one may seek privacy to increase his understanding of nature, culture, and society, to appreciate or create objects of beauty, to devise or experiment with modes of social relations, or to quest for apprehension of his existence. In each of these cases the claim is not made that all uses of privacy are necessarily moral. One may become an aesthete and renounce his responsibilities, seek understanding of how to construct better gas chambers, attempt to contrive effective propaganda, or become intoxicated with Being. The notion of query does, however, provide a reason why people regard highly the condition of privacy. They believe that it is essential if certain goods are to be realized through query. Further, the notion of query is helpful in understanding why privity, secrecy, and solitude are often treated in a similar fashion. Some kinds of query may be most effectively carried on by a small group, while others may be most suitably effected by a single person. Are people correct in believing that some kinds of query demand privacy for their proper conduct?

Part of the relationship between satisfying query and the condition of privacy can be explained simply by the consideration that most query demands undisturbed concentration. At least some kinds of information must be screened out if the person is to keep his mind on the task he has set for himself. All sorts of activities, from reflection on the consequences of a sales report to criticism of a philosophical argument, require that the person does not have other interests aroused by signals impinging from the outside. Thus, the condition of solitude is essential for the conduct of much query. More interesting are the reasons why secrecy or privity may be prerequisites for carrying on query. All of the components of query—contrivance, risk, a wide range of alternatives, and rigor of selection and choice—define this process as indefinite. Until the person is satisfied that query has resulted in an object which he wants to reveal to others, he will have good reasons to desire secrecy. First of all, if his product is incomplete he will not want others to waste their time judging it. Further, he will not want others to misjudge his capabilities and thereby prejudice them against his final product. The process of query issues in mistaken assertive judgments, ugly exhibitive judgments, and inharmonious active judgments, along the way. If these are allowed to die in secrecy or privity, social communion will be all the more probable. For example, a discussion is much more satisfying when the participants have thought out the problems beforehand than when they come unprepared and rehearse easily resolved difficulties before others. Also, the moral man presumably seeks to minimize the exposure of others to misunderstanding, ugliness, and conflict. Insofar as it is possible he will not burden his fellows with his inferior products. Of course, this does not mean that he will not call upon others for aid when they might help him in his query. Rather, he will recognize that others also have their projects and should not be disturbed without good reason. If, however, others seek to learn about his process of query, he may still have good reasons for maintaining secrecy. The dignity of the human being requires that he be judged only on the basis of those products he decides to make public so long as he is fulfilling his moral obligations. Of course, the person is obligated to maintain secrecy when the other desires information for immoral purposes.

In summary, query necessitates privacy because query demands concentration and implies incompletion and indefinition which may be remedied by the person or the small group. Query itself is justified so long as compelling assertive judgments, beautiful exhibitive judgments, tenable active judgments, and spiritual growth are part of the good life. The experimental nature of query demands that the burden of proof be placed on the person who would deny privacy to an individual who is fulfilling his other moral obligations. Some minimum grant of privacy for each person is morally necessary if only because contemplation is a part of the good life. The human being who understands the full range of his consciousness will be more fit to participate as a full person in his social relations than one who does not have such knowledge. William Ernest Hocking stated the position best when he identified privacy with adventure: ". . . suppose a community which admits privacy for every member, thus adding to the prior common property the now-common property of privacy. In that case there is also added the possibility of making common the experience of the private adventure. The total scope of community is by so much the greater; without the common privacy, no one would have a good story to add to the common experience!"[26]

Phenomenologically, privacy is a condition of being-apart-from-others. It is voluntary limitation of communication to or from others for the purpose of undertaking activity in pursuit of a perceived good. Perhaps it is because privacy is a condition of being that so much of the discussion about it has been confused. A condition is not moral or valuable in itself. Rather, a condition is an opportunity for conducting an activity which may realize value in process or issue in a moral outcome. The two primal conditions of man are being-with-others and being-apart-from-others. Certain activities are possible in each; some activities are excluded in one or the other. There is no guarantee that being in the condition of privacy will result in valuable query. It is maintained that only in the condition of privacy can certain types of query, which may be valuable, go on. To say this, however, is to strictly distinguish privacy from alienation, loneliness, ostracism, isolation, and anonymity. In the interplay between public and private, private states may provide the preparation for communion just as public states may provide the means to spiritual experience.

[26] William Ernest Hocking, "Response to Professor Krikorian's Discussion," *Journal of Philosophy*, 55 (March 1958), 278.

6

SECRECY VERSUS PRIVACY: THE DEMOCRATIC DILEMMA

CARL J. FRIEDRICH

In the legal perspective, the problem of privacy is primarily that of protecting the private sphere against intruders, whether governmental or other. In their well-known article eighty years ago, Louis D. Brandeis and Samuel D. Warren made that the focal point of their treatment of "The Right to Privacy."[1] In this paper, it is intended not to deal with this private range of privacy, but to concentrate upon the public or political implications. Privacy here is linked to secrecy.

Secrecy belongs to the group of phenomena which while ubiquitous in politics are considered morally objectionable or at least dubious, such as corruption, violence, and betrayal (treason).[2] Secrecy has traditionally been condemned by the more

[1] Samuel D. Warren and Louis D. Brandeis, "The Right to Privacy," *Harvard Law Review,* IV (1890), 193–220.

[2] See my "Political Pathology," in *The Political Quarterly* (London), 37 (1966), 70–85. See also on the problem of democracy Francis Rourke, *Secrecy and Publicity–Dilemma of Democracy* (1961).

radical liberal and democratic thinkers, and publicity has been claimed to be essential to desirable public life. Immanuel Kant was inclined to make publicity the touchstone of one's acting morally; secrecy carried the implication of something questionable and presumably morally obnoxious.[3] Bentham thought that parliamentary debates required publicity and was prepared to make it an absolute standard.[4] The argument about secrecy and publicity has continued and is a live subject of controversy in discussions over parliamentary procedure and governmental operations.[5]

It is evident from all this literature that secrecy is found throughout public life, and that some kinds of secrecy, that is, secrecy under some circumstances in some situations, is functional, whereas in others it is disfunctional. When the American constitution-makers provided for publicity as a norm, they recognized that sometimes secrecy might be needed, and it is fairly universally accepted that the fields of foreign and military policy are especially likely to require secrecy, especially in negotiations and in the area of weapons. These are not matters of privacy, obviously, but then privacy is private secrecy, and it is a question whether certain kinds of information or action though private should not be made public. An illustration is Congress requiring that membership in the Communist Party be made a matter of public record.[6] The excesses to which such a line of reasoning

[3] In arguing against rebellion in the essay "On Eternal Peace," Kant argues in Appendix II for a formal publicity, because "without publicity there can be no justice, and hence no law." Every law and rightful claim must be capable of being publicized. He calls it the transcendental formula of public law and states it as follows: "All actions which relate to the rights of other men are contrary to right and law when their maxim does not permit publicity." For the essay, see my *The Philosophy of Kant* (1949), pp. 470–471; a slightly different translation is found in Lewis White Beck's *Immanuel Kant—Critique of Practical Reason and Other Writings in Moral Philosophy* (1949), pp. 340–342. Kant derives from this principle an argument against rebellion.

[4] See my *Constitutional Government and Democracy*, 4th ed. (1968), pp. 363–367, where Bentham is cited and quoted. Cf. also the discussion in Robert Luce, *Legislative Procedure* (1922), pp. 150–151.

[5] James L. McCamy, *Government Publicity—Its Practice in Federal Administration* (1939), chap. I, and pp. 210 ff.

[6] The National Security Act of 1951; see also John Lord O'Brian, *National Security and Individual Freedom* (1955).

may be carried is manifest in the practice of totalitarian regimes which encourage children to report remarks uttered in the family circle to the authorities, if such remarks disclose a hostility to the regime.[7] The great variety in legal rules and actual practice are analyzed by Herbert J. Spiro in another essay of this volume.[8]

Constitutional democracies have, in spite of considerable variations in detail, been inclined to provide privacy (functional secrecy) where such privacy serves the process of democracy (secret ballot, etc.), and also where it does not impinge upon the public sphere (freedom of religion, etc.), or so it seems, but constitutional democracy has been invading this sphere where the safety and security of the political order appears to require it (wiretapping and the like).[9] Such tendencies may be reinforced or obstructed by particular religious and cultural beliefs and traditions, such as the Puritans' moral snooping, and the continental Europeans' acceptance of state supervision and control, as described by Spiro, but such special deviants must not be allowed to obscure the inherent logic of the standard of public interest as the yardstick for striking a sound balance between too much and too little privacy. The dignity of the individual is so crucial a constituent element of the democratic belief system that it calls for recognition except in a clear case of disfunctional secrecy, such as hiding a fugitive from justice or betraying official secrets. In his interesting study *The Torment of Secrecy*, Edward Shils has depicted some of these dilemmas and one can only applaud his conclusion that

> Ideological extremism is the enemy of the privacy and publicity which support our liberties. It is the progenitor of the combination of symbolic secrecy and universal publicity which is so hurtful to them.[10]
>
> The pluralistic society is the society of privacy and publicity. Privacy and publicity are the parallels in the focus

[7] See my *Totalitarian Dictatorship and Autocracy* (with Z. Brzezinski), 2nd ed. (1965), pp. 295 ff.

[8] "Privacy in Comparative Perspective," pp. 121–148.

[9] U.S. Congress, Senate, Committee on the Judiciary, Subcommittee on Constitutional Rights, Summary—Report of Hearings, 1958-1961, "Wiretapping and Eavesdropping," 1962. Cf. also Edward V. Long, *The Intruders—The Invasion of Privacy* (1967).

[10] Edward A. Shils, *The Torment of Secrecy* (1956), p. 238.

of knowledge and sensitivity, of autonomy and cooperation based on affinity.[11]

Functional secrecy, of which allowable privacy is an important part, can only be system-maintaining. It is obviously the heart of the argument in support of secrecy in diplomacy and military policy that is such. The Wilsonian slogan of "open covenants openly arrived at" seems to assume that secrecy in diplomacy is in itself objectionable. But, of course, Wilson himself practiced secrecy, at the Paris Peace Conference and whenever necessary in domestic politics, or he would never have been able to hold the posts of university president, governor, and president. In his *Congressional Government* he recognized a limited sphere for such secrecy, in connection with Congressional committee work.[12] Even so, Wilson bitterly condemned the secrecy of committee deliberations. But such a position has not gone unchallenged. Robert Luce, in his exhaustive work on procedure, after citing Wilson's writings, asserts that "the complete justification of privacy is that its absence would inure to the injury of the public business." Here, then, the functionality is related to the Congressional system. Luce stresses the privacy of Cabinet meetings in England and America. Such arguments, however, do not face the hard core of Wilson's objections to secrecy. In *Congressional Government,* Wilson had put the matter this way: "Legislation, as we nowadays conduct it, is not conducted in the open. It is not thrashed out in open debate upon the floor of our assemblies. It is, on the contrary, framed, digested, and concluded in committee rooms. It is in committee rooms that legislation not desired by the interests dies. . . . There is *not any legitimate privacy* about matters of government. Government *must,* if it is to be pure and correct in its processes, *be absolutely public* in everything that affects it"[13] These last phrases are evidently a radical overstatement. The sound core of it is that secrecy (privacy) should be avoided as disfunctional in the democratic process, unless a convincing

[11] *Ibid.,* p. 235.
[12] Woodrow Wilson, *Congressional Government* (1885), pp. 81 ff. For Luce's criticism, see *Legislative Procedure* (1922), p. 152.
[13] *Ibid.*

case can be made out for its functionality. It is worth noting that Wilson's argument is cast in moralistic terms: "pure" and "correct," rather than "effective" and "successful," are the terms used as measuring tapes for determining the issue.

It has been authoritatively stated that Congress, "although opposing secrecy as a principle of government or of diplomacy, in fact attempts to accommodate its behavior to the existing situation by establishing whatever controls it can over certain areas of secrecy."[14] Departments like State, Defense, and the Atomic Energy Commission, as well as the CIA, are urged to maintain close liaison with the committees of Congress concerned with their work, and the committee work has itself to become secret. CIA has been particularly difficult to control, and the desire of Congress to be "fully and currently informed with respect to its activities" has not been fulfilled.[15] As present the tendency toward, and the willingness to condone, secrecy has been greatly increased in recent years in the United States as well as in other constitutional democracies by the fear that information will be transmitted to Communist powers and their agents. Nor can this fear be treated lightly by any reasonable man who is interested in the maintenance of the political system. All governments are committed to secret service and espionage work. A member of the first Labor government in Britain, the then parliamentary undersecretary for foreign affairs, once gave vivid account to the writer about his inability to learn from the officials of the Foreign Office about these activities. All inquiries were met with stony silence or a "Nice weather today, isn't it?" The background for this attitude is to be found in the Official Secrets Acts.[16] "In sum, the acts make it, firstly, a felony for any person to obtain or communicate secret documents or information for a purpose prejudicial to the safety or interest of the state . . . information that might be useful, directly or indirectly, to an enemy, actual or poten-

[14] Roland Young, *The American Congress* (1959), p. 190.

[15] *Congressional Record,* July 20, 1953, p. 9185 as quoted in Young, *The American Congress,* p. 191.

[16] *Official Secrets Act,* 1911, 1 & 2 Geo. 5, and *Official Secrets Act,* 1920, 10 & 11 Geo. 5, as amended; *Official Secrets Act,* 1939, 2 & 3, Geo. 6.

tial."[17] This even applies to members of Parliament, and is further discussed below.

Intelligence functions have been growing fast in all countries. Confronted with a government openly committed to the espousal of world revolution, all other governments are faced with the problem of how to avert their overthrow by these revolutionary forces. How far can one go in combating them and how much of one's own policy can one permit the agents and accomplices of such a revolutionary organization to know about? These are tormenting questions, which are ultimately an aspect of "reason of state."[18] It is particularly tough for constitutional orders when such combating involves the invasion of privacy as it is likely to do. The protection of the privacy of letters, often a firm constitutional principle,[19] the privacy of telephone communications are in jeopardy, and other similar invasions of the private sphere are part of that world of "intelligence" which has been growing by leaps and bounds. It is characteristic for this world that even the names of the organizations concerned with it are often under restrictions; thus the CIA forbade its officials to state, on calling cards and the like, that they were employed by it.[20] This is a far cry from the publicity which the ideologues of democracy at one time expected to prevail.[21] Instances like the 1967 "scandal" over secret manipulations by the CIA in the field of international education are indicative of the unresolved complexities. In this case the clash between the need for secrecy from the governmental and political view-

[17] Clive Perry, "Legislatures and Secrecy," *Harvard Law Review,* 67 (1954), 768 ff. This article contains a very interesting discussion of these acts, as well as of the secret sessions of Parliament and their relation to parliamentary privilege.

[18] Cf. my *Constitutional Reason of State* (1957).

[19] Art. 10 of the *Grundgesetz* of the German Federal Republic. Judge Leibholz states in his commentary (1966) that no cases had come before the Constitutional Court. The secrecy (privacy) of letters, the telephone, and telegraph *(Brief -und Postgeheimnis)* are declared "inviolable."

[20] See the rather careless but informative *The Invisible Government* by David Wise and Thomas B. Ross (1964); see also Allen B. Dulles, *The Craft of Intelligence* (1963).

[21] Jeremy Bentham, *Essays on Political Tactics,* which begins with the proposition that "at the head of its [an assembly's] regulation the fittest law for securing the public confidence . . . is the law of publicity." (*Works,* vol II, pp. 310 ff.)

point, and the right of the researcher for privacy was particularly pronounced.[22]

The German Basic Law, seeking to anticipate this problem and the need for restricting privacy in security cases, provided in its Article 18 that anyone who "abuses" the privacy of correspondence, telephone, and telegraph by "struggling" *(Kampf)* against the liberal democratic basic order forfeits these basic rights. But such loss and its extent are decided upon by the Constitutional court. The court has been inclined to interpret these provisions very restrictively, so that even an open call for revolution on a broadcasting facility by Dutschke did not give rise to any such restriction of his rights. In the one case that came before the court the government's claim was rejected, because the person had ceased to be "politically active."[23] Besides communications, the Basic Law also protects the home; in its Article 13 it is declared inviolable; it resembles the guarantee in English-speaking countries against searches and seizures, which Article 13 also severely restricts (requirement of judicial order, etc.). Legal restrictions of a general sort are limited to cases of acute danger to persons or to public order and security. This particular right to privacy on the whole is not considered subject to the kind of abuse to which the right of privacy in the field of communications is subject, and that is, presumably, the reason that it cannot be suspended.[24]

In the heated debates over these issues it is often overlooked that secrecy is a main behavior aspect of an effective bureaucracy, whether governmental or private. A good many arguments on behalf of privacy are in fact meant to protect the secrecy of industrial and commercial operations. Rules and regulations looking toward secrecy have played a considerable role in the development of bureaucracy.[25] The determined efforts of all organizations to secrete their more important evidence in controversial and competitive situations shows that such secrecy (privacy) is functional.

[22] See 89th Congress, 2d Session, House Report 1224, "Behavioral Sciences and the National Security," January 25, 1966, especially pp. 30 ff.

[23] Gerhard Leibholz, H. J. Rinck, *Grundgesetz—Kommentar* (1966), p. 211.

[24] *Ibid.*, pp. 183 ff.

[25] See my *Constitutional Government and Democracy,* 4th ed. (1968), pp. 55 ff., for a fuller treatment.

Secrecy was defined very broadly in Great Britain at the outbreak of the two world wars in the Official Secrets Acts. The principal activities forbidden under these acts are (1) the obtaining and (2) the communication of material which is secret provided these are done with the intent of injuring the state. It is furthermore made a misdemeanor (1) for any person holding or having held a Crown office to communicate to anyone "official" documents or information without authorization, (2) for any person having reason to believe it is communicated in contravention of the statute to receive "official" information voluntarily, and (3) ordinarily, for anyone having received such information to communicate it further.[26] The problems raised by this kind of legislation affected even Sir Winston Churchill and other prominent members of Parliament. The "privacy" (secrecy) of the government has here, and in other similar legislation elsewhere, been very widely extended. Similarly in the United States, official secrets have, in conjunction with the nuclear arms race, been extended to cover a good deal of industrial activity. The need for official secrecy has, under the heading of security, been extended at the expense of private secrecy (privacy) as investigatory activities, prying into the private life of individuals, have become ever more aggressive. Fear of Soviet spies, heightened by the presence of Communists, has not only led to the exclusion of members of this party and its sympathizers from government work in "sensitive" areas, but to more and more elaborate policing by highly secretive organizations such as the Federal Bureau of Investigation. An analysis of the National Security Act of 1951 shows how far privacy has been sacrificed to official secrecy, to put it apodictally.

The secrecy of the bureaucracy under monarchical absolutism was a source of irritation to the liberal forces contending against them. The totalitarian regimes of the twentieth century have not only revived this secrecy, but carried it to an extreme. The secret police is an important feature of these systems.[27] As in the past, these exaggerations have made it difficult to recognize

[26] Cf. C. Perry, "Legislatures and Secrecy," p. 770, whose summary we largely follow here.

[27] C. Friedrich and Z. Brzezinski, *Totalitarian Dictatorship and Autocracy*, 2nd ed. (1965), chap. 14 and throughout.

the functionality of secrecy by the very forces which clamor for the protection of a private sphere. The extent to which the working of bureaucracy depends upon secrecy (and the discretion of its members) is a measure of the extent to which secrecy (and privacy) are functional. Secrecy serves real needs, and its ubiquity is an indication of the extent of such needs. Indeed, human relations would become unmanageable without it, as several other contributions in this volume undertake to argue in detail.

To give an example: a supervisor reporting on his subordinates should be able to speak with complete frankness. If his views are not kept confidential, he will not be able to do so, since he has to continue satisfactory working relationships with the men. All investigatory work requires secrecy for its effectiveness. On the other hand, such operations have a way of expanding beyond what is functional, because of their secrecy. It was recently revealed that 28,000 persons are engaged in intelligence work in Southeast Asia for the United States. Their operational value has been questioned by Congress. But such questioning is itself conceivably highly disfunctional, if such a force is in fact needed for securing necessary information. That such an army of secret agents is likely to invade the privacy of many persons, both of their own country and of foreigners, is more than likely.

One feature of such proliferation of secrecy (and privacy) is that matters are considered secret which are or could be known to everyone. When such secretiveness takes the form of forbidding high officials of the government to express in print their critical views of matters of grave public concern, it becomes disfunctional in a democracy, because this system depends upon an adequately informed public opinion. The much discussed "credibility gap" of the American government in regard to the Vietnam war is largely traceable to the secretiveness with which vital data have been withheld—the allegations of atrocities have found widespread belief among a disaffected public which feels that anything might be true since "they have not been told." The government's rejoinder that much of this information would give "aid and comfort to the enemy" (the traditional formula for describing treason) aggravates the difficulty. At this point secrecy and propaganda may also be closely linked. For not only may the withholding of important information be a part of a propaganda campaign, but certain lines of propaganda may presuppose secrecy, such as the withholding of information about reverses.[28]

In general, it may be said that the inclination of officials and party functionaries to include information on issues of *public* policy under the classification of official secrets is both widespread and harmful. Such information cannot be compared with information about strictly private matters which a doctor or lawyer is obligated to secrete, as is often done. The tendency under the party system to "privatize" policy deliberations by withdrawing the drafting into the secrecy of the upper echelons of the party bureaucracy threatens the functioning of a democratic system. On the other hand, the demand, now often heard in connection with the management of private institutions, such as business enterprises and universities, that their proceedings, such as board and faculty meetings, should be publicized (the meetings of the Harvard Faculty are now broadcast to outsiders over the radio) is a very questionable invasion of privacy that can only be rationalized in terms of socialization (nationalization). The need for privacy (secrecy) was part of their effectiveness, and so great is the functional value of such secrecy that separate informal bodies are formed for the purpose of arriving at the consensus which decisions call for. Bodies are often "defunctionalized" by ill-considered publicity, as happened to the British Parliament and to the plenary sessions of Congress. Many important points cannot be stated in the lamplight of such publicity, and either the party leadership (Britain) or the committee (U.S.) will enable those responsible for policy decisions to maintain the necessary secrecy (privacy). The sphere of secrecy depends upon the task at hand and the setting within which it must be executed, with a presumption in favor of publicity under democratic conditions.

Orwell has, in *1984,* painted a distressing picture of the almost total lack of privacy in a fully developed and technologically advanced totalitarian regime. Through the bugging of all walls

[28] See the Bibliography in chap. XXIII of my *Constitutional Government* (1968), especially the writings of Harold D. Lasswell and his pupils.

in private dwellings the secret police is enabled to ascertain what people say to one another in the intimacy of the home. This particular trend, of which wiretapping is a less extreme case, as is postal censorship, for example, in the armed forces of many countries for the alleged purpose of detecting traitors, defectors, and indiscretions, points to the fact that privacy is closely related to individualism. The idea of the sacredness of privacy grew with the growth of individualism.

To repeat, I am not concerned here with the private aspect of this privacy, individualistic and libertarian, but with the political interest that may be involved. Has it a distinctive function in particular political orders? The privacy of property clearly has in a competitive economy of advanced industrialism. For it serves this very competition, as is demonstrated by the extent to which industrial firms will go in protecting their innovations, such as automobile manufacturers in regard to their car design. But this range of issues is not my concern now. The privacy of the home, of correspondence, and the like is protected and the individual's private sphere thus guaranteed—what value has this for the political order? Perhaps the most patently functional of these privacies is the secrecy of the ballot. The function here is that of insuring that each voter is genuinely *free* to express his or her preference, that neither community pressures nor other forms of intimidation, such as losing one's job or the esteem of one's fellow townsmen, and so forth should interfere with the individual's freedom of choice. It seems in a way contradictory to provide for the secreting of an individual's views on public issues; the traditional American saying "Stand up and be counted" echoes an older and less individualistic conception of a democratic community. Indeed, it has been argued that the secret ballot is a survival of a time when liberal forces in Europe were struggling against an autocratic monarchical state, as in many parts of continental Europe throughout the first half of the nineteenth century. A truly democratic community, so the collectivist argument runs, would not need such secrecy. The argument has a Utopian ring, for the pressures of interest and group continue and in fact become more vocal in an open society.

From the privacy of a man's political convictions, the individual's privacy needs (and hence the functionality of such privacy) spread to other facets of the individual's convictions, more especially in religious matters. Religion in turn involves most of a man's personal conduct and habits, more especially in matters of family and sex. And the argument is essentially the same: only an individual free to shape his own life and that of his immediate human relations is capable of fulfilling the vital function of a citizen in a democratic community, and thus privacy becomes the corollary of democracy.[29] Hence the security needs may come to clash with this personal freedom and produce the torment of which Shils has spoken. But he is more concerned with another torment which results, he believes, from the traditional readiness for publicity characteristic of American society—a trait de Tocqueville had noted.[30] He would contrast it with the British: "The equilibrium of publicity, privacy, and secrecy in Great Britain is more stable and its deviations from the normal state are smaller than they are in the United States." Probably so; I am not here concerned with such national deviations, which are in process of becoming less pronounced all the time. If it is true that the "acceptance of hierarchy in British society permits the Government to retain its secrets, with little challenge or resentment," one wonders what might be the reason for this being increasingly true in the United States. And if "the British ruling class is unequaled in secretiveness and taciturnity," and if "no ruling class [in any democracy] discloses as little of confidential proceedings as does the British,"[31] it may well be a manifestation of the strong individualism of the British tradition, an expression of the sense of privacy which is characteristic of a people for whom their home is their castle, and in turn expressive of the democratic sense of human rights,

[29] E. A. Shils, in *The Torment of Secrecy,* pp. 36 ff., argues that privacy has declined in the United States, in contrast to Great Britain, and that is undoubtedly true. It is also true that this sense of privacy has something to do with Britain's aristocratic past. Georg Simmel, cited below, relates private secrecy to aristocratic conditions.

[30] Alexis de Tocqueville, *Democracy in America,* tr. J. P. Mayer and Max Lerner, pp. 580 ff. De Tocqueville speaks of "private circles" rather than individuals here.

[31] E. A. Shils, *The Torment of Secrecy,* pp. 49 and 47.

and hence rather a sign of the strength of democracy than the reverse. But if so, it is in strong contrast to present-day lines of thought, especially as manifest in youthful protests everywhere, made in the name of democratization. For to these states of mind, democracy means publicity; it is carried to the extreme of insisting that faculty meetings and similar private gatherings be made public[32] in an indiscriminate way. Is this possibly a return to the snooping which characterized the Puritan communities of old New England?[33]

The functionality of privacy and secrecy is inversely related to betrayal and treason. For when in a certain situation the secreting of an act or of an information becomes disfunctional, its betrayal becomes thereby functional. In psychological terms, it may be true, as Simmel has argued, that the lure of secrecy is for the possessor of a secret partly involved in the possibility of betraying it.[34] It gives the possessor of a secret a certain sense of exclusivity to be thereby set apart from ordinary mortals; this may in turn be the cause of the proliferation of secret societies and fraternal orders with their secret rituals and signs in a democratic, egalitarian society. The privacy is in such groups and organizations restricted, however, to the group as such. Between the individual members there is usually a marked lack of privacy.[35] Schindler has argued that the publicity and egality of a democratic society is typically counterbalanced by the ubiquity of clubs and other kinds of exclusive groupings[36]

[32] These broadcasts make it inevitable that one is accosted at unexpected moments, in social gatherings, by persons not belonging to the university faculty about matters on which one has commented in a meeting. Such statements have thereby lost their privileged character, and the cautious man will avoid speaking his mind, having these "galleries" in mind.

[33] Perry Miller, *The New England Mind* (1939). Horrible examples in George L. Kittredge, *Witchcraft in Old and New England* (1928).

[34] Georg Simmel, *Soziologie* (1922), pp. 274–275. Simmel's entire section on the *Geheimnis* is most germane to our subject. This treatise also available in English.

[35] *Ibid.*, pp. 281 ff., discusses the secret societies, under the general assumption that "generally speaking, the secret society appears everywhere as a corollary of despotism and police restrictions." (p. 283), but while this is true, secret societies are also common in the U.S.

[36] Dietrich Schindler, *Verfassungsrecht und Soziale Struktur* (Zurich, 1932), Pt. V, 2; pp. 135 ff.

Simmel, on the other hand, insists that secret groupings are the characteristic of aristocratic and oligarchic societies, and cites in support of his argument the fact that in Venice, for example, the state inquisitors were unknown, and that in certain Swiss towns in their aristocratic days some of the leading families were known as "secret families."[37]

Georg Simmel has formulated another general hypothesis concerning privacy (secrecy), relating it to the degree of civilization. "It seems," he suggests, "that with increasing cultural utility public affairs become steadily more public, while the affairs of individuals become more secret."[38] It seems to me that this development is related to democratization, rather than to civilization in general. For no such trend is observable, for example, in Imperial China or Rome. The "progress" of culture and civilization did not cause any increasing publicity of public affairs; rather the opposite. Hence the Chinese proverb "Those who talk, do not know, those who know, do not talk." And when Simmel writes that "politics, administration, and courts lost their secrecy, while the individual gained the chance of ever greater withdrawal," it seems from the perspective of the *political* observer that both of these trends are the response to democratization; for secrecy loses systemic functionality in a democracy, while it gains such functionality in the private sector, especially if the economy is a competitive market economy. It is not the historical development as such, as Simmel is inclined to surmise, but the growth of participation in politics under increasingly democratic conditions which causes the fact that "what is in its very nature public and concerns all, becomes . . . increasingly publicized; and what has according to its inner meaning a separate being *(Fuersichsein),* the personal affairs of each individual, becomes increasingly private, and thus the chance to remain a secret."[39]

In totalitarianism our century has experienced a sharp reaction in the opposite direction. What concerns all has become increasingly again *arcana imperii,* the secret of rule, as under absolutism in the sevententh century when the doctrine was

[37] Simmel, *Soziologie,* pp. 296 ff.
[38] *Ibid.,* p. 276.
[39] *Ibid.,* p. 277.

developed,[40] while the affairs of individuals are being deprivatized and made a part of "public" records and subject to official inspection.[41] To some theorists this destruction of the private sphere appears to be the core of totalitarianism,[42] although it is in fact a concomitant of other more central political features of these regimes. We have already remarked that in the nightmare of Orwell's *1984* this feature is highlighted, as it is in Solzhenitsyn's *The First Circle*. It is the consequence of the fact that in such a regime privacy has lost most of its functionality, while the secrecy of public affairs has become highly functional once more, rationalized as it is in terms of a revolutionary ideology and its implications. One is tempted to say that the rulers in such a regime find their thought patterns on constant exhibit through the official ideology which reduces the functional need of being "public" on matters of political detail.

In sum, privacy is a special form of secrecy, and secrecy is endemic in all social relations, and hence in all politics. But the functionality of privacy and secrecy are dependent upon the system of which they form a part, and hence their evaluation must vary. At the same time, secrecy acts as a factor of systems influencing each other, and the destruction of privacy and enlargement of official secrecy, and indeed the entire apparatus of the secret police state, has forced democratic states to adapt to the world of totalitarian competition, to increase official secrecy, and reduce privacy by the institution of police and investigatory methods resembling those of the autocratic order. Thereby they have endangered their systemic order and hence their internal security. Some years ago I wrote: "To make the innermost self secure is more vital to the security and survival of a constitu-

[40] Friedrich Meinecke, *Die Idee der Staatsräson in der Neueren Geschichte* (1924). (English ed., *Machiavellism,* 1957, chap. 6.)

[41] A vivid portrayal of this state of affairs is given by Merle Fainsod in his *Smolensk under Soviet Rule* (1958), especially chaps. 7, 13, and 16. A more recent general assessment, but still preoccupied with the Stalinist period, is found in Alex Inkeles and Raymond A. Bauer, *The Soviet Citizen—Daily Life in a Totalitarian Society* (1959), especially chap. IX, pp. 210 ff.

[42] E. G. Hans Buchheim, *Totalitaere Herrschaft* (1962) (Engl. ed. *Totalitarian Rule—Its Nature and Characteristics,* 1968). Concerning this see the discussion by Barber in Friedrich, et al., *Totalitarianism in Perspective: Three Views* (1969).

tional order than any boundary or any secret. It is the very core of constitutional reason of state."[43] Insight into this need for maintaining privacy against all clamor for official secrecy is still missing in many quarters and the trend has been in the opposite direction. The functionality of official and of private secrecy is in a delicate balance. It is difficult at the present time to assess the eventual outcome of the conflict between these two claims for secrecy.

[43] From my *Constitutional Reason of State* (1957), p. 119.

7

PRIVACY IN COMPARATIVE PERSPECTIVE

HERBERT J. SPIRO

James Thurber recalls a French dime novel

> in which, as I remember it, Billy the Kid, alias Billy the Boy, was the central figure. At any rate, two strangers had turned up in a small western town and their actions had aroused the suspicions of a group of respectable citizens, who forthwith called on the sheriff to complain about the newcomers. The sheriff listened gravely for a while, got up and buckled his gun belt, and said, *"Alors, je vais demander ses cartes d'identité!"* There are few things, in any literature, that have ever given me a greater thrill than coming across that line.[1]

The French authors and readers of "Westerns" evidently found it entirely plausible that Americans, even on the frontier, should

The research reported here was assisted by a grant from the Committee on Faculty Grants of the Social Science Research Council.

[1] James Thurber, "The French Far West," *Alarms and Diversions* (New York: Harper & Brothers, 1957), p. 174.

carry identity cards on their persons and be prepared at all times, like continental Europeans, to show them on demand to agents of properly constituted public authority. As a matter of fact, however, United States citizens have not been required to carry any such identification, whether on the frontier of the nineteenth or in the megalopolis of the twentieth century. Indeed, contrary to the practice of continental governments, American governments even today do not supply their citizens with standardized means of identification which, like the German *Personalausweis,* bear both signature and photograph. (Social Security cards specifically carry the legend "Not for identification.") The driver's license seems to be the most frequently used government-issued means of identification—a great handicap to nondrivers, as the humorist Art Buchwald has described. He wanted to pay by check for a typewriter in a Washington discount store, but even his White House Press Corps card was found inadequate as identification by the manager, who somehow regarded nonpossession of a driver's license as un-American.

Credit cards, issued by private firms, probably run a close second to driver's licenses as a means of identification. This is appropriate, since Americans are required to identify themselves more often for private and business purposes than for public and state purposes. It even seems safe to assert, subject to empirical verification, that Americans are readier to respond to demands for identification, and other information about themselves, when these demands come from private organizations or individuals, than when they come from governmental organizations or officials. In continental Europe, the preferences seem to be reversed. The state is entitled and enabled to know all about the private individual, who, in his social relations, even within the family, practices strict privacy or even concealment.[2]

The contrast does not end there. European observers of American mores have often commented upon the narrow scope of privacy, if not the total lack of a *sense* of privacy, on the part of the common man in the United States. On the other hand, American students of continental European societies are occasionally surprised by the reluctance of private individuals to "reveal" the

[2] See Arnold Simmel, "Privacy," *International Encyclopedia of the Social Sciences* (New York: Macmillan and Free Press, 1968), vol. 12, pp. 480–487.

kind of information which their counterparts in the United States would cheerfully broadcast in the interest of good public relations. The same contrast also extends to the behavior of governments and their officials, only that the characteristics are reversed. In Europe—for this purpose including Great Britain but excluding Sweden—secretaries of state still conduct themselves in keeping with the etymology of their title. The activities of government, especially of administration, are secret to a much greater extent than in the United States, where the President's departmental secretaries operate, comparatively viewed, in the glare of publicity.

GERMANY AND THE UNITED STATES

These differences can be illustrated by way of a few German-American comparisons. The German citizen is supposed to carry his *Personalausweis* at all times. He also has to be registered with the Registry Office *(Meldeamt)* and must notify the district registry—until recently the police station—when he moves his residence, even within the same town. There are no similar obligations incumbent upon the United States citizen—a reason, incidentally, why it is much easier in the United States, and also in Canada and Great Britain, to disappear in the sense of the German expression *spurlos verschwunden* (which possibly reflects wishful thinking on the part of those who coined it).

Germans working for wages are required by law to turn over to their employer their personal wage-tax card and insurance record, which list previous employers, periods of employment, and gross pay received in each position. Employees in the United States are required by law to furnish new employers only with their Social Security number. In recent years, as a result of initially controversial federal legislation, American taxpayers have had to disclose, and have had disclosed about them by their banks, dividend-paying corporations, and other sources of income, to the government, for tax purposes, a great deal more information than in the past, when tax-dodging was viewed almost as a sport and getting caught was considered a sign of being unintelligent rather than unethical. Even today, the taxpayer discloses and is expected to disclose to the Internal

Revenue Service only the minimum of information directly asked of him on the relevant forms. So-called loopholes exist to be used, and taxpayers as well as the IRS appear actually to enjoy recurrent battles of wits within the law. An English judge, Lord Clyde, opined in a well-known British tax case that

> No man is under the smallest obligation, moral or other, so to arrange his legal relations to his business or his property as to enable the Inland Revenue to put the largest possible shovel in his stores.
>
> The Inland Revenue is not slow—and quite rightly—to take every advantage open to it under the taxing statutes for the purpose of depleting the taxpayer's pocket. And in a like manner the taxpayer is entitled to be astute to prevent, so far as he honestly can, the depletion of his means by the Revenue . . . (*Ayrshire Pullman Motor Services v. Commissioners of Internal Revenue,* 1929).

In Germany, the *Finanzamt* knows more about the taxpayer to begin with, will suspect dishonesty at a point at which its British or North American counterpart might begin merely to spar, and is therefore likely to initiate official investigations earlier.

To exaggerate the differences: the German state knows all about its citizens, but they know very little about it and very little about one another. The United States government knows very little about its citizens, but they know all about it and perhaps too much about one another. Before a German child leaves home to spend the day with friends or even relatives, his mother typically warns him not to reply to "inquisitive" questions about "family secrets" which will surely be asked of him. The warning is, in a sense, superfluous, because chances are that the child does not know the secrets: his parents have kept them hidden from him. The American child in a similar situation does not receive the warning, although he is likely to have the information—father's income, value of home, cost of vacation—and may be subjected to similar questioning (which will be less inquisitive because of easier access to the "data" inquired about and lower desire for concealment). On a more political level, Americans positively like to be interviewed by attitude surveys and opinion polls and generally respond frankly if superficially to questions, while Germans have tended to view interviewers somewhat more suspiciously and to respond to their queries with greater circumspection, in terms of both their own constitutionally guaranteed right to the secret ballot (*Wahlgeheimnis*)[3] and the possible results of the poll when published. The German federal government, as a result of its citizens' duty to register their residence, has such regular and reliable sources of information that it need not conduct anything like the decennial United States Census, provided for by Article I, Section 2 of the United States Constitution, which regulates the apportionment of representatives.

Americans, otherwise almost yearning to be polled, surveyed, and interviewed, recently protested through their representatives in Congress against invasions of privacy and discrimination, allegedly threatened by the quantity and scope of questions proposed for the Census of 1970. There has also been a great deal of concern in the United States about the risks to privacy of establishing a central government data bank. The abuse of the information or misinformation held by private credit bureaus has also been debated. In Germany, on the other hand, since long before the day of memory banks and electronic computers, and to this day, the state, through the police, and more recently also the registry offices, compiled dossiers on every individual which contained standard vital data and all "legally negative" information available about him, including denunciations by other private persons to the police. When applying for a position involving a modicum of risk, in terms of confidence or money and other valuables, the applicant is normally required by German employers to furnish a police certificate of good conduct (*polizeiliches Führungszeugnis*). Characteristically, German private enterprise relies upon public authority to qualify or disqualify a person for private employment. In the United States, police files, like those of the FBI, are only exceptionally made available to private companies, while governments, in screening their prospective officials and other employees, do normally avail themselves of information gathered by private agencies like credit bureaus.

[3] Article 38, Basic Law. See also Article 10: "Secrecy of the mails as well as secrecy of postal and telecommunications are inviolable. Restrictions may be ordered only on the basis of a law."

PRIVACY AS THE GOLDEN MEAN

Great Britain seems to lie between these two apparent extremes on the spectrum that runs from secrecy and concealment to publicity and public relations. The Englishman's home was his putative castle, in which he sat firmly protected against invasion from the real castles of the Crown by its agents, long before the Supreme Court of the United States held, in 1969, that citizens have the right to own and watch pornographic movies in their homes and are protected against police searches and seizures in at least this private respect. However, the Crown and its agents know as well as their counterparts on the Continent how to guard the secrets of government. In London, the deliberations of the Cabinet are much less likely to "leak" to the press and the general public than in Bonn, Paris, or Rome. As members of Her Majesty's Right Honourable Privy Council, Cabinet members are sworn to preserve what used to be the monarch's privacy and has long since become the public's secrecy. In general, however, the government keeps secret only matters to which "functional requirements" of secrecy actually apply. In the House of Commons, the ("official") Opposition in general debate, as well as private members on both sides of the aisle during the Question Period, will bring out into the open most matters of controversy to which the royal prerogative of privacy-secrecy, as extended by, among other things, the Official Secrets Act, does not apply. As a result, British citizens know more about their government than German citizens know about theirs. They probably think that they know less about their government than American citizens believe themselves to know about theirs, but because of the much lower importance in Britain of government by leak and by public relations, both Britons and Americans may be wrong. In any case, what the former do know about their government—whether it be less or more than what Americans know about theirs—is likely to be more accurate.

The British government knows less about its citizens than the German government about its. Even the National Health Service asks the millions of patients to whom it gives free treatment for a minimum of data. If the United States government knows still less about its citizens, then that may be due more to the greater size and federal structure of the country than to any difference in basic attitudes. People in the United Kingdom know and want to know less about one another in their social relations than people in the United States. This means that Britons are relatively more protected in their privacy against obtrusion from their fellows than Americans, and against intrusion from their government than Germans. These two barriers positively reinforce each other. It does the American little good to know that his government is constitutionally and legally barred from prying into his private affairs as long as a credit bureau or the communications media can both pry and publicize their "findings." It does the German little good to feel confident about his ability to exclude relatives, acquaintances, and unofficial strangers from his private affairs as long as the state knows almost literally all about these and makes some of the information—for example, his previous employment record, including pay received and periods of unemployment—available to certain unofficial citizens like prospective employers.

These superficial comparisons raise certain questions and suggest a tentative refinement of the concept of privacy. Privacy should not be understood as the polar opposite of publicity. The privacy of the individual and publicity for the government seem rather to stand in a dialectical relationship to one another. Unless the activities of government are subjected to the searchlight of publicity, government secrecy can easily serve as a cloak for invasion and destruction of the individual's privacy. Privacy and publicity are not the pathological extremes; secrecy and the manipulation of "news"—or, ultimately, propaganda[4]—are. The same distinction is also applicable to the nonpolitical dimension of "social" relations among individuals. Privacy and publicity—in the sense of openness about activities whose consequences may affect others—stand in a positive dialectical tension with each other. Concealment of other-regarding actions and exhibitionism about self-regarding matters stand in a negative reinforcing relation to each other. This is as true of the discriminatory practices of a "private" country club as of the commercialized self-advertisement encouraged on a television program like "Queen

[4] See Carl J. Friedrich, "Political Pathology," *Political Quarterly*, 37 (1966), 70–85.

for a Day." It applies equally to pollution of the atmosphere by privately manufactured and operated automoblies, and to unsolicited mailings of pornography. The following illustrates the spectrum of attitudes with regard to privacy:

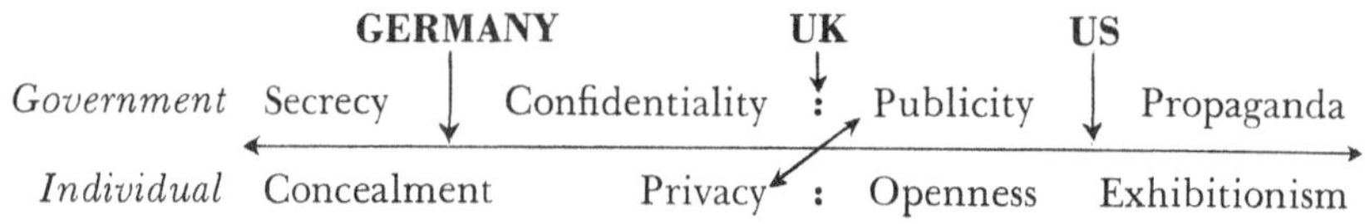

With this preliminary refinement of the concept *privacy,* we can now ask two sets of comparative questions: what accounts for the different locations on this spectrum of the United Kingdom and the United States, and of continental Europe and England?

UNITED STATES AND UNITED KINGDOM

The question about the "uniqueness" of the United States has often been asked. Here I am concerned with only one aspect of that question, and my comparison is not between the United States and all of Europe, but only between the United States and the United Kingdom, or, more accurately and more narrowly, England and Wales. They have shared the Common Law from the beginning, when it was brought to North America by the English colonists who founded their "splinter society."[5] It seems safe to assume that, until the American Revolution, English subjects in the thirteen colonies generally shared attitudes toward privacy with their relatives back home in England, and that Crown officials generally conducted themselves on the secrecy-propaganda spectrum as did their counterparts at home. However, beginning with the Declaration of Independence, individual attitudes and official behavior in the United States have been moving toward the extreme of propaganda/exhibitionism. In case the objection should here be raised that such a movement can also be detected in England itself, as a corollary of technological change, the answer is that it has been much slower

[5] Louis Hartz and others, *The Founding of New Societies: Studies in the History of the United States, Latin America, South Africa, Canada and Australia* (New York: Harcourt, Brace and World, 1964).

in England. On the Continent, technological change seems to have led in the other direction, toward more secrecy by governments and more concealment by individuals. On the other hand, the addition to the population of the United States of millions of immigrants and their descendants from continental Europe has apparently not reduced the trend toward propaganda and exhibitionism here. The central question therefore remains, Why the Anglo-American differences?

By contrast with all their contemporaries in Europe, the United States and certain of its preceding colonial governments were actually *founded.* The acts of founding lent substance to the kind of social contract posited by John Locke, who, in turn, had been influenced by his familiarity with these colonial foundations. Locke *seemed* to draw a distinction between "society" and "government."[6] His work easily lent itself to such an interpretation by people whose experience suggested to them that society would go on more or less the same, after one government had been overthrown and replaced by another government, which is precisely what happened in the course of the American Revolution. That Locke intended to distinguish between the two was made especially plausible by the adversary relations which he posited between a rebellious people and its government, apparently the legislature unfaithful to its trust. Since the legislature is normally supposed to function as impartial umpire in disputes between other adversaries, it cannot perform this role of judge in a dispute to which it is a party itself. Therefore, "Heaven" becomes the judge to which the two adversaries—the people and the government—appeal.[7] Victory in the rebellion gives the verdict of Heaven, whereupon the people, if victorious, can institute a new government.

In the American revolutionary and postrevolutionary context,

[6] See Peter Laslett, ed., *Locke's Two Treatises of Government* (Cambridge: Cambridge University Press, 1960), p. 155 and *passim.*

[7] "241. But farther, this Question, *(Who shall be Judge?)* cannot mean, that there is no Judge at all. For where there is no Judicature on Earth, to decide Controversies amongst Men, *God* in Heaven is *Judge;* . . ." *Ibid.,* chap. 19, "Of the Dissolution of Government," p. 445. See also the *Declaration of Independence:* "We, therefore, the Representatives of the United States of America, in General Congress, Assembled, appealing to the Supreme Judge of the world for the rectitude of our intentions . . ." in the struggle against the "present King of Great Britain."

where "the great Mr. Locke" enjoyed enormous popularity at least until the Civil War,[8] these teachings, so understood, may have led to an exaggeration of Locke's apparent distinction between society and government—which he, in turn, may have derived from the Christian tradition of conflict between temporal and spiritual authorities. American "society" had actually defied the English Crown in the revolutionaries' appeal to Heaven. From thence forward, relations between the "people" and the Crown's successors, that is, government, were seen in, and constitutionally molded into, adversary opposition. The Constitution of the United States can be interpreted to have permanently opposed to each other, in an adversary relationship, "society" —that is, the people—represented by the legislative power in the Congress, and "government"—that is, the executive power—represented by the President. The impartial umpire to which these two adversaries can appeal is the judicial power, the Supreme Court.

Subjects of English kings, starting with the barons of King John, gradually won their rights, including those to privacy in its manifold, expanding aspects, as a result of adversary fights. The Bill of Rights, which was added to the American Constitution, lists several of these: against the quartering of soldiers (Article III), violated by George III according to the Declaration of Independence; against unreasonable searches and seizures of citizens' persons, houses, papers, and effects (Article IV); and against self-incrimination (Article V). In their homes and in their minds, the Founders meant to maintain at least as much privacy as they were supposed to have been enjoying previously as English subjects. And this was *pri*vacy in the original meaning given by the *Oxford English Dictionary:* status *de*prived of the public and official.[9] On the other hand, they were not going to permit their new government, that is, the President, to operate with as much secrecy as had been available, in their view, to the Crown. For example, the Constitution requires that the Presi-

[8] Merle Curti, "The Great Mr. Locke: America's Philosopher, 1783-1861," *Huntington Library Bulletin,* No. 11 (1937), 107-151.

[9] *The Oxford Universal Dictionary on Historical Principles* (Oxford: Clarendon Press, 1955), pp. 1586 ff.

dent "shall from time to time give to the Congress Information of the State of the Union . . ." (Article II, Section 3). The Congress, on the other hand, as the people's representative in its continuous adversary struggle with the executive, was constitutionally commanded "from time to time to publish" the "Journal of its Proceedings" ("except such Parts as may in their Judgment require Secrecy") (Article II, Section 3).[10] And Congress was given adequate instruments for enforcing publicity upon the executive. Since it has always been exposed to a stronger searchlight of public scrutiny than the English Crown and its agents, or its continental counterparts—except in Sweden[11]—the American President and his agents have often used what is now called "news management" as an instrument of government and a substitute for secrecy. They have done this even in recent decades, when the requirements of national defense enabled them to make claims for the increasing need for secrecy. Such claims were often advanced by means of the manipulation of news, including, paradoxically, leaks of allegedly secret information.

The arts of "public" relations and advertising were first developed, and are most advanced, in the United States. The publics with which private firms carry on their "public" relations consist of millions of "private" individuals. These "privates" seem to enjoy and to demand a good deal less privacy than their counterparts in England. Compared to their fellows in Germany, they seem quite incapable or unwilling to conceal information about themselves from other individuals or from the general unofficial public. Why this relative lack of a sense of privacy?

[10] The West German Basic Law provides: "The Bundestag conducts its business in public. Upon request of one tenth of its members or upon request of the Federal Government, the public can be excluded by a two-thirds' majority. The request is resolved by nonpublic session" (Article 42, Section 1). The Rules of Procedure of the Bundestag provide: "The deliberations of Committees are not public" (Paragraph 73, Section 1). *Amtliches Handbuch des Deutschen Bundestages—4. Wahlperiode* (Darmstadt: Neue Darmstädter Verlangsanstalt, n.d.).

[11] "All administrative agencies must keep their records open for public inspection; exceptions to this rule, . . . regarding foreign office and military documents, are defined by law." (Dankwart A. Rustow, *The Politics of Compromise: A Study of Parties and Cabinet Government in Sweden* [Princeton: Princeton University Press, 1955].)

Louis Hartz's and Frederick Jackson Turner's theses may complement one another to provide a partial answer.[12] In England, where consciousness of the existence of antagonistic classes left over from the encounters between feudalism and its successors is still firmly embedded, members of each class demand protection of its social peculiarities; hence the clubbiness of all English life, including even modern business and labor organizations. Relatively un-class-conscious Americans, on the other hand, are unaware of social peculiarities, except those caused by economic differentials, which the rich advertise and the poor try to overcome, not to conceal. Some of these habits may have begun on the frontier with the egalitarian atmosphere and the obstacles that its underpopulated, mobile, and physically open environment would have placed in the path of developing any broadly cast concept of privacy. (Erving Goffman defines "private places" as "soundproof regions where only members or invitees gather," and there were few of those on the frontier, as also in most premodern nonurban societies, especially in tropical climates, usually characterized by underdeveloped notions of privacy.)[13]

Like most deterministic explanations, the frontier and feudalism theses do not carry us far enough. Why should habits formed on the frontier more than a century ago still persist in the most highly urbanized society in history, today? Why should people acutely conscious of economic gradations (not to speak of racial and religious differences) act as though unaware of the possible group protection afforded by the barriers of social privacy? The answer may be found in the exaggerated distinction made in the United States, since its founding, between government and society. For long periods of American history, progress was believed to have been made through the more or less spontaneous freeing of *social* energies, unrestrained by, and often in an adversary opposition to, the forces of government. If anything about the individual or groups to which he belongs is to be

[12] Louis Hartz, *The Liberal Tradition in America: An Interpretation of American Political Thought Since the Revolution* (New York: Harcourt, Brace, 1955). Frederick Jackson Turner, "Significance of the Frontier in American History," in *Frontier and Section: Selected Essays* (Englewood Cliffs, N.J.: Prentice-Hall, 1961), pp. 37–62.

[13] Erving Goffman, *Behavior in Public Places: Notes on the Social Organization of Gatherings* (New York: The Free Press, 1963), p. 9.

concealed, then it must be concealed from government, the principal adversary. On the other hand, since government itself is enjoined from operating in secret—and in criminal, as in some civil and regulatory, proceedings from using secret or private information about individuals and corporations unless it was openly obtained, in court or other "hearings" that normally employ adversary procedures—why keep anything private from other members of the society? Presumably all members of society are together in the continuous struggle against government. They therefore have nothing—at any rate little, certainly less than their European counterparts—to conceal from one another, but everything to conceal from the government. One's neighbors, pollsters, interviewers, casual travel acquaintances—these are entitled to know, or forced to hear, all about your "private" life. In this context, psychoanalysis and its vulgar offshoots became popular fads only in the United States. But the government is entitled to a minimum of information. The British government is not entitled to much more, but because Englishmen are less inclined than the American heirs of John Locke to erect "boundaries" between government and society,[14] they are more likely to treat unofficial individuals and institutions analogously to government and to maintain as much privacy in their social relations as in their relations with their government.

On the Continent, the state knows all about the individual, who does not object, because the state, for the most part, keeps this and other information secret, and because he is simply accustomed to it from time immemorial as part of the traditions of the police state. This total exposure of one's nakedness vis-à-vis the state, however, leads by way of compensation to total concealment vis-à-vis one's fellows in family, society, economy. The "Fifth Amendment" is, as it were, turned around. Since the individual has so little protection against the state, he needs more protection against his peers, if he is to maintain any sphere of personal autonomy at all. In the United States, the individual enjoys sufficient or, according to some, excessive, legal and constitutional protection against a government conceived of

[14] For a critique of the concept of boundaries, see my "Evaluation of Systems Theory," in *Contemporary Political Analysis*, James C. Charlesworth, ed. (New York: The Free Press, 1967), p. 168 and *passim*.

as segregated from society, so that, out of the need to create feelings of community, he "overcommunicates." Private individuals, to borrow a phrase from private finance, "go public," sometimes to the extreme of the kind of self-exhibitionism that, when viewed by Europeans, strikes them as an invasion of *their* privacy as members of the viewing public. In England, where government and society are not considered separate compartments, governmental privacy (confidentiality) and publicity, as well as their equivalents at the level of the individual, privacy and openness, stand in dialectical tension with each other, so that the opposites degenerate neither into secrecy and concealment nor into propaganda and exhibitionism.

ENGLAND AND THE CONTINENT

So far, the comparison suggests more marked differences between the Anglo-American countries on the one hand and the continental European countries on the other than between the United States and England. One obvious reason for this has already been hinted at. It is the separate development of, and the notion of privacy peculiar to, the English Common Law. The growth of the Common Law has been studied—indeed, it has often been celebrated—by legal historians, lawyers, and comparative students of law from Sir John Fortescue to Sir William Holdsworth. Comparativists among them have usually stressed that lawyers and the Common Law have been relatively independent of the Crown and the central apparatus of government, whereas jurists and the Roman Law, after its reception and still more after the great recodifications, have been relatively dependent upon royal rulers and their successors. The Roman Law, in Justinian's comprehensive codification, easily lent itself as an instrument of comprehensive centralizing rule. It may therefore have facilitated establishment of the traditional type of police state in countries like France and Prussia, where subjects could conceal very little in their private lives from agents of the central government. Cameralism did not develop in England. On the Continent, by contrast, collection of the *camerale* and other taxes, recodification of the Roman Law, and the growth and training of the legal profession, and later of the police, were inextricably related to one another.[15] We might, as a result, simply explain the major differences with respect to privacy between England and the Continent in terms of the growth of cameralism in the continental countries. In Germany, and especially in Prussia, cameralism was intimately linked with *Kabinettsregierung*: "This system of personal government from the royal study or cabinet was called in Germany *Kabinettsregierung,* which reflects the contrast to the development in England [governed at the time by men who were also Kings of Hanover], where a different 'cabinet system' became the vehicle of parliamentary government."[16]

David Hume called an explanation the point at which the mind comes to rest, and cameralism does not yet seem satisfying as such a resting place. Why did cameralism develop in the continental monarchies and not in England? It is not enough simply to attribute this to the inventive genius of a few rulers, who were enabled by circumstances to put together certain ingredients, including the Roman Law, that were lying at hand, ready to be properly combined. Why were these ingredients lacking in England? Or, if they were present, why did English political genius fail to put them together in a similar fashion?

Before the publication of Montesquieu's *Esprit des Lois* in 1748, and its pervasive influence especially in what was to become the United States, most comparative students of government perceived the unity, rather than the separation, of judicial, legislative, and executive "functions." They were aware that procedures commonly applied in the judicial process were likely to be used also in the other activities of government—what

[15] On cameralism, see Carl J. Friedrich, "The Continental Tradition of Training Administrators in Law and Jurisprudence," *Journal of Modern History,* XI: 2 (June 1939). On certain aspects of the police state, see Yves Lévy, "Police and Policy," *Government and Opposition,* 1 (1966), 487-510, and Howard C. Payne, *The Police State of Louis Napoleon Bonaparte, 1851–1860* (Seattle: Washington University Press, 1966).

[16] Hajo Holborn, *A History of Modern Germany, 1648-1840* (New York: Alfred A. Knopf, 1964), p. 192.

our contemporary jargon calls rule making and rule application, in addition to rule adjudication.[17] However perceived, this is, of course, as true today as in the sixteenth or seventeenth centuries, since many if not most or even all of the men who make, apply, and "judge" laws have undergone the same training and, often, engage in these *more or less* differentiated activities at different times of their careers. Moreover, in the history of the differentiation of functions of government, adjudication precedes legislation or execution.[18] In the Old Testament, the Book of Judges precedes the Book of Kings.

Sir Thomas Smith, in comparing English and French government in the sixteenth century, noted that, in criminal trials, only the indictment was in writing under Common Law procedure, whereas under Civil Law procedure a great deal more was committed to the written records. In England, all the rest was done "openlie."[19] Three centuries later, a student of English and French court procedure commented upon the "staggering orality" of Common Law courts.[20] I am tempted to describe the Civil Law counterpart with the Freudian opposite: staggering anality.[21] In English and American courts, then as now,

[17] See the review of Gabriel A. Almond and G. Bingham Powell, Jr., *Comparative Politics: A Development Approach,* in *Journal of Politics,* 29 (1967), 903–905.

[18] See also Charles H. McIlwain, *The High Court of Parliament and Its Supremacy: An Historical Essay on the Boundaries between Legislation and Adjudication in England* (New Haven: Yale University Press, 1934). Professor McIlwain himself, in his entry in *Who's Who,* lists as his first professional activity, admission to the bar of Allegheny County, Pennsylvania, 1897.

[19] "This is to be understood although it will seem straunge to all nations that doe use the civill Law of the Romane Emperours, that for life and death there is nothing put in writing but the enditement onely. All the rest is doone openlie in the presence of the Judges, the Justices, the enquest, the prisoner, and so manie as will or can come so neare as to heare it, and all depositions and witnesses given aloude, that all men may heare from the mouth of the depositors and witnesses what is saide." (Sir Thomas Smith, *De Republica Anglorum,* chap. 23, "Of the sessions of gaole delivery, and the definitive proceedings in causes criminal.")

[20] C. J. Hamson, in *The English Trial and Comparative Law,* T. F. T. Plucknett and C. J. Hamson, eds. (Cambridge: W. Heffner & Sons, 1953), p. 22. See also Sir Maurice Amos, "A Day in Court," *Cambridge Law Journal,* 2 (1926), 343.

[21] For reflections on the connection between privacy and social responsibility within a psychoanalytic context, see Philip Rieff, *The Triumph of*

everything is expressed publicly in open court if it is to be taken notice of. In Civil Law courts, much more is repressed into documents if it is to become a part of the written record, which is more important than statements made in open confrontation and altercation between contending parties to a suit. The people who conduct these judicial proceedings have received the same training as those who are members of legislatures and of bureaucracies. Often, they are simply the same people at different stages of their careers. And even where they are neither the same people nor have received the same *formal* training, they are, as a matter of course, members of the same culture (or "political culture"), "socialized" (more appropriately, perhaps, "politicized") to believe either that oral and open, or that documentary and closed, materials constitute better evidence. They share these views or preferences with other members of the political system, including, I suspect, historians in their adherence to canons of evidence.

More than a century before Sir Thomas Smith, another English public servant who compared the Common and the Civil Law in their political effects, Sir John Fortescue, remarked upon the French practice of torture, not to be found in Common Law courts, and upon the examination of accused and witnesses, under the Civil Law, "in private places."[22] Even in the fifteenth century, the percipient participant-observer noticed certain obvious differences that may be relevant to the development of both cameralism and the continental state's peculiar access to total information about its subjects, which complements the state's own relatively secret mode of operating. What are the origins of these differences?

---

the Therapeutic: Uses of Faith after Freud (New York: Harper & Row, 1966), pp. 139 and 259.

[22] "The law of France, therefore, is not content to convict the accused in capital cases by witnesses, lest innocent blood be condemned by the testimony of liars. But that law prefers the accused to be racked with tortures until they themselves confess their guilt, than to proceed by the deposition of witnesses who are often instigated to perjury by wicked passions and sometimes by subornation of evil persons. By such precaution and disingenuousness, criminals and suspected criminals are afflicted with so many kinds of tortures in that kingdom that the pen scorns to put them in writing." (Sir John Fortescue, *De Laudibus Legum Anglie,* chap. XXIII, S. B. Chrimes, ed. [Cambridge: Cambridge University Press, 1949].)

What we know of the customs and the laws of the Anglo-Saxons prior to the Norman Conquest suggests that the individual enjoyed little privacy vis-à-vis either other individuals or agents of public authority—as in most primitive societies, including Christian ones. After the Conquest, his right to privacy from, not to speak of concealment against, the government was further reduced, partly as a result of the introduction from the Continent of the Norman inquest, that instrument of administrative control whose greatest monument is the Domsday Book, an inventory of landholdings in King William's new realm.[23] Within a century after 1066 A.D., a new version of the inquest or inquisition began to be used by the King's itinerant judges in the settlement of disputes involving land. In about another fifty years, the jury, which had developed out of the originally administrative Norman inquest, started to perform its judicial function in criminal (as distinguished from civil) trials.[24]

Meanwhile, in the Duchy of Normandy itself, the inquest developed in its own way, ultimately influenced by the institutionally and etymologically related procedure of the Canon Law, the inquisition.[25] This procedure had been refined toward the end of the twelfth century, by decretals of Pope Innocent III.[26] Church courts using the inquisition interrogated the accused and other witnesses in secret.[27] Testimony and other depositions

[23] George W. Keeton, *The Norman Conquest and the Common Law* (New York: Barnes & Noble, 1966), chap. VIII, "Domesday Book," and *passim.*

[24] Theodore F. T. Plucknett, *A Concise History of the Common Law*, 5th ed. (London: Butterworth & Co., 1956), pp. 111-126.

[25] A. Esmein, *A History of Continental Criminal Procedure with Special Reference to France* (Boston: Little, Brown, and Co., 1913 [written in 1877-80]), pp. 39 ff. "Under the pressure, however, of various causes, the accusatory procedure of the nations of the Germanic race becomes inquisitorial, written, and secret, taking its inspiration from the two learned legislations of Europe, the Roman Law and the Canon Law. An ordinance of St. Louis . . . [of 1260 A.D. or earlier] helps this movement by substituting, in the domains of the crown, the *procedure by inquest* or jury ('enquête') for the proof by *wager of battle.*" While the nobles persisted in demanding the old procedures, "the citizens ('bourgeois') and the peasants ('vilains') readily enough accept these innovations which proscribe the duel and replace the wager of battle ('en champ clos') by oral or written pleadings."

[26] *Ibid.*, pp. 79 ff.

[27] Under the *processus per inquisitionem*, the judge "can summon and arrest the accused, bring witnesses against him, and condemn him if proof of his guilt is furnished by this means." *Ibid.*, p. 80.

were, in the first instance, taken down in writing, and thereafter courts considered for all practical purposes only documentary material.[28] Since the inquisition was a procedure of the Canon Law, it was confined to church courts, and secular courts continued also to use other, less rationalized methods of arriving at decisions. These included trial by combat and other ordeals, which, since they were regarded as giving divine judgment, required for their efficacy the participation of priests. In 1215 A.D., Innocent III, in the Fourth Lateran Council, forbade participation of the clergy in ordeals.[29] In consequence, secular courts, especially in criminal trials, relied increasingly upon adaptations of the inquisition. In Normandy, as gradually elsewhere in France and eventually the rest of the Continent, "the office of judge became so intellectualized that it came to consist almost entirely in the perusal of documents, and instead of seeing the witnesses testify in open court, the judge could only read their depositions taken by commissioners."[30]

The accused was interrogated in secret, by the forerunner of the *juge d'instruction,* often under torture. The investigating magistrate passed on his file to the collegial court which would render judgment, and of which he might be a member. The accused often faced his judges only when they pronounced his sentence, and sometimes not even then, so that the clerk of the court would tell him at the prison doorkeeper's lodge what it was.[31] There could be no confrontation or cross-examination, no mutual disclosure of charges or evidence under such a system. The court, acting for the government, was unrestricted

[28] Under the Ordinance of Villers-Cotterets (April 1539) of Francis I, a very long examination of the accused was conducted by a single judge. When the accused finally appears before the bench, the "tribunal has for its enlightenment only the written proceedings and the last interrogation of the accused. Everything is in writing; and everything is secret, both examination and judgment; and in the majority of cases the latter is not evidentially grounded." *Ibid.,* pp. 148 ff.

[29] T. F. T. Plucknett, *A Concise History of the Common Law,* pp. 118 ff., Sir William Holdsworth, *A History of English Law,* 6th ed., vol. I (London: Methuen & Co., 1938), p. 323.

[30] T. F. T. Plucknett, in Plucknett and Hamson, *The English Trial and Comparative Law,* p. 42.

[31] A. Esmein, *A History of Continental Criminal Procedure,* pp. 39 ff., 160 and 308; Arthur Engelmann and others, *A History of Continental Civil Procedure* (London: John Murray, 1928), pp. 71 ff.

in its efforts to discover all about the accused, the accuser, the delict, and anything remotely connected with it.[32] On the other hand, the accused and other persons involved in the proceedings—the continental languages characteristically lack an equivalent for the word "trial"—were unable to find out anything about the court's secret business or, as for that matter, about each other. This was true even of civil suits, after the distinction between them and criminal cases was clearly recognized. Civil cases, in their nature, generally depend upon the private parties for initiation and continuation (though there was a brief period in Prussian legal history when Frederick the Great established a code under which civil suits had to be prosecuted *and* defended by official, not private, jurists).[33] When the Roman Law penetrated to the German territories, courts, before their complete professionalization, developed the practice of sending the complete file of a case to a university law faculty for its opinion, which was usually accepted by the lay judges.[34] It was in this period that we must look for the origins of the saying *quod non est in actis, non est in mundo*.[35] This dictum still puts in a nutshell continental attitudes, as does its corollary that whatever is in the individual's official and secret file is true or, at any rate, more to be relied upon than what he says

[32] The judge's task was to "find out the truth for himself, even if the parties were reluctant to help him." As a result, he became "a true inquisitor," even "Hunting up witnesses" himself. These developments led to "taking the conduct of the case out of the hands of the parties and putting it entirely into the hands of the judge," who therefore needed a sizable trained staff (T. F. T. Plucknett, *The English Trial and Comparative Law,* p. 42).

[33] Arthur Engelmann and others, *A History of Continental Civil Procedure,* pp. 17–19.

[34] Adolf Stölzel, *Die Entwicklung des gelehrten Richterthums in deutschen Territorien: Eine rechtsgeschichtliche Untersuchung* (Stuttgart: J. G. Cotta, 1872), pp. 187–231. Some courts even developed the practice of reducing their own work by accepting verdicts and sentences *(Urtheilssprüche)* from the juristic faculties. *Ibid.,* p. 219. See also John F. Dawson, *A History of Lay Judges* (Cambridge: Harvard University Press, 1960), *passim.* Also Myron P. Gilmore, *Argument from Roman Law in Political Thought, 1200–1600* (Cambridge: Harvard University Press, 1941), pp. 3 ff.: "Finally, there was the complete reception of the Roman law in Germany, a development which was the logical extreme of the process which was elsewhere a matter of degree, with the minimum represented by England."

[35] Arthur Lenhoff, "The Law of Evidence: A Comparative Study Based Essentially on Austrian and New York Law," *American Journal of Comparative Law,* 3, 315.

about himself or about others, for example, in oral public altercation.

The papal prohibition of clerical participation in trials by ordeal was as effective in England as on the Continent, but it was to have very different effects. The Conquest had introduced to England not only the Norman inquest but also trial by battle. However, both before and after 1066, the English preferred the ordeal by fire or water to judicial combat.[36] In one of the few "statutes" left of his English reign, King William provided that an Englishman challenged to trial by combat by a Norman could opt for one of the other forms of ordeal (or vice versa).[37] The provision suggests that all these trials were initiated with public accusations *of* private persons *by* private persons.[38] The inquest imported from Normandy, on the other hand, was at first used by royal agents for the purpose of discovering and getting on the record certain facts about the king's new and old subjects.[39] Within a hundred years of its introduction to England, the inquest or jury began to be used also by the royal justices in eyre, that is, on circuit, to get decisions in disputes about landholdings.[40] And after Innocent's prohibition of the ordeal—by water, fire, or combat—the king's judges came to rely upon the jury for rendering verdicts when they went on circuit for gaol delivery, that is, in criminal cases.[41] The procedure used in both criminal and civil trials was and continued to be accusatory. It pitted the parties against each other in the posture of private adversaries, contending before the impartial, singular, public judge, who enforced the rules of procedure, and the impartial, plural jury, who, in secret,

[36] George Neilson, *Trial by Combat* (Glasgow: William Hodge & Co., 1890), p. 72 and *passim.*

[37] F. Pollock and F. W. Maitland, *The History of English Law Before the Time of Edward I,* 2nd ed. (Cambridge: Cambridge University Press, 1898), vol. I, pp. 50 ff. For the statute, see *Die Gesetze der Angelsachsen,* F. Liebermann, ed. (Halle: Max Niemeyer, 1903), vol. I, pp. 483 ff.

[38] See A. Esmein, *A History of Continental Criminal Procedure,* especially p. 11.

[39] G. W. Keeton, *The Norman Conquest and the Common Law,* pp. 114 ff.

[40] T. F. T. Plucknett, *A Concise History of the Common Law,* p. 111, on "Inquisitions in England" and "Assizes in England," especially the Assizes of Clarendon of 1164 and 1166 and the Assize of Northampton of 1176.

[41] *Ibid.,* pp. 118 ff.

arrived at the simple, substantive verdict—"guilty," or "not guilty." In England, the notion of the equality of prosecution with defense in criminal cases is maintained even today, when the prosecution is still conducted by private barristers retained for the purpose, *ad hoc,* by the Crown.

What are the causes, and what the consequences, of the unique English response to the problems created by the decree of the Lateran Council? Chief cause must have been the use of the home-grown Common Law in the King's Courts, and the fact that the English universities taught only the Roman Law, not the Common Law—until Blackstone's lectures in the eighteenth century.[42] The University of Paris and other continental unversities also taught the Roman Law, but in France it was or was to become the law of the land. As a result, the "intellectualization" of the office of judge could proceed apace after—and probably even before—abolition of the ordeal, because there was enough trained personnel on hand to provide not only judges but also clerks for the normally collegial courts. Lay judges in the continental countries were replaced by professional judges, of whom there has usually been a plethora.[43]

In England, there was, from the outset, a dearth of professional judges, drawn from the *serjeants-conteur,* forerunners of the barristers, who still provide all of England's approximately two hundred professional judges today.[44] (West Germany, with a similar-size population, has more than 12,000 professional judges.)[45] Because English professional judges in the thirteenth century were overworked, they relied increasingly upon the jury —"lay judges" in Professor Dawson's terminology—to find the verdict for them. The jury consisted of true and good men of the country, who probably knew the parties and the circum-

[42] Blackstone's lectures were delivered between 1755 and 1765. See William Blackstone, *Commentaries on the Laws of England. Of Public Wrongs* (Boston: Beacon Press, 1962).

[43] J. F. Dawson, *A History of Lay Judges,* pp. 105–111.

[44] On serjeants-at-law and barristers, see Alan Harding, *A Social History of English Law* (London: Penguin Books, 1966), pp. 172–175. See also Brian Abel-Smith and Robert Stevens, *Lawyers and the Courts: A Sociological Study of the English Legal System 1750–1965* (London: Heinemann, 1967).

[45] On January 1, 1967. *Statistisches Jahrbuch der Bundesrepublik Deutschland.*

stances, who indeed started out more as witnesses (originally oath witnesses) than as judges of the facts in the contemporary sense.[46] At any rate, they were good and true, but also generally illiterate. The best way to get a verdict out of them, and incidentally also to reduce the workload of the professional judge, was to force the adversaries to boil down their dispute to a single, simple point, the issue, and then to let *them* argue, alternately and orally, in open court, to this point. Documents might indeed not "confuse the issue"—a very English phrase—but they would certainly confuse an illiterate jury and not help the man who was having "his day in court."

The jury deliberated in secret, but that was and is the only part of the trial not held in the open,[47] and it deals with the matter previously presented by the adversaries in open court. The judge confines himself to the procedural role of guarding

[46] W. Holdsworth, *A History of English Law,* 3rd ed. (1944), vol. IX, p. 130.

[47] While the deliberations of collegial courts of appeal in Common Law countries do not take place in public, the practice of publishing dissents throws open to public scrutiny even this most august stage of the judicial process. The contrast with France is marked: "Since the bench is normally composed of at least three judges . . . , the individual responsibility of each member is limited. The requirement of French law that all decisions be *per curiam,* dissenting or concurring written opinions being prohibited, acts as a formal deterrent to a French judge's assertion of his own views or convictions. Moreover, he is under a duty not to violate the principle of secrecy, or *secret des délibérations.*" René David and Henry P. de Vries, *The French Legal System: An Introduction to Civil Law Systems* (New York: Oceana Publications, 1958), p. 19.

When the constitution of the German Imperial Supreme Court was being drafted, about 1883, the publication of dissenting opinions was considered, only to be decisively rejected: "It was incompatible with the authority of the courts and good relations between the judges. . . . The proposal would lead to Byzantinism and to the seeking of publicity. It would foster vanity and disputatiousness. As few decisions would be unanimous, dissenting opinions would become the rule. The development of law and of legal science will be fostered by careful reflection in the libraries, but not through violent discussions following expressions of polemically motivated dissenting opinions. The court faces the outside world as a single authority, whose decisions are the decisions of the court. A court's principal function is to decide the individual case justly and to uphold the authority of the laws, not to provoke scientific discussion over legal questions." The possibility of publishing dissenting opinions was again considered and rejected by the Bundestag when it was debating the constitution of the Federal Constitutional Court in 1949, because trust in justice was believed to be insufficiently developed. See Arthur von Mehren, "The Judicial Process: A Comparative Analysis," *American Journal of Comparative Law,* 5 (1956), pp. 208 ff.

the "rules of the game" and instructing the jury about the law: "The law is for me, the facts are for you." The judge cannot, and the judiciary as a whole does not want, to find out all about a defendant or other parties to a trial. They do not even want to find out all about the crime or quarrel that led to the trial. To exaggerate the differences, we could say that the Common Law court wants to arrive at a decision, while the Civil Law court wants to find the truth. Even in the United States, where, by contrast to England, the office of public prosecutor is as highly differentiated as on the Continent, the typical district attorney does not want to tell the court all about a defendant and the crime of which he stands accused, but only enough to "win his point."[48] The court itself—which includes the jury—is not allowed to take notice of matter that is not brought up openly and according to proper procedures, allowing for adversarial cross-examination. In England until the sixteenth century, persons who volunteered information at a trial to which they were not parties, or to which they had not been brought as witnesses by one of the parties, could be charged with the crime of maintenance.[49]

[48] For a comparison of English and American prosecution, see Delmar Karlen, *Anglo-American Criminal Justice* (Oxford: Clarendon Press, 1967), p. 18 and *passim*.

[49] "Thus in 1450 Fortescue, C. J. is reported as saying: 'If a man be at the bar and say to the court that he is for the defendant or plaintiff, that he knows the truth of the issue, and prays that he may be examined by the court to tell the truth to the jury, and the court asks him to tell it, and at the request of the court he says what he can in the matter, it is justifiable maintenance. But if he had come to the bar out of his own head, and spoken for one or the other, it is maintenance and he will be punished for it. And if the jurors come to a man where he lives, in the country, to have knowledge of the truth of the matter, and he informs them, it is justifiable; but if he comes to the jurors, or labors to inform them of the truth it is maintenance, and he will be punished for it; so Fortescue said, and it was admitted by the court.' This shows both that the jurors were expected to make their own inquiries and that the law discouraged the volunteer witness.

"It is clear, however, that in the sixteenth century, when Sir Thomas Smith wrote, witnesses held a far more important place than they held in the time of Fortescue. (Footnote to *Republic* 147, 148: 'Witnesses be sworn and heard before them, not after the fashion of the civil law, but that not only the twelve, but the judges, the parties, and so many as be present may hear what each witness doth say. The adverse party or his advocates . . . interrogateth sometimes the witnesses and driveth them out of contenance.')" (W. Holdsworth, *A History of English Law*, vol. I, p. 335.)

Anthropologists have shown us the great, in many ways crucial, importance of court procedure in the lives of premodern peoples.[50] Where the community is relatively tight, horizons parochial, and other forms of entertainment scarce, court proceedings can be among the most dramatic and impressive events in the lives of ordinary persons. Everyone, at least indirectly through his family, is bound to be touched by court proceedings in successive stages of his life. This is true especially of communities that are, for whatever related reasons, litigious. We know that the English were quite litigious, among other periods, around the year of 1300 A.D., when litigation was being encouraged by the then rather unpopular advocates.[51] By participating in court proceedings or by observing them—observers *are* participants, in the anthropological if not the legal sense—ordinary people become familiar with court procedures and they are likely to adopt aspects of these procedures, quite unconsciously, into their own day-to-day habits of action and thought. Court procedure, thus internalized, can become a model, even *the* model, for procedures of action in other, quite different, entirely nonjudicial situations—bargaining in the marketplace, arguments between spouses, teaching in school, even problem-solving as it goes on within the mind of the individual.

The adversary procedure of their courts and of the rest of their politics, to which this procedure was gradually transferred,[52] accustomed the English to discover about (and to disclose to) one another only such information as was demonstrably relevant to a clearly formulated issue. Everything else remained private. In this respect, the Crown, as represented by prosecuting counsel or by the king's judges, was in the same position, both actively and passively, as its subjects.[53] However, the Crown

[50] See, for example, Max Gluckman, *The Judicial Process among the Barotse of Northern Rhodesia* (Manchester: Manchester University Press, 1955).

[51] Herman Cohen, *A History of the English Bar and the Attornatus to 1450* (London: Sweet & Maxwell, 1929), p. 160.

[52] On the transfer of adversary proceedings from the law courts to politics, see my *Government by Constitution: The Political Systems of Democracy* (New York: Random House, 1959), pp. 225-230 and *passim*.

[53] After the judge, "The second dominant figure in an English trial is the defense counsel. The barrister who prosecutes is inhibited by tradition from vigorously seeking a conviction, for the philosophy that the government can

was of course more powerful than its subjects, except in their occasionally successful rebellions—when, in fact, they appealed to Heaven, as did the Barons against King John, the authors of the Glorious Revolution and the Bill of Rights against James II, and the American rebels against George III. That is why these rebellions against the Crown sought to protect the individual's right to privacy by placing special prohibitions upon the Crown, or its successors overseas. The connection between the adversary method of the Common Law and origins of the Fifth Amendment has already been demonstrated by Leonard W. Levy.[54] The danger of moving in the other, Roman Law direction was explained, in exile, by Chief Justice Fortescue to his royal tutee, the heir apparent, at a time when it must have seemed clearly in Fortescue's interest not to criticize, but to praise the Prince's ancestors:

> From these things an understanding of the effects of that law, which certain of your ancestors tried to abrogate, is clear to you. Above all, also, the effects of that other law appear to you, which they tried, with so much zeal, to introduce in place of that law, so that by their fruits you shall know them. Was it not ambition, lust, and license, which your said ancestors preferred to the good of the realm, that incited them to this commerce?[55]

PRIVACY AND POLITICAL DEVELOPMENT

In the course of the modernization of England, the scope of privacy was gradually expanded, as an unintended consequence of the formulation, deliberation, and resolution of a whole series of issues, all of them fought over according to the

---

neither win nor lose a criminal case, being as concerned an innocent man go free as to see a guilty man convicted, is taken very seriously in England." (D. Karlen, *Anglo-American Criminal Justice,* p. 176.) This, taken together with the rules requiring virtually full disclosure in the preliminary hearing (*Ibid.,* p. 145), may put the Crown today at a disadvantage vis-à-vis its subjects.

[54] Leonard W. Levy, *Origins of the Fifth Amendment: The Right against Self-Incrimination* (New York: Oxford University Press, 1968), chap. I, "Rival Systems of Criminal Procedure," and *passim.*

[55] J. Fortescue, *De Laudibus Legum Anglie,* chap. XXXV.

rules of the adversary game. In other modernizing or modern systems, privacy seems to be one fruit yielded by the *development of politics,* more than by the *institutionalization of government.* This distinction, incidentally, is more useful than the exaggerated post-Lockean American compartmentalization of *society* and *government,* of which "social mobilization" and its opposite, "institutionalization" of government or the single party, are obvious descendants.[56] Privacy is generated, and its scope can be expanded, precisely through the continuous tensions between government and politics, which enable human beings, as individuals and in unofficial groupings, to *deprive* government of access to and control over them. In privacy, the individual procreates and also creates new ideas and ideals, out of which are formulated novel issues that then lead to the expansion of politics. The process is not a unilinear, steadily onward, upward, forward one. Premodern communities knew little privacy; certain modern political systems like England offer an optimum—not a maximum—of it; while the "post-modern" United States (and the Soviet Union, possibly "converging" in this respect) seems to be moving away from privacy,[57] although the Supreme Court has been making brave attempts to stem the tide.

If privacy arises out of the dialectical tension between government and politics; between pursuit of the basic goals of stability and flexibility, of effectiveness and efficiency; between the procedures of government and the substance of policies; between fundamental, long-term considerations and circumstantial short-term needs, then it should be possible to locate privacy and its pathology within the dimensions of an approach to comparative politics that purports to be comprehensive:[58] privacy accom-

[56] But in their attitudes toward the so-called developing countries, most American social scientists reverse traditional American preferences by rejecting social mobilization in favor of governmental institutionalization. See, for example, Samuel P. Huntington, "Political Development and Decay," *World Politics,* XVII: 3 (April 1965), 386–430, especially 419 ff. See also H. J. Spiro, *Patterns of African Development: Five Comparisons* (Englewood Cliffs, N. J.: Prentice-Hall, 1967), pp. 134–137.

[57] See also my "Totalitarianism," *International Encyclopedia of the Social Sciences* (New York: Macmillan and Free Press, 1968), vol. 16, pp. 106–113.

[58] "Comparative Politics: A Comprehensive Approach," *American Political Science Review,* LVI: 3 (September 1962), 577–595.

panies the dialectically and dynamically equilibrated "politics of purposive compromise." The pathological style of legalism has its parallel in secrecy; pragmatism, in manipulation; violence, in torture; and ideologism, in confession. Regimes nowadays usually described as totalitarian are sometimes characterized by all of these, which reinforce each other negatively.

At the level of the individual, the corresponding pathology of privacy consists of concealment, exhibitionism, sadism, and masochism. These, too, can be combined in the psychotic individual. This suggests two interesting concluding questions: Can we define certain "natural" needs of optimal privacy for different stages of civilization? And what is the relation, with respect to privacy, between the health and pathology of individual and political system?

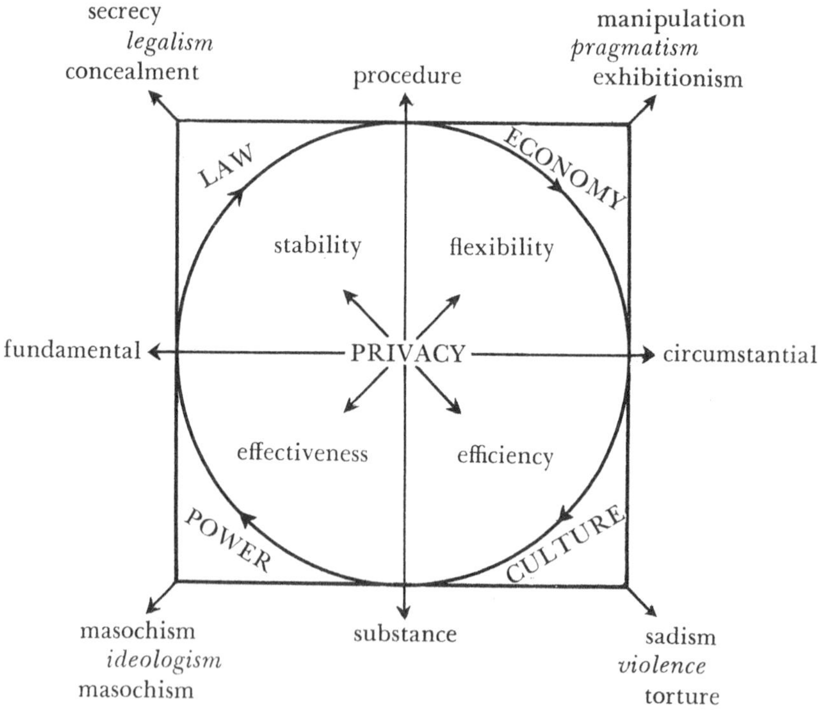

8

ON PRIVACY

ERNEST VAN DEN HAAG

DEFINITION: THE NATURE OF PRIVACY

Privacy is the exclusive access of a person (or other legal entity) to a realm of his own. The right to privacy entitles one to exclude others from (a) watching, (b) utilizing, (c) invading (intruding upon, or in other ways affecting) his private realm.

The protection of everybody's life, property, and convenience (including privacy itself), and the enforcement of laws generally, requires some limitation of any right in favor of other rights and of the rights of others. (Except for Mr. Justice Black, no one has discovered absolute rights.)[1] Hence the rights and duties of law-enforcement agencies and of private citizens must be balanced against each other.

Prescriptive (ultimately legislative and legal) authorities de-

[1] See Sidney Hook, *The Paradoxes of Freedom* (Berkeley, Calif.: University of California Press, 1962), chap. 1 *passim*. (I am using "rights" colloquially as synonym for "claims.")

fine the relation of the right to privacy to other rights: what is to be regarded as private, when, where, and by whom? what is a violation? who is entitled to define whose privacy? what limitations are legitimate? what should be regarded as implicit or involuntary consent to limitations?[2] what (and whose) rights are super- or subordinate to the right to privacy, to what degree, in what manner, on what occasion?

Descriptive studies concern the natural and social conditions which generate the desire for privacy and determine the manner and degree of fulfillment. Social conditions also determine largely, although perhaps not exclusively, what is regarded as within the private area, and what legal protection is given to it.

The right to privacy has long been indirectly protected by outlawing offenses such as trespass, or burglary, which can scarcely be committed without violation of privacy. But the need to protect privacy per se has become salient now, because technology has made it possible to violate privacy without trespass; and because powerful communications media find it more and more profitable to violate privacy in the service of public curiosity; and, finally, because new technologies threaten privacy from ever new directions.

Just as in the past the right to privacy was often protected indirectly through the protection granted other rights, so a number of other (claimed or emerging) rights now are protected indirectly by the protection granted the right to privacy—which has to be violated to interfere with them. Thus, in *Griswold et al. v. Connecticut* (380 U.S. 530) a law prohibiting the use of contraceptives was declared unconstitutional because, according to Mr. Justice Douglas, the law violated a "right to privacy older than the Bill of Rights." (Mr. Justice Stewart, in his dissent, asked "What provision of the Constitution does make this State law invalid?" and found none. Such a provision might be indeed desirable. But, unlike the majority of the Court, I cannot convince myself that desirability implies existence.)

Privacy is best treated as a property right. Property grants

[2] I shall neglect the question of whether some privacy should be regarded as inalienable by either law or consent.

an owner the exclusive right to dispose of what he owns. Privacy is the exclusive right to dispose of access to one's proper (private) domain. The *genus* is the same; the *differentia* lies in the origin and nature of what is owned. Privacy is not (though its extent may be) the product of specific transactions. Rather, it is an extended part of the person. The private realm is less tangible, therefore, and less separable from the owner than other properties; it is more immediately part of his definition.[3] Privacy then refers to control over one's own psychic area, with such dimensions as living space, image, expression, mentation, communication.[4] Others may be excluded from observing, or utilizing, these dimensions, or from invading them with their own sounds, images, etc.; they may not control our image, or our experience and comfort.

Privacy is still largely a moral norm; it is only in part defined by legislation and is best regarded as a right inherent in the person, with violation a *malum in se*. The nature of that right may be clarified by considering three classes of violation, which also indicate the additional legislation needed.

(a) Mere unauthorized *watching* of a private realm or activity deprives the watched of his mental property by curtailing the exclusiveness of his access to, or disposal of, his self. Being watched in one's private area therefore violates one's privacy, regardless of whether there is public exposure of what has been observed, and regardless of whether such exposure leads to loss of reputation, embarrassment, or indeed to any loss to the observed (or benefit to the observer) other than the loss of a mental property: privacy. The right to privacy entitles me to withhold the contribution of my private realm to the contents of someone else's mind—to his image of me—even if no further use of it is contemplated.

The formation of an image of me in the minds of others, which includes involuntary contributions of my private realm,

[3] Privacy covers a specific personal domain. In contrast, "secrecy" refers to the withholding of information on anything (a secret treaty is not a private one). Unlike privacy, secrecy requires intent and a transaction which need not be personal. Thus: "I discovered his secret by violating his privacy" or "official secrets." "Secret" involves not necessarily private transactions kept from others.

[4] Mentation may be invaded by "brainwashing," or involuntary disclosures in certain psychological procedures.

may also force me to modify my private acts, or otherwise to attempt to control the image being formed by others so as to gain the approval of my fellows or, at least, to avoid their contempt or anger. But such an effect need not occur, or be likely, to make unauthorized observation a violation. However, it must be stressed that restrictions, or systematic violations, of privacy weaken the major defense available to individuals against the social pressure to conform. Individuation rests on privacy.

(b) *Utilization* of the private realm concerns publications about it, true or false. Utilization requires neither actual observation nor actual information. I am entitled to make my private domain inaccessible even to the fantasies of others when these are published and may appear to the unwary to convey actual information. Only when these fantasies are clearly fiction, unlikely to be linked with my actual person, is my privacy not violated. The violation of the private area lies in the publication of private matters, which contribute to an image of the person whose privacy is utilized in the mind of others; the violation does not depend on whether material loss, inconvenience, or loss of reputation, or embarrassment, is suffered. It lies solely in the utilization of what is private; it is independent of any disadvantage to the violated or advantage to the violator.

Publications about my private acts—true or false—may also lead to interpretations of my public acts which may restrict my freedom or force me to respond. However, such publications violate my privacy even when they do not compel me to react to them, because they diminish that control over my image in other people's minds, to which I am entitled by virtue of my exclusive disposal of access to my private domain.

(c) *Intrusion* by persons, or animals, or machines, or by any objects under the control of others, violates my privacy, as do noises, odors, images, or communications which others are in duty bound to control when they affect my private domain. Any invasion of my senses in my private area is a violation thereof, regardless of whether it is deliberate or incidental to some activity controlled by others, and of whether it actually or tangibly interferes with my activities or comforts.

The right to privacy protects me against becoming an involuntary participant (or sufferer) in the activities of others, just as it protects me against having to suffer their participation in (or observation of) my activities.

PRIVACY AND LAW ENFORCEMENT: WHEN TO SHIFT THE BALANCE

To balance the right of protection from violations of privacy against other rights is to decide (*inter alia*) how much law-enforcement agencies should be allowed to infringe on the privacy of suspects, in order to protect the right of other citizens not to be victimized by burglars, murderers, *et al.* What degree of suspicion of what kind of crime is required to permit the police to spy on suspects, by what means? How far can police go in attempting to induce suspects to reveal evidence or to confess?

Courts have always had to decide when to superordinate the claims of law enforcement to those of privacy and when to subordinate them. They do so by interpreting principles (often constitutional provisions) as though to establish a permanent order of priorities. Thus in the last twenty years the courts have found that the Constitution grants certain (hitherto undiscovered) rights to suspects and defendants. Evidence previously admitted in court no longer is, and conviction, to that extent, has become harder to obtain.[5] Unfortunately, such changes in interpretation are quite independent of the factors on which the priorities *ought* to depend: in time of social danger—for example, in time of war or when the crime rate is high—measures of social defense must be strengthened, and individual rights subordinated to them, to a greater degree than is desirable when the social danger recedes. The rights of suspects and those of police should not be treated as fixed forever, in their relation

[5] The greater difficulty in obtaining convictions is not necessarily reflected in the disposal of cases by the courts. Lack of admissible evidence may prevent prosecution; or lead to the acceptance of guilty pleas to lesser offenses. Minor burglaries, shopliftings, and muggings may not even lead to police investigation.

Punishment of the convicted has become less and less harsh since (about) the Enlightenment. The argument in the text may apply to this development as well.

to each other, by the Constitution. Nor should the balancing depend only on the changing attitudes of the courts. Within broad constitutional limits these rights should be changed *automatically* in response to circumstances, just as, for instance, the penalty for espionage changes automatically in wartime.

Expenditures on defense and police forces usually are changed with circumstances, and new legislation is passed in response to changes in conditions and attitudes. Yet the legal balance between the right to privacy and the powers of law-enforcement agencies is not systematically shifted in accordance with circumstances. The conflicting claims are treated as though their priority is determined exclusively by permanent constitutional principles. However, if wire tapping by law-enforcement agencies is always a threat to privacy, so is law violation by criminals, which threatens privacy no less than other values. Citizens want protection from both threats, and at any time most protection against what is most threatening at that time. It follows that they want protection of the privacy of suspects to be reduced (where it impedes law enforcement) when the crime rate is high, and to be increased when the crime rate is low.

There is no reason for the law not to gratify this desire. Claims—for example, of the private versus the public interest—are permanent. The order of priorities is not; it depends on fluctuating quantities or urgencies. A general legal rule could automatically increase (or decrease) police surveillance powers (and change related matters) as the crime rate, determined by official authority, increases (or decreases) beyond certain predetermined points. A constitutional interpretation permitting as much is not beyond the ingenuity of the Supreme Court. At present, because neither the law nor its interpreters acknowledge the need to meet quantitative changes by shifting the priorities of rights, we often find the powers of law enforcement curtailed when they should be expanded, and vice versa.

It is often urged that subordination of privacy to the public interest by law-enforcement agencies is a "police state method," which should not be countenanced in a democracy under any circumstances. "Police state" here probably means a state in which the rulers enforce their wishes by using the police, without sufficiently limiting the means available to it.

There are nearly pure instances of "police states" extant at the present time in the Communist world and somewhat less pure ones in Africa, South America, the Caribbean, the Near East, and the Iberian Peninsula. Since one cannot reasonably identify the political system of the United States with that of any of the "police states" listed, protesters probably intend to stress that the American "police state methods" protested bear an uncomfortable resemblance to those generally applied in actual "police states." If this be so, it is of little relevance to the evaluation of the methods in question.

However, the protester may also wish to suggest that the acts protested may lead to a "police state" or indicate that we are on the way to becoming one. This would be a factual observation, or prediction, which as far as past experience goes, is incorrect. The known "police states"—including Nazi Germany and Fascist Italy, as well as all those mentioned before—have all been preceded either by a period of nonenforcement of law and general social disorder (with or without civil war, revolution, or coup d'état) or by a period in which the means available proved unequal to the task of enforcing the law and were not sufficiently improved in time.[6] No "police state" has ever followed a timely enlargement of the powers of law enforcement within a democracy, let alone grown from or been caused by it. No "police state" has ever been the effect of "police state methods."

A good case may be made—although I shall not make it—for the contrary contention: whenever there is a rise of general crime and of activity directed against a democratic system, severe laws strictly enforced and increased power for law-enforcement agencies, even at the cost of temporarily impairing privacy, serve to prevent a "police state"; insistence on the right to privacy at all costs does not.

In the light of the foregoing considerations some recent court decisions appear to have doubtful merit. In *Miranda v. Arizona* (384 U.S. 436) the Supreme Court found that, beyond heeding a request for counsel by a suspect in custody (*Escobedo v. Illinois,* 378 U.S. 478), the police must, even if unrequested,

[6] "Police states" which become such as a result of conquest are here disregarded.

offer him counsel and notify the suspect that he need not make any statements. The decision protects the privacy of suspects by helping them to avoid disclosing information they might not want to disclose when advised by counsel.[7] If heeded fully, *Miranda* would probably eliminate confessions as well as revealing statements to the police altogether: counsel seldom will advise a client to talk when doing so might help the police. Thus the Court brought about a radical shift of the balance in favor of privacy and against law enforcement.

The decision is usually justified by arguments aptly expressed by Joseph W. Bishop, Jr., Ely Professor of Law at Yale University: "[*Miranda*] gave the poor, unskilled criminals what mafiosi . . . had all along—the means to exercise their constitutional right to keep silent and talk to a lawyer. . . . Rich, sophisticated criminals [do not] deserve a better chance than poor, ignorant criminals."[8] Thus the argument for *Miranda* is that since "rich, sophisticated criminals" may escape conviction by not confessing on advice of counsel, "poor, ignorant criminals" also must be enabled to escape conviction by not confessing on advice of counsel. If one group of (rich) criminals escapes conviction, another group of (poor) criminals ought to be helped to do likewise.

The equality betwen the two groups is regarded as more important than the conviction of those criminals who are "ignorant" enough to confess their guilt. The purpose of court action is no longer to protect the innocent and punish the guilty, but to make sure that the guilty rich and the guilty poor get an equal chance to escape conviction. Shouldn't we correct the inequality between rich and poor criminals by making sure that the guilty rich will not escape conviction, rather than by helping the guilty poor to escape because the rich might? And should it prove impossible to prevent the rich from escaping conviction—which I doubt—should we really help one group of criminals to escape conviction because another might or did?[9]

[7] For a defense of *Miranda* and protection of privacy see R. S. Gerstein, "Privacy and Self-Incrimination," *Ethics*, 80 (January 1970), 87–99.

[8] *New York Times Magazine*, September 7, 1969.

[9] The case for *Miranda* is not improved much if, unlike Professor Bishop and most supporters, one assumes the suspects to be innocent. Even in the

DEGREES OF PRIVACY

Once its scope has been defined, legal priorities determine the protection accorded privacy against encroachment by police. However, privacy is often a matter of degree: one forfeits some part, but not all of it, with regard to everybody, or, at least, to somebody, by placing oneself in a position which requires or permits some loss of privacy.

Participants in public occasions give up some of the privacy to which they are otherwise entitled. So do persons who volunteer for a lawful or unlawful role in public life. The criminal, the columnist, the actor, or the public official, all become public figures and thus volunteer to forego some degree of privacy. Finally, institutional or contractual arrangements may provide for abridgment of privacy. Spouses each renounce some privacy with regard to the other; so do business partners. Yet neither gives up privacy with regard to anyone else, or to the public at large; nor does either give up all privacy even with regard to the other.[10]

Users of a public thoroughfare, or carrier, must expect to be seen by others and cannot claim the immunity from observation they might claim at home. However, if the user's image is flashed on a TV screen or his picture published in a magazine, his privacy is violated—unless he voluntarily participated in a public occasion which may be reasonably expected to be attended by such publicity.

Thus, one's privacy is violated if it is abridged beyond the

---

absence of counsel they would be unlikely to confess to what they have not done. But should they, and should trial counsel be unable to show the confession to have been extracted by illegitimate means and thus inadmissible, defendants can always repudiate their confession in court. The jury, then, would have to determine whether the confession was extracted by overeager police or the repudiation by overzealous defense counsel. I do not see how a repudiated confession, unless corroborated by independent evidence, would greatly influence the jury. On the other hand, failure to confess on advice of counsel might indeed help as many "poor, ignorant criminals" to escape conviction as it does help "rich, sophisticated criminals" to do so. And that would be a calamity. (The Bazelon-Katzenbach letters [*The Journal of Criminal Law, Criminology and Police Science,* December 1965] are pertinent here.)

[10] "Giving up" privacy is, of course, the same as authorizing the sharing of the private realm or deprivatizing it, for someone, in some respect.

degree which might be reasonably expected, required, or risked by one's activity. If one's image, voice, or activity is displayed to a wider public (or to a different one, in some cases) than could reasonably be expected to perceive it, one's privacy is violated. Sitting in a restaurant or walking along a street, one has no reason to expect that his filmed image will be made available to TV viewers. Such a filming or recording violates one's reasonable expectations of limited privacy, even if unreleased or unused—although in practice the matter is likely to come to notice only if some use is made of the material.[11] At present the law permits release of such pictures as "news," although (other) commercial uses require consent.

The degree of privacy does not depend only on the occasion but also on the person. A candidate for office, a public official, an actor, or a criminal may not intend his activity to be divulged. Yet, if one voluntarily engages in activities which, by their nature, require, or risk, public exposure, or exposure to the public, he must be deemed to have volunteered to forego his privacy to the degree required or risked by his activity. The public figure gives up at least two aspects of privacy: the right to anonymity in public places and the right to keep the observation of his public activities confined to those in attendance.[12] This abridgment of privacy is inherent in the activity volunteered for. The criminal may no more intend the loss of privacy than he intends the loss of liberty. The voluntary act leads to an unintended effect.[13]

[11] A description from memory does not violate privacy. One must expect to enter other people's memory; and their memory is theirs to dispose of; whereas any part of my action, or voice, or image not incorporated in someone's memory—existing independently of it—is not anyone else's property. It cannot be displayed without my consent.

[12] As mentioned, under present law the images of a private person can be published as well. The public figure in addition can be defamed with little hope of recovering libel damages. (The private person has a reasonable chance.)

[13] Paradoxically in some respects present legal practice grants more protection to the privacy of the criminal than to that of the noncriminal. Evidence unlawfully procured, e.g., by eavesdropping, will be excluded and, possibly, other evidence tainted thereby. Thus the criminal is well protected from unlawful search. If the police eavesdrop on a law-abiding citizen he may bring an action—but nobody so far has recovered damages. Since no evidence is presented none is excluded. In short, violating the privacy of a nonsuspect

Similarly, the candidate for employment, credit, or welfare payments volunteers to give up as much privacy as is relevant to the position applied for, although he need not intend or anticipate the effects of this abridgment.[14] It does not follow that even relevant information should always be required; nor does anything follow about the means employed to verify it. The importance of the information sought must be balanced against the importance of not reducing the privacy of its object.

Altogether voluntary public disclosures also have the effect of limiting privacy in the areas disclosed. The octogenarian, who proclaims that he never smokes or drinks, permits publication of information on his smoking and drinking habits which may confirm or falsify his proclaimed abstention. Else the right to unchecked misinformation would be granted to those who volunteer, for whatever purpose, to publicly reveal their private habits.

Whereas the criminal foregoes privacy by voluntarily acting against the public interest, of which, therefore, he becomes an object, his victim does not. Yet often the victim's privacy is abridged far beyond what is already inherent in the criminal act suffered. Similarly, the victim of a traffic accident does not volunteer to have his (or her) picture in the newspaper. The public may be interested in pictures. But only the data required for identification of those involved and a description of the event can be justified as being in the public interest. An excellent case may also be made for restricting the excessive latitude of reporting on judicial proceedings. Again, pictures of the protagonists cannot, by any stretch of the imagination, be required for any justifiable purpose.

Even if one volunteers to reveal part of one's private life, one does not volunteer to surrender all privacy. Only as much is lost as bears on the information given or the role assumed.

---

is less of a risk for the police than violating the privacy of a suspect. There is no reason why the violation of privacy could not be penalized separately without necessarily excluding evidence thereby. This would discourage violation of *anyone's* privacy. Yet evidence of guilt would not have to be disregarded.

[14] The agency which insists on information about the private realm, not relevant to the position applied for, acts irrationally. This irrationality itself may be enough of a restraint; it may make legal restrictions unnecessary, although they would not be improper.

Unfortunately, this limitation is nearly impossible to enforce. The actress who needs publicity may wish to publicize only her professional activities. Yet the publicity she needs may be denied her unless she also permits and even helps publicity about her marital affairs. Short of outlawing publication of certain kinds of information altogether, regardless of consent, no protection is available against being forced to authorize publicity on private matters for the sake of publicity on professional matters.

Stricter protection of privacy from the prying curiosity of the public and from those whose business it is to satisfy this curiosity may nonetheless be possible. Too little effort has been directed to such protection. All too often any interest of the public is equated with the public interest. The public is entitled to information relevant to the formation of opinion on public issues, but not to be entertained, or to have its curiosity satisfied, at the expense of the privacy of some of its members. The interest of the public is one thing; the public interest another. It is difficult, therefore, to agree with the view expressed by Justice Charles E. Clark (Second Circuit Court of Appeals, New York, 1940):

> Regrettably or not, the misfortunes and frailities of neighbors and public figures are subjects of considerable interest and discussion to the rest of the population and when such are the mores of the community, it would be unwise for a court to bar their expression in the newspapers, books, and magazines of the day.

That "the mores of the community" make it "unwise" for a court to set a different, constitutionally, or even morally, more justifiable norm, is a doctrine which would make it hard to understand the legal history of the last decades.

THE WANING OF PRIVACY: INVASION CAUSED BY CROWDING, AFFLUENCE, EQUALITY, AND INSENSITIVITY

So far privacy has been dealt with as the right not to let others participate in one's activities, be it only by watching or publicizing them. But privacy also grants us the right not to participate in the activities of others. It is violated whenever, through suffering, in our private domain the noises, tremors, odors, lights, images, or communications produced outside we are forced to participate in activities we do not choose. This violation of privacy actually interferes with our freedom to do, or be, as we want, whereas being watched or publicized only threatens to do so.

To be forced, even while in one's private domain, to share in the activities of others, if only by suffering from incidental effects, is now perhaps the most rapidly rising threat to privacy. To say that our private area often reverberates with intrusive noises, reeks with intrusive odors, is assailed by intrusive communications, lights, and images is to exaggerate but little. A radical change of social policy would be required to control the intrusion of odors and noxious fumes, the invasion by incessant noises of traffic, the obtrusion of airplanes flying overhead.[15] Without such change privacy is doomed and therewith the motivation and protection of individuation.

Some legal protections against these intrusions are possible and certainly desirable. Yet they are likely to be futile in the end. Legal protections of privacy become illusory unless effective measures are taken to control the social developments which ineluctably undermine and nullify them.

Crowding

Owing to increased productivity, decreased mortality, and unchecked fertility, the population of this planet continues to rise at an unprecedented pace. In 1925 it was two billion; in 1960 three billion; in 1970 3.5 billion; by 1975 it will be four billion—an increase of one billion in fifteen years; by 1980 there will be five billion people; one dare not project further.

So far the rate of growth has been accelerating. As leaders of many countries begin to propose measures to reduce fertility,

[15] The spoiling or pollution of public resources—by spewing sewage into rivers, spilling oil on beaches, strewing landscapes with debris—is certainly a grave problem. However, though overlapping, it is not identical with invasion of privacy. In the case of air pollution the distinction becomes nugatory. But it would be farfetched to call the pollution of a public beach an invasion of privacy.

as the means to do so become simpler and cheaper, and the inclination stronger, the rate of population growth may well decelerate. Perhaps the resources available will satisfy the needs of future populations as much as before.[16]

However, privacy—at least that aspect of it which entitles each person not to participate in the activities of others, or to suffer the intrusion of these activities in his private domain—is likely to shrink greatly. And it will become more and more porous. Places not flown over by planes and crisscrossed by other transportation, not contaminated by noise and fumes, not crowded with people and activity, will be rare. Privacy will become a privilege available to only a few who are willing to pay a high price in money, effort, and sacrifice of amenities. Even so it will be incomplete.

The chances of privacy diminish roughly (and unevenly) as crowding increases. The increase of population ineluctably intensifies crowding. Modern economies require few people to devote themselves to farming and many to engage in industrial production and tertiary services concentrated in metropolitan areas. To support a population of five billion or more, the world will have to be industrialized and urbanized quite rapidly. The physical distances among residences will be shortened as will distances among work places, while the distance between residential and work areas will be lengthened. This crowded locational pattern produces—and modern means of transportation make possible—steady streams of traffic from and to residential and work areas.

Traffic necessarily abridges the privacy of participants and that of everyone affected by the noise and the fumes. Thus, even though urban residences can be built so as to protect privacy almost as well as rural residences might (walls can be thickened, for example) privacy actually cannot be preserved in urban life. The urban resident must join streams of traffic as soon as he leaves his residence. Moreover space, and thick walls, are quite

[16] It is highly misleading to compare world resources (anyway, on the whole, unknown) with world population. The world is divided into quite impermeable compartments: underpopulated Canada will not allow sizable masses from overpopulated China to enter. Moreover, such transfers are costly. (Siberia is more likely for the Chinese—but they have to win a war first.)

costly; an apartment or house protected from noise is a luxury few can afford.

The loss of privacy is not offset by a greater sense of community or by more friendly mutual involvement. On the contrary, there is alienation, mutual indifference, and even hostility. Little mutual involvement is desired. Others are felt as impositions on one's senses, as irritations. City dwellers become "blasé," that is, unresponsive, because of the multiplicity and frequency of transitory contacts and stimuli to which crowdedness exposes them. When there are too many of them, others are perceived largely as anonymous demands on one's time and sentiments, or as objects to be controlled and exploited.[17] Individual relations and mutual toleration of individuality require comparative permanence, shared objects, and a feeling of singularity and nonrecurrence. Under crowded conditions people are less likely to become significant to one another; each person relates to the crowd. The effect is isolation, a "lonely crowd" of people who have few ties to one another, and whose ties come too easily undone.

Affluence and Equality

It might be possible to construct an index measuring the physical and social space occupied per capita and therewith the distance remaining among persons and the degree of privacy. The index would be governed by such matters as average population density, and actual distribution, income level and actual distribution, technology, etc. Without such an index the following hypotheses and illustrations will have to suffice.

Given the population and size of a city and the external circumstances, the higher the income of the inhabitants, the larger —*ceteris paribus*—the physical space each requires and the shorter the physical distances among inhabitants in residential and in business areas: *affuence intensifies crowding.*

[17] John B. Calhoun's experiments with Norway rats ("Population Density and Social Pathology," *Scientific American*, February, 1962) shows that crowding leads to social pathology among rats. It is not impossible that such effects may occur among humans too. But we do not know whether they do or what degree and kind of crowding would produce them.

Further, *the more equally distributed a high income is, the greater the crowding effect*—the larger the space required per capita, the smaller the distances between people in most locations and occasions—shopping, going from and to work, leaving the city, recreation, eating, etc. Affluence and equality also add significantly to the public services and to the private activities which intensify noise and air pollution. The activities of all in the aggregate tend to invade the privacy of each.

The advantages of industrialization, of prosperity, and of equality are obvious. Although obvious too, the effect on privacy usually is neglected. Privacy becomes unattainable in most respects for the average citizen who will not be able to escape crowding, traffic noises, and fumes. He will become an involuntary participant in the activities of others wherever he is, even in his private domain. The very rich may be able to afford the constantly rising price of protecting their privacy by living on estates outside the city, but even they will not be able to avoid invasions such as airplanes overhead. And they must, on occasion, travel to the city.

Specifically, high and widely spread income tends to reduce privacy because money is spent on privacy-reducing implements—which often are purchased to increase the privacy of the owner. (Isn't that part of the motivation for the car, the boat, the week-end cottage?) Yet in the aggregate they tend to be self-defeating.

Most people who can afford to have cars. Wherever kept, cars increase physical space requirements by a multiple of the space they actually displace at any time. To make their use possible, roads must be built and parking spaces at their various temporary destinations. When used, cars produce traffic noise and air pollution. These affect the prosperous city and country far more than the one which is not. Of two areas with equal population density, the area in which people drive cars will always be more crowded. Nothing reduces the uninvaded space available to each person more than the rapid and always possible movement of cars and, to a lesser extent, planes. (Travelers from prosperous countries are now in the process of destroying the beauty, the character, and the privacy of the less developed countries.) Because cars enable the population to move rapidly from place to place, one scarcely is alone anywhere.

Cars usually are driven to about the same places at the same time. If it is accessible by car, therefore, there will be no attractive place which remains uncrowded on a holiday, with congested roads leading to and from it. The end product, therefore, of providing a car for everybody is self-defeating. Accessibility produces crowding and reduces privacy. This effect can be avoided in prosperous countries only by taxing cars heavily and providing mass transportation to selected points.

Widely shared prosperity also increases general consumption. Increased consumption means more production per capita—this is indeed part of the definition of prosperity—and therewith more noise and pollution per capita, as well as more traffic and greater space requirements.

It has often been pointed out that the U.S. uses a disproportionate share of the world's resources, far more, per capita, than other countries. This very fact—also an index of prosperity—means that the problems of noise pollution and crowding, even of garbage disposal, multiply. And these problems affect privacy. Garbage must be removed. But garbage disposal produces noise as well as odors and air pollution, all of which affect private areas. High consumption means more garbage. High income—which causes high consumption—also seems to mean elaborate packaging, newspapers and magazines thick with advertising, and many additional sources of garbage, of traffic, of air, and of noise pollution.

Although intensified by it, the problem is not caused altogether by prosperity. Propensity and technical possibility are to blame as well. Transistor radios are a major source of noise pollution even in the poorest areas. Since they are used for the sake of noise, one must conclude that privacy, or at least the right to be protected against the intrusion of noise, is far from popular.

The threat to privacy from invasion arises from the nature of our economy, the policies committed and omitted by political authorities, and the social style of urban living that has been adopted. The remedies can only be suggested summarily.

(1) Every inducement to stop the increase of population must be used. This involves (a) free distribution of semipermanent (removable) contraceptive agents; (b) fiscal rewards for not having offspring, including bounties for the acceptance of con-

traceptive agents, and (c) fiscal penalties (taxes) for having offspring.

(2) Heavy taxation of all private means of transportation.

(3) Penalizing taxation for anything that pollutes the air or produces noise. This will lead to the adoption of noise- and pollution-reducing devices. Where these are not feasible, it will lead to the reduction of the invasion-producing activities.

(4) Thought must be given to the restriction of undue packaging and generally of disposable, that is, garbage-producing objects. The cost of disposal ought to be included in their price by fiscal means.

Even though the producers of noises, odors, and images can be held responsible for the invasive effect by taxation, ultimately, the cost of protecting privacy will be shifted to the public. It remains to be seen whether the public is willing to pay it. Ways can be found to minimize the activities which produce invasions of privacy, such as private cars. Will the public accept them? Nothing will really help if the population continues to increase at the present rate.[18] Will this rate be reduced soon enough?

Insensitivity

One kind of invasion of privacy might be controlled by legislation without radical changes of social policy. No taxation, or restriction on public or private services, would be required.

Privacy is violated whenever, in public places or in places of public accommodation (such as restaurants, lobbies, elevators) which are difficult or impossible to avoid, we are forced to listen to broadcast or otherwise reproduced messages or music. Sometimes prefabricated noise is piped in by owners or sponsors; sometimes it issues from the radios, etc., of fellow riders of the bus, or of fellow users of the public park, restaurant, etc. Whatever the source of the canned noise, we are forced to suffer it, if we want to use the taxi, elevator, beach, etc.[19] What degree

[18] The technology of garbage disposal and of noise and pollution control is in its infancy. Yet I doubt that we can hope for more than some mitigation of the effects of prosperity and population increase.

[19] Actual public speaking, singing, or playing should not be regarded as a violation of privacy, even when the audience is captive. The activity enjoys

of privacy we might otherwise enjoy in public places is impaired: we are made to participate in activities we do not wish and do not need to share. The broadcast enjoyed by one person intrudes upon the privacy of another. We have been spared official broadcasts in public carriers by means of hard-fought judicial decisions. However, if a passenger wishes to play his own radio in a public bus, few drivers will interfere. Thus all passengers will have to suffer the broadcast desired by any.

It is not hard to legislate protection against this type of invasion. But to do so would require far more sensitivity to the problem than has been shown hitherto.

In New York there is a regulation forbidding taxi drivers to play their radios while driving passengers. It is totally unenforced. There is no regulation against receiving signals from a central dispatcher, which produce a highly irritating noise. Passengers who dare asking the driver to turn down the noise meet with more hostility than success. The possibility of actually separating the driver and passenger compartments, so as to ensure mutual privacy, is excluded as "undemocratic." (When partitions are installed, they are carefully made ineffective.)

Such examples could be multiplied. The point is simple. The protection of privacy depends on social policies, on legislation, and on enforcement. None of these will occur unless the public indicates an interest in the preservation of privacy strong enough to induce the needed changes of policy, the needed legislation, and the needed enforcement. Beyond public pressure, there must also be a public willingness to pay the monetary price and to make the personal sacrifices of convenience that would be required.

However, it seems that the less privacy most people have, the less they miss it. Some indeed seem to feel threatened by any

---

some First Amendment protection. At any rate the actual threat to privacy comes from broadcast, or mechanically reproduced, activities. By themselves people are not able to produce as persistent a disturbance as a radio can. In a sense, billboards which preempt the landscape, and skywriting which preempts the sky, also invade privacy since they force participation. So do many public "nuisances," noises, odors, etc., in excess of what is required by the activity which takes place. These violations, however, can be dealt with fairly easily by legal and fiscal measures (see my "What to Do About Advertising," *Commentary*, May 1962).

privacy—their own as well as that of others. The high decibel levels of discotheques, and the intentional crowding of the floor, suggest that the customers want to be submerged by sound (and light) waves and by one another. They want to be shorn of privacy, each lost in sound, lights, and the crowd.

With the loss of privacy, however, the most effective defense of the individual against the pressure of the public will disappear. For it is by our ability to avoid being observed by others and to avoid having to share in their activities that individuality is preserved and the pressure to conform limited. Compared to the danger to individuality, which comes from the invasion of the private area by public activities, by crowding, by noise, by pollution, the danger which arises from invasions by law-enforcement agencies is minor.

9

PRIVACY AND AUTONOMY

HYMAN GROSS

Why is privacy desirable? When is its loss objectionable and when is it not? How much privacy is a person entitled to? These questions challenge at the threshold our concern about protection of privacy. Usually they are pursued by seeking agreement on the boundary between morbid and healthy reticence, and by attempting to determine when unwanted intrusion or notoriety is justified by something more important than privacy. Seldom is privacy considered as the condition under which there is *control* over acquaintance with one's personal affairs by the one enjoying it, and I wish here to show how consideration of privacy in this neglected aspect is helpful in answering the basic questions. First I shall attempt to make clear this part of the idea of privacy, next suggest why privacy in this aspect merits protection, then argue that some important dilemmas are less vexing when we do get clear about these things, and finally offer a cautionary remark regarding the relation of privacy and autonomy.

I

What in general is it that makes certain conduct offensive to privacy? To distinguish obnoxious from innocent interference with privacy we must first see clearly what constitutes loss of privacy at all, and then determine why loss of privacy when it does occur is sometimes objectionable and sometimes not.

Loss of privacy occurs when the limits one has set on acquaintance with his personal affairs are not respected. Almost always we mean not respected by *others,* though in unusual cases we might speak of a person not respecting his own privacy—he is such a passionate gossip, say, that he gossips even about himself and later regrets it. Limits on acquaintance may be maintained by the physical insulation of a home, office, or other private place within which things that are to be private may be confined. Or such bounds may exist by virtue of exclusionary social conventions, for example, those governing a private conversation in a public place; or through restricting conventions which impose an obligation to observe such limits, as when disclosure is made in confidence. Limits operate in two ways. There are restrictions on what is known, and restrictions on who may know it. Thus, a curriculum vitae furnished to or for a prospective employer is not normally an invitation to undertake a detective investigation using the items provided as clues. Nor is there normally license to communicate to others the information submitted. In both instances there would be disregard of limitations implied by considerations of privacy, unless the existence of such limitations is unreasonable under the circumstances (the prospective employer is the CIA, or the information is furnished to an employment agency). But there is no loss of privacy when such limits as do exist are respected, no matter how ample the disclosure or how extensive its circulation. If I submit a detailed account of my life while my friend presents only the barest résumé of his, I am not giving up more of privacy than he. And if I give the information to a hundred employers, I lose no more in privacy than my friend who confides to only ten, provided those informed by each of us are equally restricted. More people know more about me, so my *risk* of losing privacy is greater and the threatened loss more serious. Because I am a less private person than my friend, I am more willing to run that risk. But until there is loss of control over what is known, and by whom, my privacy is uncompromised—though much indeed may be lost in secrecy, mystery, obscurity, and anonymity.

Privacy is lost in either of two ways. It may be given up, or it may be taken away. Abandonment of privacy (though sometimes undesired) is an inoffensive loss, while deprivation by others is an offensive loss.

If one makes a public disclosure of personal matters or exposes himself under circumstances that do not contain elements of restriction on further communication, there is loss of control for which the person whose privacy is lost is himself responsible. Such abandonment may result from indifference, carelessness, or a positive desire to have others become acquainted. There are, however, instances in which privacy is abandoned though this was not intended. Consider indiscretions committed while drunk which are rued when sober. If the audience is not under some obligation (perhaps the duty of a confidant) to keep dark what was revealed, there has been a loss of privacy for which the one who suffers it is responsible. But to constitute an abandonment, the loss of privacy must result from voluntary conduct by the one losing it, and the loss must be an expectable result of such conduct. If these two conditions are not met, the person who suffers the loss cannot be said to be responsible for it. Accordingly, a forced revelation, such as an involuntary confession, is not an abandonment of privacy, because the person making it has not given up control but has had it taken from him.

Regarding the requirement of expectability, we may see its significance by contrasting the case of a person whose conversation is overheard in Grand Central Station with the plight of someone made the victim of eavesdropping in his living room. In a public place loss of control is expectable by virtue of the circumstances of communication: part of what we mean when we say a place is public is that there is not present the physical limitation upon which such control depends. But a place may be called private only when there is such limitation, so communication in it is expectably limited and the eavesdropping an offensive violation for which the victim is not himself responsible. And consider the intermediate case of eavesdropping on a conversation in a public place—a distant parabolic microphone focused on a street-corner conversation, or a bugging device planted in an airplane seat. The offensive character of such practices derives again from their disregard of expectable limitations, in this instance the force of an exclusionary social convention which applies to all except those whose immediate presence enables them to overhear.

So far there has been consideration of what constitutes loss of privacy, and when it is objectionable. But to assess claims for protection of privacy we must be clear also about *why* in general loss of privacy is objectionable. This becomes especially important when privacy and other things we value are in competition, one needing to be sacrificed to promote the other. It becomes important then to understand what good reasons there are for valuing privacy, and this is our next item of business.

II

There are two sorts of things we keep private, and with respect to each privacy is desirable for somewhat different reasons. Concern for privacy is sometimes concern about what of us can become known, and to whom. This includes acquaintance with all those things which make up the person as he may become known—identity, appearance, traits of personality and character, talents, weaknesses, tastes, desires, habits, interests—in short, things which tell us who a person is and what he's like. The other kind of private matter is about our lives—what we've done, intend to do, are doing now, how we feel, what we have, what we need—and concern about privacy here is to restrict acquaintance with these matters. Together these two classes of personal matters comprise all those things which can be private. Certain items of information do indeed have aspects which fit them for either category. For example, a person's belief is something which pertains to him when viewed as characteristic of him, but pertains to the events of his life when viewed as something he has acquired, acts on, and endeavors to have others adopt.

Why is privacy of the person important? This calls mainly

for consideration of what is necessary to maintain an integrated personality in a social setting. Although we are largely unaware of what influences us at the time, we are constantly concerned to control how we appear to others, and act to implement this concern in ways extremely subtle and multifarious. Models of image and behavior are noticed, imitated, adopted, so that nuances in speech, gesture, facial expression, *politesse,* and much more become a person as known on an occasion. The deep motive is to influence the reactions of others, and this is at the heart of human social accommodation. Constraints to imitation and disguise can become a pathological problem of serious proportions when concern with appearances interferes with normal functioning, but normal behavior allows, indeed requires, that we perform critically in presenting and withholding in order to effect certain appearances. If these editorial efforts are not to be wasted, we must have a large measure of control over what of us is seen and heard, when, where, and by whom. For this reason we see as offensive the candid camera which records casual behavior with the intention of later showing it as entertainment to a general audience. The victim is not at the time aware of who will see him and so does not have the opportunity to exercise appropriate critical restraint in what he says and does. Although subsequent approval for the showing eliminates grounds for objection to the publication as an offense to privacy, there remains the lingering objection to the prior disregard of limits of acquaintance which are normal to the situation and so presumably relied on by the victim at the time. The nature of the offense is further illuminated by considering its aggravation when the victim has been deliberately introduced unawares into the situation for the purpose of filming his behavior, or its still greater offensiveness if the setting is a place normally providing privacy and assumed to be private by the victim. What we have here are increasingly serious usurpations of a person's prerogative to determine how he shall appear, to whom, and on what occasion.

The same general objection applies regarding loss of privacy where there is information about our personal affairs which is obtained, accumulated, and transmitted by means beyond our control. It is, however, unlike privacy of personality in its untoward consequences. A data bank of personal information is considered objectionable, but not because it creates appearances over which we have no control. We are willing to concede that acquaintance with our reputation is in general not something we are privileged to control, and that we are not privileged to decide just what our reputation shall be. If the reputation is correct we cannot object because we do not appear as we would wish. What then are the grounds of objection to a data bank, an objection which indeed persists even if its information is correct and the inferences based on the information are sound? A good reason for objecting is that a data bank is an offense to self-determination. We are subject to being acted on by others because of conclusions about us which we do not know and whose effect we have no opportunity to counteract. There is a loss of control over reputation which is unacceptable because we no longer have the ability to try to change what is believed about us. We feel entitled to know what others believe, and why, so that we may try to change misleading impressions and on occasion show why a decision about us ought not to be based on reputation even if the reputation is justified. If our account in the data bank were made known to us and opportunity given to change its effect, we should drop most (though not all) of our objection to it. We might still fear the danger of abuse by public forces concerned more with the demands of administrative convenience than justice, but because we could make deposits and demand a statement reflecting them we would at least no longer be in the position of having what is known and surmised about us lie beyond our control.

Two aspects of privacy have been considered separately, though situations in which privacy is violated sometimes involve both. Ordinary surveillance by shadowing, peeping, and bugging commonly consists of observation of personal behavior as well as accumulation of information. Each is objectionable for its own reasons, though in acting against the offensive practice we protect privacy in both aspects. Furthermore, privacy of personality and of personal affairs have some common ground in meriting protection, and this has to do with a person's role as a responsible moral agent.

In general we do not criticize a person for untoward occurrences which are a result of his conduct if (through no fault of his own) he lacked the ability to do otherwise. Such a person is similarly ineligible for applause for admirable things which would not have taken place but for his conduct. In both instances we claim that he is not responsible for what happened, and so should not be blamed or praised. The principle holds true regarding loss of privacy. If a person cannot control how he is made to appear (nor could he have prevented his loss of control), he is not responsible for how he appears or is thought of, and therefore cannot be criticized as displeasing or disreputable (nor extolled as the opposite). He can, of course, be condemned for conduct which is the basis of the belief about him, but that is a different matter from criticism directed solely to the fact that such a belief exists. Personal gossip (even when believed) is not treated by others as something for which the subject need answer, because its existence defies his control. Responsible appraisal of anyone whose image or reputation is a matter of concern requires that certain private items illicitly in the public domain be ignored in the assessment. A political figure may, with impunity, be known as someone who smokes drinks, flirts, and tells dirty jokes, so long (but only so long) as this is not the public image *he* presents. The contrasting fortunes of two recent political leaders remind us that not being responsible for what is believed by others can be most important. If such a man is thought in his private life to engage in discreet though illicit liaisons he is not held accountable for rumors without more. However, once he has allowed himself to be publicly exposed in a situation which is in the slightest compromising, he must answer for mere appearances. And on this same point, we might consider why a woman is never held responsible for the way she appears in the privacy of her toilette.

To appreciate the importance of this sort of disclaimer of responsibility we need only imagine a community in which it is not recognized. Each person would be accountable for himself however he might be known, and regardless of any precautionary seclusion which was undertaken in the interest of shame, good taste, or from other motives of self-regard. In such a world modesty is sacrificed to the embarrassment of unwanted acclaim, and self-criticism is replaced by the condemnation of others. It is part of the vision of Orwell's *1984*, in which observation is so thorough that it forecloses the possibility of a private sector of life under a person's exclusionary control, and so makes him answerable for everything observed without limits of time or place. Because of this we feel such a condition of life far more objectionable than a community which makes the same oppressive social demands of loyalty and conformity but with the opportunity to be free of concern about appearances in private. In a community without privacy, furthermore, there can be no editorial privilege exercised in making oneself known to others. Consider, for example, the plight in which Montaigne would find himself. He observed that "No quality embraces us purely and universally. If it did not seem crazy to talk to oneself, there is not a day when I would not be heard growling at myself: 'Confounded fool!' And yet I do not intend that to be my definition." Respect for privacy is required to safeguard our changes of mood and mind, and to promote growth of the person through self-discovery and criticism. We want to run the risk of making fools of ourselves and be free to call ourselves fools, yet not be fools in the settled opinion of the world, convicted out of our own mouths.

III

Privacy is desirable, but rights to enjoy it are not absolute. In deciding what compromises must be made some deep quandaries recur, and three of them at least seem more manageable in light of what has been said so far.

In the first place, insistence on privacy is often taken as implied admission that there is cause for shame. The assumption is that the only reason for keeping something from others is that one is ashamed of it (although it is conceded that sometimes there is in fact no cause for shame even though the person seeking privacy thinks there is). Those who seek information and wish to disregard interests in privacy often play on this notion by claiming that the decent and the innocent have no cause for shame and so no need for privacy: "Only those who have done or wish to do something shameful demand privacy."

But it is unsound to assume that a claim for privacy implies such an admission. Pride, or at least wholesome self-regard, is the motive in many situations. The famous Warren and Brandeis article on privacy which appeared in the *Harvard Law Review* in 1890 was impelled in some measure, we are told, by Samuel Warren's chagrin. His daughter's wedding, a very social Boston affair, had been made available to the curious at every newsstand by the local press. Surely he was not ashamed of the wedding even though outraged by the publicity. Or consider Miss Roberson, the lovely lady whose picture was placed on a poster advertising the product of Franklin Mills with the eulogistic slogan "Flour of the family," thereby precipitating a lawsuit whose consequences included the first statutory protection of privacy in the United States. What was exploited was the lady's face, undoubtedly a source of pride.

Both these encroachments on privacy illustrate the same point. Things which people like about themselves are taken by them to belong to them in a particularly exclusive way, and so control over disclosure or publication is especially important to them. The things about himself which a person is most proud of he values most, and thus are things over which he is most interested to exercise exclusive control. It is true that shame is not infrequently the motive for privacy, for often we do seek to maintain conditions necessary to avoid criticism and punishment. But since it is not the only motive, the quest for privacy does not entail tacit confessions. Confusion arises here in part because an assault on privacy always does involve humiliation of the victim. But this is because he has been deprived of control over something personal which is given over to the control of others. In short, unwilling loss of privacy always results in the victim being shamed, not because of what others learn, but because they and not he may then determine who else shall know it and what use shall be made of it.

Defining the privilege to make public what is otherwise private is another source of persistent difficulty. There is a basic social interest in making available information about people, in exploring the personal aspects of human affairs, in stimulating and satisfying curiosity about others. The countervailing interest is in allowing people who have not offered themselves for public scrutiny to remain out of sight and out of mind. In much of the United States the law has strained with the problem of drawing a line of protection which accords respect to both interests. The result, broadly stated, has been recognition of a privilege to compromise privacy for news and other material whose primary purpose is to impart information, but to deny such privileged status to literary and other art, to entertainment, and generally to any appropriation for commercial purposes. Development of the law in New York after Miss Roberson's unsuccessful attempt to restrain public display of her picture serves as a good example. A statute was enacted prohibiting unauthorized use of the name, portrait, or picture of any living person for purposes of trade or advertising, and the legislation has been interpreted by the courts along the general lines indicated. But it is still open to speculation why a writer's portrayal of a real person as a character in a novel could qualify as violative, while the same account in a biographical or historical work would not. It has not been held that history represents a more important social interest than art and so is more deserving of a privileged position in making known personal matters, or, more generally, that edification is more important than entertainment. Nor is the question ever raised, as one might expect, whether an item of news is sufficiently newsworthy to enjoy a privilege in derogation of privacy. Further, it was not held that the implied statutory criterion of intended economic benefit from the use of a personality would warrant the fundamental distinctions. Indeed, the test of economic benefit would qualify both television's public affairs programs and its dramatic shows as within the statute, and the reportage of *Life* magazine would be as restricted as the films of De Mille or De Sica. But in each instance the former is in general free of the legal prohibition while the latter is not. What, then, is the basis of distinction? Though not articulated, a sound criterion does exist.

Unauthorized *use* of another person—whether for entertainment, artistic creation, or economic gain—is offensive. So long as we remain in charge of how we are used, we have no cause for complaint. In those cases in which a legal wrong is recognized, there has been use by others in disregard of this authority, but in those cases in which a privilege is found, there is not *use* of personality or personal affairs at all, at least not use in the sense of one person assuming control over another, which is the gist of the offense to autonomy. We do indeed suffer a loss of autonomy whenever the power to place us in free circulation is exercised by others, but we consider such loss offensive only when another person assumes the control of which we are deprived, when we are used and not merely exposed. Failure to make clear this criterion of offensiveness has misled those who wish to define the protectable area and they conceive the problem as one of striking an optimal balance between two valuable interests, when in fact it is a matter of deciding whether the acts complained of are offensive under a quite definite standard of offensiveness. The difficult cases here have not presented a dilemma of selecting the happy medium, but rather the slippery job of determining whether the defendant had used the plaintiff or whether he had merely caused things about him to become known, albeit to the defendant's profit. The difference is between managing another person as a means to one's own ends, which is offensive, and acting merely as a vehicle of presentation (though not gratuitously) to satisfy established social needs, which is not offensive. Cases dealing with an unauthorized biography that was heavily anecdotal and of questionable accuracy, or with an entertaining article that told the true story of a former child prodigy who became an obscure eccentric, are perplexing ones because they present elements of both offensive and inoffensive publication, and a decision turns on which is predominant.

There remains another balance-striking quandary to be dismantled. It is often said that privacy as an interest must be balanced against security. Each, we think, must sacrifice something of privacy to promote the security of all, though we are willing to risk some insecurity to preserve a measure of privacy. Pressure to reduce restrictions on wiretapping and searches by police seeks to push the balance toward greater security. But the picture we are given is seriously misleading. In the first place we must notice the doubtful assumption on which the argument rests. It may be stated this way: the greater the ability to watch what is going on, or obtain evidence of what has gone on, the greater the ability to prevent crime. It is a notion congenial to those who believe that more efficient law enforcement contributes significantly to a reduction in crime. We must, however, determine if such a proposition is in fact sound, and we must see what crimes are suppressible, even in principle, before any sacrifice of privacy can be justified. There is, at least *in limine,* much to be said for the conflicting proposition that once a generally efficient system of law enforcement exists an increase in its efficiency does not result in a corresponding reduction in crime, but only in an increase in punishments. Apart from that point, there is an objection relating more directly to what has been said here about privacy. Security and privacy are both desirable, but measures to promote each are on different moral footing. Men ought to be secure, we say, because only in that condition can they live a good life. Privacy, however, like peace and prosperity, is itself part of what we mean by a good life, a part having to do with self-respect and self-determination. Therefore, the appropriate attitudes when we are asked to sacrifice privacy for security are first a critical one which urges alternatives that minimize or do not at all require the sacrifice, and ultimately regret for loss of a cherished resource if the sacrifice proves necessary.

IV

In speaking of privacy and autonomy there is some danger that privacy may be conceived as autonomy. Such confusion has been signaled in legal literature by early and repeated use of the phrase "right to be let alone" as a synonym for "right of privacy." The United States Supreme Court succumbed completely in 1965 in its opinion in *Griswold v. Connecticut,* and the ensuing intellectual disorder warrants comment.

In that case legislative prohibition of the use of contraceptives was said to be a violation of a constitutional right of privacy, at least when it affected married people. The court's opinion relied heavily on an elaborate *jeu de mots,* in which different senses of the word "privacy" were punned upon, and the legal concept generally mismanaged in ways too various to recount here. In the *Griswold* situation there had been an attempt by government to regulate personal affairs, not get acquainted with them, and so there was an issue regarding autonomy and not privacy. The opinion was not illuminating on the question of what are proper bounds for the exercise of legislative power, which was the crucial matter before the court. It is precisely the issue of what rights to autonomous determination of his affairs are enjoyed by a citizen. The *Griswold* opinion not only failed to take up that question in a forthright manner, but promoted confusion about privacy in the law by unsettling the intellectual focus on it which had been developed in torts and constitutional law. If the confusion in the court's argument was inadvertent, one may sympathize with the deep conceptual difficulties which produced it, and if it was deliberately contrived, admire its ingenuity. Whatever its origin, its effect is to muddle the separate issues, which must be analyzed and argued along radically different lines when protection is sought either for privacy or for autonomy. Hopefully, further developments will make clear that while an offense to privacy is an offense to autonomy, not every curtailment of autonomy is a compromise of privacy.

10

PRIVACY: ONE CONCEPT OR MANY

PAUL A. FREUND

This paper is an inquiry into the formation and possible disintegration of a legal concept, right of privacy, inviting comparison with the life history of a scientific concept like "ether" or "atom."

FORMULATION OF THE CONCEPT

The law, like other branches of thought, lives by metaphor, moves by simile, and organizes itself by concepts. Centuries ago eavesdropping (itself a metaphor) was regarded as a misdemeanor, involving an element of trespass. Offensive shadowing in a public place also came to be treated as a wrong, "like" eavesdropping, though without the element of trespass. These can be characterized as instances of distressing intrusion into the private domain of living or into the sphere of a person's autonomous movement. What is the position, then, of unwelcome publicity concerning private affairs, which causes similar mental distress but is not marked by any physical intrusion?

This was the question dealt with by Samuel Warren and Louis D. Brandeis in the seminal article entitled "The Right of Privacy," published in the November, 1890, issue of the *Harvard Law Review*.[1] The occasion for the paper was the unwelcome publicity accorded the social activities of Warren's family, proper Bostonians of the Victorian era. Not for the first time did a highly personal trouble stimulate original minds to powerful generalizations of principle: witness John Milton's domestic situation as the impetus for his tracts on divorce, leading in turn to his great manifesto on the liberty of unlicensed printing.

The term "right of privacy" had been used and endorsed in an article published in *Scribner's* in July 1890, written, surprisingly enough, by a journalist, but an exceptional one, E. L. Godkin. The article was cited by Warren and Brandeis. Under the title "The Rights of the Citizen: To his own Reputation," Godkin castigated the overzealous reporters and profit-minded publishers who exposed to public view a person's folly, misfortune, indiscretion, or weakness that had never got beyond the domestic circle. But Godkin was not sanguine about relief:

> In truth, there is only one remedy for the violations of the right of privacy within the reach of the American public, and that is but an imperfect one. It is to be found in attaching social discredit to invasions of it on the part of conductors of the press. At present this check can hardly be said to exist. . . . As long as the money-getting talent holds the field against all other competing talents, in the race for distinction of every kind, we shall probably not see any great change in the attitude of the press on this subject.

What to the publicist was a cause for despairing lament was a challenge to the resourcefulness and creativity of the two lawyers. They undertook to fashion a new legal concept, one that would operate as a deterrent by reason of liability-incurring sanctions, and to do so out of theretofore disparate legal phenomena. Moving beyond the analogy of eavesdropping and shadowing, they took a fresh look at the well-established protection of literary rights in letters and other unpublished works and the recognized protection of studio photographs against un-

[1] 4 *Harv. L. Rev.* 193.

authorized publication. The former had been treated as a species of "property," but Brandeis (for internal and other evidence indicates his dominant authorship) argued that this rationale was simply circular and conclusory;[2] that the substantial interest protected in the case of letters and manuscripts, protected regardless of their material value or lack of it, was the interest of personality; and that the causing of mental distress, rather than the deprivation of a material possession, was the gravamen of the offense. Similarly, in the case of the release of studio photographs, the conventional legal treatment—breach of trust or of a confidential relation—was regarded by Brandeis as putting the emphasis on an accidental rather than an essential element of the right.

Why had it been more comfortable for the law to absorb certain claims of personality into existing rules protecting property or confidential relations than to recognize these claims more forthrightly by amending or supplementing the rules? There was a certain apprehension that legal recognition of personality as such, and of injury to feelings, would open up a nest of claims that would be too insubstantial, too numerous, and too difficult of verification for legal sanctions to be employed. There was, as a special case, the maxim that equity protects only property rights. Preventive relief, that is, by injunctions, was not available for interests simply of personality, in a court of equity that acted on the basis of written evidence and through a judge without a jury. Infringement of property rights and breaches of trust were the staple business of equity courts. And there is always a strong pull to accommodate change to continuity in an ongoing, revered institution by preserving the rule or dogma and utilizing an assimilative fiction to encompass the new demand within its traditional terms.

The law responded no differently than institutions like universities and churches. Harvard has had an old rule that only graduates of Harvard are eligible to vote in certain university elections. With the strong infusion of non-Harvard men on the faculty, the rule has not been abrogated but an honorary Master

[2] Compare: "Do the gods love piety because it is pious, or is it pious because they love it?" Plato, *Euthyphro*.

of Arts degree is quietly bestowed where it is necessary for compliance. When a fundamentalist Catholic priest in Boston persisted in preaching that since only members of the Church are saved, non-Catholics are incapable of salvation, the demands of ecumenism led his superiors to insist that, while the dogma remained true, membership in the Church embraced all who had not after the benefit of full instruction rejected it.

There was, to be sure, some hint of the protection of an interest in privacy in a celebrated English case brought by Prince Albert on behalf of himself and the Queen.[3] The royal couple, having made some drawings for the enjoyment of themselves and intimate friends, delivered them over to an engraver for limited reproduction. Somehow the plates came into the possession of another subject of the realm, an enterprising exhibitor named Strange, who prepared a catalogue with a fulsome announcement of a public showing: "The royal and most interesting collection is now submitted to the inspection of the public, under the firm persuasion and in the full confidence that her Majesty's loyal and affectionate subjects will highly admire and duly appreciate the eminent artistic talent and acquirements of both her Majesty and her illustrious consort his Royal Highness Prince Albert." There followed a passage from *Coriolanus,* as unctuous as, for Strange's purposes, it was apt:

> You must not be the grave of your
>   deserving; England must know
> The value of her own. 'Twere a
>   concealment
> Worse than a theft, no less
>   than a traducement,
> To hide your doings.

The judges were not impressed, and Strange was enjoined from proceeding with his venture. It would doubtless have been undignified and inappropriate to dwell on the monetary value of the artistic creations and of the dominion over them enjoyed by the creators. The indignity involved in the scheme cried

[3] *Prince Albert v. Strange,* 2 DeGex & Sm. 652 (1849).

out for condemnation stronger than would be meet for impairment of property values or even for participating in a breach of trust. The Vice Chancellor, Knight Bruce, was able to glide smoothly, if portentously, from property to propriety:

> I think, therefore, not only that the defendant here is unlawfully invading the plaintiff's rights, but also that the invasion is of such kind and affects such property as to entitle the plaintiff to the preventive remedy of an injunction; and if not the more, yet, certainly, not the less, because it is an intrusion—an unbecoming and unseemly intrusion—an intrusion not alone in breach of conventional rules, but offensive to that inbred sense of propriety natural to every man—if intrusion, indeed, fitly describes a sordid spying into the privacy of domestic life—into the home (a word hitherto sacred among us), the home of a family whose life and conduct form an acknowledged title, though not their only unquestionable title, to the most marked respect in this country.

It was for us a germinal historical episode. In a country where the law boasts that it is no respecter of persons, privacy is not reserved for royalty, nor is the recognition of mental and emotional distress confined to a ruling class. There is too great a gap between the first Elizabeth's time and Victoria's, at least on this side of the water, for us now to be much moved by some other Shakespearean lines:[4]

> A sight most pitiful in the
> meanest wretch,
> Past speaking of in a King.

To have stressed the rationale of breach of confidential relationship, moreover, would have arrested the development of the law artificially in one area of unwelcome publicity: the unauthorized publication of a photographic likeness. So long as the art was confined to still photography this rationale was adequate, but with the development of the instantaneous camera, and the resulting hazard of the street photographer, a relation of trust or even of simple contract was no longer an appropriate requisite.

[4] *King Lear,* Act IV, sc. vi, l. 205.

The difference between distressing disclosure caused by the behavior of a studio photographer and by that of a street photographer hardly seems significant for the recognition of legal rights; indeed, reproduction of the unposed, unguarded likeness, exploitable for advertising or for amusement, seems if anything to be the more egregious offense.

And so, looking back, one can say that the formation of a distinct concept of privacy, in preference to working with the traditional categories of property and breach of trust, reflected claims of democracy and pressures of technology. The pioneering American statute on the subject, that of New York in 1902, was in fact enacted to overcome a decision that denied recovery to a young lady of exceptional beauty but no special position or fame, whose likeness had been captured by a street photographer and used in advertising posters.[5]

Democracy and technology point, at the same time, to crucial limitations on the claims of privacy. The right pertains to one's "private" affairs, but the scope of that domain will be affected by the nature of one's public calling as well as by the prevailing standards of legitimate exposure. Warren and Brandeis recognized, without elaboration, that a right of privacy would be limited by a legitimate public interest in becoming informed. In a democracy those who hold or actively seek public office relinquish a portion of their self-sanctuary by holding themselves out as deserving of public trust. What might otherwise be deemed immune from revelation or inquiry, or subject to disclosure merely to a private employer, becomes relevant information to be assessed by the members of a larger constituency in the process of judging their agents. It could be said, in general, that the more exalted or sensitive the office, the greater the shrinkage in the domain of private affairs.

Technology, too, makes a difference. Urbanization, to be sure, on balance probably enhanced the opportunities and respect for privacy. In contrast to rural and village life, the urban setting lessened curiosity about neighbors' behavior, diffused personal relationships, and increased attention to the affairs of the "pub-

[5] See note 9, below.

lic" world. This was true at least for upper- and middle-class persons; the poor, huddled into crowded quarters, were stripped of a large measure of privacy. But in the last generation technology and institutional pressures have greatly threatened the sense of privacy—through the common employment of private investigators in labor and family conflicts; governmental security checks; psychological testing, sociological interrogations, and psychoanalytical probings; and the mass curiosity catered to by popular journalism.[6] Techniques such as fingerprinting, or electronic photography in a bank, come to be tolerated as they become commonplace; the teaching hospital is accepted as offering medical services that compensate for the loss of the isolation of the domestic sickbed; the increased capacity of applied sciences, whether psychosomatic medicine or computer technology, to utilize more and more kinds of data, and the consequent calls for such data, may weaken traditional resistance to disclosure. As the area of relevance, political or scientific, expands, there is strong psychological pressure to yield some ground of privacy.

Another limitation on privacy, one recognized by Warren and Brandeis, was the principle of privileged occasion, drawn from the law of defamation. Even a false and damaging statement will be innocent in law if it is made in an honest belief in its truth and made on an occasion that calls for uninhibited candor—a request by a prospective employer or a credit agency, for example, for information concerning another's reliability. Other false and damaging statements may be privileged absolutely, as when they are made in a pleading in a lawsuit or in the verdict of a jury. These encouragements to disclosure in the law of defamation are all the more applicable as qualifications on a right to privacy, since the latter encompasses statements that are truthful.

The law of defamation might inded have served as a base for the concept of a right of privacy itself. In one aspect—the unauthorized use of a name or photograph for advertising purposes —the right to be free from defamation has been found adequate

[6] The preceding sentences draw on Edward Shils, "Privacy: Its Constitution and Vicissitudes," 31 *Law and Contemporary Problems* 281, 288–301 (1966).

in English law to protect the interest of privacy.[7] A well-known amateur golfer was depicted in an advertisement as carrying a package of a certain brand of chocolate. The falsity damaging to reputation, for purposes of the law of libel, consisted in the innuendo that he had permitted himself to be used thus for purposes of notoriety and gain. There was, to be sure, a dissenting opinion arguing that a caricature so offensively vulgar could not possibly have misled anyone knowing anything of the complainant.

Beyond this special class of cases, the law of defamation might have been adapted more generally to the interest of privacy through a reworking of the defense of truth. At least since Lord Campbell's Act in 1834, and generally earlier in American law, truth has been held to be a defense to a claim of libel when uttered or published for justifiable ends and with good motives. Through a strict construction of these conditions it might have been possible to treat the claim to privacy as a branch of the law of libel dealing with truthful statements made for improper purposes.

Why Warren and Brandeis did not choose this course can only be conjectured. The law of defamation is, to begin with, one of the most artificially complex areas of legal doctrine: it is rife with distinctions between libel and slander, general and special damages, conditional and absolute privileges, damage to reputation and to feelings, libel *per se* and libel *per quod*. Even more important, doctrinal development was in the direction of enlarging, not contracting, the defense of truth in actions for defamation. This liberalization of the defense was a hard-won liberty in the struggle against the eighteenth-century law of seditious libel. To have developed a law of privacy by engrafting new constraints on the defense of truth as an appendage to the law of libel would have introduced distorting complexities and might have had a regressive effect on the law of libel itself. Had this course been taken, had privacy been accommodated through patchwork on

[7] Cyril Tolley v. Fry and Sons Ltd. [1931] A.C. 333 (House of Lords). A bill to establish a broader right of privacy against unwarranted publicity was debated in the House of Lords on March 13, 1961, but foundered on the issue of freedom of the press.

classical concepts, Brandeis might have been marked as a Lorentz, certainly not an Einstein, in the history of legal thought.

CRITIQUE OF THE CONCEPT

"Seek simplicity and distrust it" is the admonition of any science. If Warren and Brandeis sought it, others have argued of late that we should distrust it. The position of the critics can be analyzed under two major propositions. First, in its original form the right of privacy is trivial and rather outdated. Today the discomfort of unwanted publicity is likely to be a mark of eccentricity or neuroticism. At best this sort of privacy is a bourgeois value, deserving of only a low priority among the pressing concerns of the law. Indeed, it is more likely that unauthorized publicity, as it centers on figures in the public eye, will offend the subject's sense of business values than of personal inviolability; exploitation without compensation is then the gravamen of the offense.

Second, in its more expansive form the concept of privacy obfuscates analysis. There are four or five distinct legal rights subsumed under the one rubric:[8]

(a) Freedom from misappropriation of one's name or picture for commercial gain. This is in substance a right of publicity in the case of those for whom public attention is a capital asset. For others, as the English case of the amateur golfer suggests, there is an innuendo in the exploitation that is false and that could readily be assimilated to the law of libel. Oddly enough, it is this interest in freedom from commercial use of a name or photograph that is the gist of the right of privacy as generally defined by statute law in the states.[9] The courts have had to

[8] See William Prosser, "Privacy," 48 *Calif. L. Rev.* 383 (1960), breaking down the concept into the first four of these categories. Cf. Harry Kalven, "Privacy in Tort Law: Were Warren and Brandeis Wrong?" 31 *Law & Contemp. Probs.* 326 (1966); Leon Green, "Continuing the Privacy Discussion," 46 *Tex. L. Rev.* 611, 750 (1968).

[9] The New York statute of 1902, the prototype, was unfortunately drafted in the limited terms of its precipitating occasion: "A person . . . [who] uses for advertising purposes, or for the purposes of trade, the name, portrait, or picture of any living person without having first obtained the written con-

generate a more expansive right by feats of statutory construction.

(b) Freedom from embarrassing publicity. This, the essence of the concern of Warren and Brandeis, has been defined in general terms under the rubric "Interference with Privacy" in the American Law Institute's Restatement of the Law of Torts: "A person who unreasonably and seriously interferes with another's interest in not having his affairs known to others or his likeness exhibited to the public is liable to the other."[10] There is a countervailing interest that may be strong enough to serve as a legal defense: newsworthiness, or in constitutional terms, freedom of the press. There is a degree of circularity in the defense, for what is newsworthy at a given time and place depends to some extent on conditioning of public expectations by the practices of the news media. In any event, the issues are likely to revolve around such questions as whether a quondam public figure can be revived with embarrassing data about him—whether, that is, there is a right of obscurity—and where, in a public figure's affairs, the public sector ends and the private begins.

(c) Freedom from being put in a false light, as by attributing to someone a belief or position he does not hold. As with certain cases under (a), the connection is with the law of libel, though damage to feelings, and not necessarily to reputation, may suffice.

(d) Freedom from intrusion into private affairs. This includes protection against eavesdropping, searches and seizures, electronic and other surveillance, intrusive questioning by employers, government agencies, experimental scientists, and the like. The scope of the right is clearly delimited by the relative importance and

---

sent of such person . . . is guilty of a misdemeanor." Civil remedies are provided in a further section.

The statute has given rise to a body of decisional law in New York not unlike that developed in a number of other states without benefit (or hindrance) of a statute on privacy. The phrase "for the purposes of trade" has been used by the judges as an astonishingly subtle differentiator of legitimate and illegitimate incursions on privacy. In *Spahn v. Messner, Inc.*, 18 N. Y. 2d 324 (1966), the court held illegitimate a "fictionalized biography [of a professional athlete] exploited for commercial benefit," while recognizing that "a public figure, whether he be such by choice or involuntarily, is subject to the often searching beam of publicity and that, in balance with the legitimate public interest, the law affords his privacy little protection." Id. at 328.

[10] Restatement of Torts, sec. 867.

exigency of the countervailing interest in the intrusive behavior. A demand that a witness reveal his political associations may be remote, prejudicial, and unwarranted in the context of a legislative investigation, but quite otherwise in an actual trial, where the bias or the knowledge of the witness may be crucial to a true verdict. Similarly with searches and seizures and with surveillance, the resolution of interests may depend on the "reasonable cause" for the intrusion and the procedures employed to establish this.

(e) Freedom from disclosure of, and privilege not to disclose, confidential communication between spouses, patient and physician, client and lawyer, penitent and priest. Efforts to secure a like privilege for communications from an informant to a journalist have thus far generally been unsuccessful.

The argument against a unitary concept underscores the imprecise analysis of legal issues that such a concept fosters. One (or possibly two) of the foregoing categories involves an element of falsity. Two raise issues of freedom of the press. Two impinge on the search for truth in the administration of justice. Given this disparity of central issues, privacy becomes too greedy a legal concept. It might give excessive protection to an interest in human dignity and sensitivity. A majority of the Supreme Court has found in the emanations and radiations from various guarantees of the Bill of Rights a right of privacy against government, and on that basis overturned a Connecticut birth-control law insofar as it penalized the giving of medical advice to married couples.[11] The result might have rested on more conventional grounds: that as applied to married couples no real secular purpose was served by the law, and that it was either an arbitrary interference with personal liberty in contravention of the due-process clause or an endeavor to establish a particular religious tenet for the whole community, in violation of the guarantee against establishment of religion. If the Court is taken at its word, however, a right of privacy exists that would confer on a witness at a trial not merely a privilege against self-incrimination but against being compelled to give any self-degrading testimony.

[11] *Griswold v. Connecticut,* 381 U.S. 479 (1965).

As a logical corollary, the right would jeopardize the validity of immunity statutes, which confer protection on the witness against future self-incriminating use of his testimony in return for overriding his present claim to remain silent. Since the immunity granted by such statutes must be coextensive with the constitutional privilege, and since they cannot confer immunity from self-disgrace, they would necessarily fall short of the protection due under the new constitutional right of privacy. Whether all the Justices who voted to establish the new right in the birth-control case meant to commit themselves to such a sequel is doubtful. The point is, the critics would say, that the judges may be needlessly and heedlessly propelling the law into obscure quagmires of doctrine through what an English judge once called well-meaning sloppiness of thought.

INTERESTS AND RIGHTS, PRINCIPLES AND RULES

What, then, are the considerations favoring a unitary concept?[12] In the first place, it may be useful to adopt a large concept in order to offset an equally large rhetorical counterclaim: freedom of inquiry, the right to know, liberty of the press, Lord Acton's "Everything secret degenerates."

Second, moving beyond the war of words, the fuzzy contours of a concept provide, despite the metaphor, a cutting and growing edge. Logical reductionism, or operationalism, which eschews concepts in favor of discrete statements of the form "if . . . then . . ." sacrifices assimilative powers. In reducing a concept it reduces too our chances of accommodating new relations. "The concepts of a growing science," as J. Bronowski has said, "must be richer and more pliable than any logical construction from the sum of its parts."[13] The value of a rich and pliable concept of privacy needs no laboring when our technology is bringing

[12] Cf. Edward J. Bloustein, "Privacy as an Aspect of Human Dignity: An Answer to Dean Prosser," 39 *N.Y.U.L. Rev.* 962 (1964); Charles Fried, "Privacy," 77 *Yale L. J.* 475 (1968).

[13] J. Bronowski, "The Machinery of Nature," *Encounter* (Nov. 1965), 45, 52.

new threats at least as menacing as instantaneous photography: computerized data banks,[14] psychological testing, electronic surveillance, truth serums and other mind-conditioning drugs. It is surely useful to have at hand a concept that alerts us to, and bespeaks a limitation on, a profusion of potential intrusions.

The more precise question—really a double question—is whether privacy has a legitimating unity as a social-psychological concept, and if so whether the legal system can embody it without undue sacrifice of clarity and good sense in making the accommodations always required among competing principles. The question can be put in slightly different form. If we define an interest as a claim, demand, need, or concern, and a right as a legally protected interest, should privacy be accorded the status of an interest and then of a right?

An analysis along functional lines might view the interest in privacy as an aspect of an interest in secrecy.[15] In its official manifestation secrecy is a state policy serving military, diplomatic, and bureaucratic needs. It is calculated to give security against hostile actions, and also to encourage full and free expression among friends. It lifts inhibitions born of fear—fear of reprisal, of mockery, of quick rejection. It affords shelter for experiment, concession, novelty, trying-out, temporary failure.

Privacy as an individual interest may seem to stand in opposition to the interest of the state in secrecy. In an interesting discussion it has been suggested that there is an inverse relation between the externally closed character of a society and the recognition of private groups and associations within it: the more

[14] Laboratory models indicate the feasibility of storing on one 4800-foot reel of one-inch material the equivalent of twenty pages of dossier material for every one of the 200 million people in the country (Paul Baran, "On the Engineer's Responsibility in Protecting Privacy" [Rand Corp. paper, presented at the Institute for Electrical and Electronic Engineers National Convention, N.Y., March 18-21, 1968]). The author stresses the obligation of engineers to point out the necessity for additional expenditures for safeguards to privacy in the design of information-storage systems.

[15] Secrecy could be viewed, more restrictively, as nondisclosure imposed by rule, while privacy is at the discretion of the person concerned. See Shils. "Privacy: Its Constitution and Vicissitudes," p. 283, n. 1. But this distinction seems to rest on attention to one or the other side of the right-duty relationship rather than on a difference in the interests protected.

closely the frontiers are shut, the less toleration will there be for isolation and group life within the larger collectivity.[16] While that may be so as a political fact, and properly reprehended, it does not obscure the essentially similar psychological functions of individual privacy and state secrecy. For the individual in his personal relations privacy offers a shelter for the loosening of inhibitions, for self-discovery and self-awareness, self-direction, innovation, groping, nourishment for a feeling of uniqueness and a release from the oppression of commonness. In a sense privacy points a way out of Hillel's riddle: "If I am for myself only, what am I? If I am not for myself, who will be for me?" Ministering as they do to a sense of uniqueness, of distinctive worth, the sacred and the sexual are traditionally associated with privacy. When Havelock Ellis speculated that "obscene" derived from behavior normally occurring off-scene or off-stage, he may have shown himself to be an indifferent etymologist but he was a sound psychologist. The sophisticated argument for some form of censorship, as Norman Mailer has observed, is the danger of loss of personality through complete frankness: "For back of the ogres of censorship and the comedies of community hypocrisy, there still rests the last defense of the censor, that sophisticated argument which might urge that sex is a mystery and men explore it and detail it and define it and examine it and eventually disembowel it at their peril."[17]

It is at least a hypothesis worth testing that privacy, though in its immediate aspect an individual interest, serves an important socializing function. An unwillingness to suffer disclosure of what has been discreditable in one's life, or of one's most intimate thoughts and feelings, reflects an intuitive sense that to share everything would jeopardize the sharing of anything. Complete openness in social life would encounter misunderstanding, inability to forgive, limited tolerance for differences. The inner

[16] Arnold Simmel, "Privacy," in *International Encyclopaedia of the Social Sciences.* Compare: "There is scarce truth enough alive to make societies secure, but security enough to make fellowships accursed. Much upon this riddle runs the wisdom of the world." (Shakespeare, *Measure for Measure,* Act III, Sc. ii, ll. 213–215.)

[17] Norman Mailer, Foreword to Charles Rembar, *The End of Obscenity* (1968).

sense of privacy, and mutual respect for it, may be a mechanism that helps to secure the conditions for living fraternally in a world where men are not gods, where to know all is not to understand and forgive all. Self-containment may be a necessary concomitant of social support, a means, to employ another form of discourse, of coming to terms with the reality principle.[18] At all events, a measure of privacy for certain affairs and sentiments seems to be a feature of social organization in all cultures; where physical privacy is not feasible various symbolic gestures or signals are utilized and respected, like the manipulation of a veil over the mouth and eyes.[19]

A special case of privacy is confidentiality, or differential sharing—with persons in a special relationship, such as spouse, priest, physician, lawyer, or colleagues. This interest is reflected in the law of confidential communications. The legal protection is based on a policy of encouraging sharing within limited relationships, reinforcing a sense of special loyalty and understanding. Recognition of these circles of intimacy represents a compromise between total self-sufficiency, which is insupportable, and complete openness, which is felt to be self-defeating.

It remains to ask whether, if privacy is a useful concept as an interest, it is viable as a legal concept as well. That it entails risks of slovenly, overbroad, and one-dimensional thinking when doing service in a variety of legal contexts, with a diversity of

[18] The paradox that significant intimacy with others requires a measure of privacy through withdrawal from them is exhibited strikingly in the kibbutz society in Israel. "Though they greet each other with a 'Shalom!' or 'How's things?' twenty times or more every day, they really have little to talk about since everyone knows everything about everyone else—good reason to withhold the really important things for oneself and to share them with no one." Bruno Bettelheim, *The Children of the Dream* (1969), p. 251. Bettelheim found that children reared in the communal environment of the kibbutz developed traits of shyness toward outsiders, a relative lack of flexibility, spontaneity, and individuality, a distaste for argumentation and large or complex ideas, while showing marked self-confidence and bravery in action, dedication to the group, and satisfaction in work, love of nature enjoyed in solitude, and an avoidance of standard childhood crises of choice, an avoidance that may be accompanied by a corresponding lack of the emotional depth that would follow upon the resolution of such crises.

[19] See Alan E. Westin, *Privacy and Freedom* (1967), p. 14 and chap. I passim.

countervailing rights, has already been acknowledged. Here the question should be refined. The choice need not be limited to simple adoption or rejection of the legal concept. There are levels or orders of statement in law as in science. There are principles and there are rules. A higher order of generality is not only tolerable in the statement of principles; it is to be encouraged, for the assimilative, magnetic effect, the shock of recognition, that it produces when new or questionable phenomena are encountered. A principle is the natural language of the theoretician of law, the jurist, while a rule is preeminently the language of legislators and counselors-at-law. A rule is a particularization that describes the state of the law in a defined context, and prescribes with a relatively high degree of immediacy and precision. A principle is a more plastic formulation, useful for predicting and shaping the course of legal development. It is in the latter context that the right of privacy is of cardinal worth. Thus when Mr. Justice Brandeis was faced on the Court with the question whether wiretapping occurring physically outside the premises was a "search and seizure" within the protection of the Bill of Rights, he was able to give an interpretation to the constitutional language, not indeed to discover a new and unstated general right apart from the text, but to fathom a meaning in the text, that would respect the "right to be let alone, the most comprehensive of rights and the right most valued by civilized men."[20] The rule remained the constitutional text, anchored to its provisions for reasonable cause and search warrants, not a floating rule embodying a right of privacy as in the Connecticut birth-control case. The essay of 1890 was highly relevant in the constitutional case of 1928, but as a direction-finder, not a computerized landing instrument. The formulation in the Restatement of Torts, quoted above at page 191, is appropriate for a statement of principle; that in the New York statute, in footnote 9, is suitable for a rule. It would be a mistake to rely on the Restatement formula for the ready resolution of any concrete controversy, and it would be equally a mistake to read the New York

[20] Dissenting in *Olmstead v. United States,* 277 U.S. 438, 478 (1928). In *Katz v. United States,* 389 U.S. 347 (1967), the dissenting position was adopted by the Court.

statute without awareness of the principle or as exhausting the principle.

If it would be misleading to incorporate a right of privacy into a legal rule, it would be impoverishing to exclude it as the term of a legal principle.[21]

[21] European counterparts to the American law of privacy are discussed in Stig Strömholm, *Rights of Privacy and Rights of Personality: A Comparative Survey* (Stockholm, 1967). Results tend to be similar, though reached under the rubric "rights of the personality." Particularly interesting is the recent development in Germany, applying against private behavior the right to "the free development of the personality" declared in Article 2 of the Constitution of 1949. See also the comparative survey in *Privacy and the Law: A Report by Justice* (London: British Section of the International Commission of Jurists, 1970), pp. 19–27.

11

PRIVACY: A CULTURAL VIEW

JOHN M. ROBERTS
THOMAS GREGOR

Simple inspection of the ethnographic literature will confirm the statement that patterns of privacy may differ quite widely from one society to another. Although it is clear that "privacy" is a promising cross-cultural variable, anthropologists have yet to state a general theory of privacy or even to begin to describe privacy systematically in the societies they study. Ethnographies discuss how actors come together and transmit information, but seldom give details of how the transmission of information is restricted.[1] Gossip networks and chains of command are closely described, but not the complementary barriers to information that bind these communication channels and give them structure. Moreover, there is no comparative treatment or cross-

[1] We are using "privacy" in this sense, as suggested by Alan F. Westin: "Privacy is the claim of individuals, groups, or instititions to determine . . . when, how, and to what extent information about them is to be communicated to others." Alan F. Westin, *Privacy and Freedom* (New York: Atheneum, 1967), p. 7. When privacy is minimal, we use the term "exposure."

cultural analysis of different systems of privacy. In short, anthropologists have not given privacy the systematic attention that the subject deserves.

In part, this relative neglect of privacy may stem from the dissimilarities between modern urban privacy patterns and those encountered in many of the societies studied by anthropologists. Thus, the household does not always appear as a central focus for the rules of privacy in many simple societies, although it certainly has this status in our own. Indeed, the rules of privacy may be closely associated with broad systems of behavior, such as kinship or religion, which are not equally salient in contemporary American culture. This is certainly true in the privacy patterns of two societies in which the authors have conducted firsthand research: the Mehinacu of Brazil and the Zuni of the American Southwest. The Mehinacu turn out to be an extreme example of a society whose privacy pattern is radically different from the one we know. Here spatial and physical barriers to penetration and surveillance are minimal. Institutionalized privacy among the Mehinacu largely relies instead on rules of kinship and religious taboos. Among the Zuni there is a quite different pattern of privacy, but even here the restrictions on the flow of information are primarily a function of the religious system. In fact, as we shall see, Zuni religion, among other things, defines a set of rules for establishing hidden regions and maintaining secret knowledge within the society. Domestic privacy appears to be only an aspect of these religious injunctions, since the most defended regions within the household invariably have religious functions.

Still, since the household is truly a cultural universal, it is reasonable to begin a consideration of privacy from the anthropological point of view by examining domestic privacy from a cross-cultural perspective. Societies differ in many ways, but they always have households of one sort or another. When a survey was made of the Human Relations Area Files, the expected finding that societies high in political integration would also tend to have high degrees of domestic privacy was borne out with such strength that it was essentially trivial. In fact, high domestic privacy has many associations indicative of general cultural complexity. In an attempt to examine a group of societies where variation in privacy could occur, a small sample of cultures possessing low political integration was selected for study.

Cultures coded as having no political integration even at the local level or as having autonomous local communities (not exceeding 1,500 population) were chosen from the Human Relations Area Files "blue ribbon" sample. A general data sheet was prepared by an experienced ethnologist for each of these cultures with a series of entries pertaining to community size, settlement patterns, and domestic privacy. The entries on domestic privacy included codes pertaining to the permeability of dwellings to sight and sound, the presence or absence of closable windows and doors, the presence or absence of partitions within the dwelling unit, and the number of persons who commonly lived together. Three anthropologists[2] used these sheets to group cultures into five privacy categories (very low, low, intermediate, high, and very high) on an impressionistic or judgmental basis. Disputed cultures and cultures with insufficient information were eliminated, leaving the following forty-two cultures:

Very High: Chukchee, Kikuyu, Lapps, Lolo, Luo, Tallensi, Tarahumara.

High: Fang, Ila Koryak.

Intermediate: Dorobo, Iban, Jivaro, Papago, Seri, Tehuelche, Tikopia, Tubatulabal.

Low: Andamanese, Chippewa, Gilyak, Mundurucu, Nambicuara, Tapirape, Toda, Trukese, Vedda, Wogeo, Yaruro, Yahgan.

Very Low: Delaware, Goajiro, Ifaluk, Manus, Mataco, Murngin, Senara, Siriono, Tiwi, Tucuna, Tupinamba, Yokuts.

This small sample was used in exploring the associations between privacy and selected variables appearing in the "Ethnographic Atlas."[3] When the scale of privacy was collapsed into three ordinal ranks—low, intermediate, and high privacy—the scale turned out to be *negatively* associated with a two rank scale (low = 15% or less; high = 16% or more) of dependence upon the gathering of wild plants and small land fauna (G = .690,

[2] The authors are grateful to Bernd Lambert for his assistance in determining relative levels of privacy.

[3] George Peter Murdock, "Ethnographic Atlas: A Summary," *Ethnology*, VI: 2 (1967), 236 pp.

$p = .003$), with a two rank scale (low = 15% or less; high = 16% or more) of dependence upon hunting ($G = -.507$, $p = .032$), and with a two rank scale (low = 25% or less; high = 26% or more) of dependence upon fishing ($G = -.559$, $p = .029$). In contrast, the same privacy scale was *positively* associated with a two rank scale (low = 15% or less; high = 16% or more) of dependence upon animal husbandry ($G = +.887$, $p = .0001$) and with a two rank scale (low = 45% or less; high = 46% or more) of dependence upon agriculture ($G = +.722$, $p = .004$). These associations suggest that even among these societies with little political integration, those with domesticated plants and animals are more likely to be higher in privacy than those dependent upon gathering, hunting, and fishing. Perhaps privacy as we know it is a neolithic development.

The strongest association is with animal husbandry. The data show that in particular privacy is strongly associated with the domestication of large animals. The association between the absence and presence of bovine animals, for example, is high ($G = +.765$, $p = .0009$). High privacy is also associated with the presence of cereal crops and probably with intensive agriculture.

Other associations suggest the presence of social structural variables with privacy. The privacy scale is associated with a two rank scale of absent and present patrilocal or virilocal marital residence ($G = +.691$, $p = .02$). Again there is a positive association of privacy with the prevailing mode of obtaining a wife, a scale ranging from low commitment through bride service to bride price or bride wealth ($G = +.613$, $p = .003$).

Finally, in the area of expressive culture there is an interesting association with a four class ordinal game scale (no games, physical skill only, chance without strategy, and strategy present) ($G = .560$, $p = .01$). There is also an association between the privacy scale and a high god scale (absent or not reported, present but not active in human affairs, present and active in human affairs but not supportive of human morality, and present, active, and specifically supportive of human morality) which shows that the higher the privacy the more likely the presence of strong high gods ($G = .628$, $p = .02$). Perhaps when human surveillance diminishes, supernatural surveillance increases.

While the above findings do not support firm conclusions, they lead to some interesting speculation. It would appear that privacy, as we know it, is largely a neolithic invention occurring primarily in the Old World and associated with the Near Eastern cultural complex which later diffused to all the centers of high culture in the Old World. Second, it is likely that the psychological variables which have already been correlated with the presence of large domestic animals, games of strategy, and high gods would also prove to have significant relationships with high privacy. Indeed, it is absolutely imperative that such comparisons be made in the future, for they may well serve to give an insight into the psychological determinants of desires for privacy and the psychological concomitants of different privacy levels. It may well be the case, for example, that the high obedience and high responsibility training for children which are correlated with such variables as big animals, games of strategy, and high gods may be necessary if a culture is also to maintain high privacy. In any event, the present small exercise in cross-cultural inquiry is enough to suggest that privacy can be studied with profit in a cross-cultural context.

From the anthropological point of view, it might be most interesting to examine particular cases from societies with low political integration, for it is at this level, apparently, that the basic patterns of privacy first developed. The Mehinacu have agriculture, but in many respects they are similar to the simpler societies in the sample. The Zuni have agriculture and large domestic animals (the last as a result of acculturation) and they have a higher level of political complexity (although the aboriginal Zuni would have properly fitted in the sample). Neither culture, however, is an example of the standard privacy culture. Both illustrate the dynamics of privacy at this lower level of political complexity in somewhat exotic settings. Both serve to illustrate the great complexity of this subject.

THE MEHINACU: EXPOSURE, SURVEILLANCE, AND SECLUSION

A good way to learn about the functions of privacy is to examine a society where everyday life must proceed in a highly exposed setting. Such societies are often found among technologically simple people who live in small communities. A small, simple community tends to be highly exposed because its members have a wide variety of relationships with one another. Any two individuals may simultaneously be work partners, kinsmen by blood and marriage, commoner and chief, shaman and client, and members of the same religious cult. This diffuseness of social relationships contrasts radically with larger societies where different types of social relationships are invariably segregated among different actors. The predominance of diffuse relationships in the setting of the small society is of considerable interest because it suggests that members of such societies are interested in learning about one another as total social personalities. A member of a small community, then, is curious about the medicine man not just as a medical practitioner but also as a kinsman and a work partner.

It is likely that this wide range of curiosity will be satisfied, because social relationships are not only diffuse in the setting of a small community but they also tend to be highly observable. Thus, many small societies live in nucleated settlements. Whatever occurs in such a settlement is usually immediately visible to the other villagers. Even when settlements are not so compact, public paths, wells, and shrines are often points of inescapable observability. The technological simplicity of some small societies also contributes to the public character of social life. In general, building materials are not wholly effective barriers to sound. Houses are often constructed without closable doors or internal partitions. They may even be open lean-tos. Such shelters provide very little privacy, and it may be possible to overhear virtually everything that occurs within the community. This possibility is augmented by the fact that a small community is generally a great deal quieter than a large modern one with its traffic, radios, television sets, and machines. The sounds that do occur—crying children, conversations, disputes—are socially relevant sounds, contributing to the deprivatization of those who utter them. Further, social events in the setting of the small community are likely to be extensively reported. Since each man is known to all his fellows his conduct is newsworthy. Relatively few transmissions of information are needed to keep the community abreast of his behavior. As a result gossip networks are unusually efficient in small societies and information about a man's whereabouts and activities is widely available.

Exposure

What is day-to-day social life actually like in the arena of a community where events may be seen, overheard, and rapidly communicated throughout the village? During ten months of 1967, the junior author systematically studied privacy among the Mehinacu, a small tribe of 57 Arawakan-speaking tropical forest horticulturalists living along the headwaters of the Xingú River in Central Brazil. In general the Mehinacu are an extreme case of the exposed small society we have been describing.

Many features of the design of the Mehinacu settlement and dwellings make social life highly observable and audible. The five houses in the village, for example, are built around an open circular plaza approximately 200 feet in diameter. Anyone crossing the plaza during daylight hours will be seen by some of his fellow tribesmen. Someone is almost always sitting in the doorway of a house, taking advantage of the light to work on a task or just staring outside to keep an eye on what is happening in the village. Paths from the community lead to a bathing area and port which are also very public regions. The Mehinacu take pride in these trails, which are the nominal property of the village chiefs. They are built long, wide, and straight. The trail to the port, for example, is so wide it could accommodate two small cars side by side. Anyone on this path is visible fifteen minutes or more before he arrives in the village. The fields surrounding the community are also highly visible. Most of these fields are contiguous, and until a new crop has matured it is possible to see from one end to the other and identify all the farmers working there. Similarly, many of the waterways around the village are public regions. A villager is nearly always getting water from the bathing area, and the network of streams around the village is heavily used for fishing and transportation. In these areas there is a good chance that a Mehinacu will be observed by one of his fellow tribesmen.

Even when the Mehinacu are not immediately visible, their

activities can often be deduced. Each person's footprint is well-known to his fellows. Since the soil on the network of paths around the village is sandy, the barefoot Mehinacu leave visible records of their whereabouts and activities, records that the villagers are astonishingly adept at reading. A few footprints are often enough for them to accurately reconstruct a fellow tribesman's activities and intentions. There are numerous other indications besides footprints that serve the same function. Personal property of all kinds can be identified with its owner. Even the few mass-produced Brazilian trade goods that have found their way into the village are usually one of a kind, and everyone knows to whom they belong. As a result, a possession left anywhere around the village is a clue to the activities of its owner. Garden tools in a field, for example, indicate that the farmer has been there earlier and intends to return shortly. Similarly, an arrow found in some reeds by the bank of a river may tell where its owner has been fishing, information the Mehinacu sometimes try to keep secret.

Even when events are neither immediately nor indirectly observable they may often be overheard. The thatch walls of the houses do almost nothing to muffle sound. Normal conversations cannot only be detected within the houses but through the walls as well. It is virtually impossible to hold a discussion (except in whispers) without some risk that a third party is silently listening nearby. Sounds other than conversations also allow the Mehinacu to keep track of their fellow villagers. Each night, after the fires have died down and it is pitch dark in the windowless houses, sounds are the only clue to the activities and whereabouts of other Mehinacu. At these hours the Mehinacu say that lovers, thieves, and witches prowl about in the darkness. They can, on occasion, be detected and identified by the sounds of their furtive movements within the houses. The Mehinacu take advantage of the permeability of their community to sound by signaling to each other with high-pitched falsetto whoops. There are distinctive calls informing the tribe that hunters and fishermen are returning with their catch, that strangers are approaching the village, that valuable goods are being traded at a barter session, and that the older men of the village are concluding a discussion on an important course of action. These and other similar signals are so effective as communication devices that they enable a Mehinacu to follow many of the major social events of the day without ever leaving his hammock.

When the Mehinacu see or overhear newsworthy activities, they often gossip about them. On one occasion there was an opportunity to observe the speed and manner in which such stories are passed along. A Mehinacu had returned from the Indian post with an unusually fine tale. One of the villagers, he related, had robbed the chief of the white men of his mosquito net; the chief was furious and disaster threatened the village. This story was spread through the community primarily by closely related women who work together in the gardens and in the tedious process of making manioc flour. Within several hours it was no longer possible to find anyone who had not heard it other than the alleged culprit and his immediate family.

By now it must be apparent that privacy is a scarce commodity within the Mehinacu community. Wherever one is, whatever one is doing, there is a chance that another person is also there, quietly listening and watching, perhaps intending to report what he has learned to the rest of the tribe. What effect does this public character of village life have on ordinary social relations within the tribe? Most obviously, the visibility of social action and the efficiency of communications tend to expose misconduct. Whatever occurs in violation of Mehinacu social rules will be widely reported. Stories of theft, extramarital liaisons, and malicious accusations of witchcraft often get back to the very persons who stand to be most offended by them. Since theft, sexual promiscuity, and allegations of witchcraft are very common,[4] important social relationships may be disrupted by their exposure. Hence, the cooperation of close relatives is seriously jeopardized when a Mehinacu learns that a kinsman has accused him of witchcraft, stolen fruit from his garden, or seduced his

[4] Petty pilfering is a daily affair. Most of the younger Mehinacu conduct extramarital liaisons with everyone else of the opposite sex unless they are of different generations or are explicitly forbidden from such a relationship by the incest taboo. Approximately one-half of the men of the tribe are considered to be witches from the point of view of an average Mehinacu.

wife. The low level of privacy thereby places pressures on the maintenance of the basic relationships upon which normal village life depends.

In a similar way, lack of privacy threatens an individual's self-esteem. Even if a villager does not regularly engage in misconduct, there are times when he would like to conceal his behavior. A Mehinacu man, for example, is expected to be a competent fisherman and an effective lover. Inevitably, there are occasions when his performance is less than adequate. At such times it is extremely damaging to have his failures become a matter of public record, but this is just what is likely to happen in the highly exposed setting.

Finally, high exposure places special pressures on relationships and roles that require private rehearsal for proper performance. Among the Mehinacu the role of shaman most dramatically illustrates this principle. The Mehinacu shaman periodically rids the community of the plagues of flies and insects which torment the villagers during the wetter months. These insects are believed to be created by local witches from small pellets of wax which they strategically seed about the community. The shaman thwarts the witches by "finding" the pellets before they have an opportunity to mature into flies and mosquitoes. Some of our informants have told us, however, that they have seen false shamans secretly planting the wax pellets themselves in advance of a highly dramatic ceremony during which they are retrieved. As the reader can well imagine, the success of this ceremony depends on the shaman's ability to spread the wax balls throughout the village unobserved. The public character of Mehinacu social life is a distinct threat with which he must cope if his performance is to be credible.

The role of the shaman is in some ways similar to more ordinary relationships within the Mehinacu community. The roles of husband and wife, for example, depend to a degree on the spouses' ability to "rehearse" their relationship in private for subsequent public performance. Mehinacu husbands and wives must make every effort to smooth over their hostilities and in-law problems away from the public eye, so that they can present a credible, conflict-free performance of their relationship to their fellow tribesmen. This presentation is difficult to manage, however, since the Mehinacu live with their in-laws in unpartitioned multifamily houses. Although spouses may attempt to restrain their disagreements until they are outside the village, they are often unable to do so. Among younger couples sexual jealousy seems to be responsible for many of these arguments, which sometimes erupt into violence. Invariably these altercations are observed and gossiped about by the villagers. When the disputes and the gossip become sufficiently frequent it acts as a divisive wedge between husband and wife, since their kinsmen may begin to put pressure on them to terminate their marriage. This pressure is usually effective because a man who lives with his spouse must be on good terms with her parents. He owes them deference and respect, which he expresses by neither touching them, passing them in doorways, nor mentioning their names. Furthermore, he must provide them with gifts at the time of his marriage and contribute his labor to the maintenance of their household. In this subordinate position he is vulnerable to their displeasure. Once a man's in-laws have decided that he is not a good husband it is not long before they begin to claim that he is also a bad son-in-law and perhaps even a witch. Demands upon his labor will increase, food will be served only after he has left the house, and he will be the victim of invidious gossip. Not surprisingly the day will come when he takes down his hammock and returns to his own residence, thereby terminating the marriage. This pattern of divorce would be less likely if marital discord could be managed privately, so that in-laws do not become part of the conflict. As it is, the public character of a couples' marriage may threaten the integrity of their relationship.

We have seen that although village social life is highly public in character, it seems to require a measure of privacy for its persistence. How, in the highly exposed setting of the Mehinacu community, is compromising information concealed?

Getting Along in a Highly Exposed Community

The Mehinacu have a number of ways of establishing a measure of privacy for themselves even though they are often hard-pressed to do so. Some of these methods are institutionalized, including well-defined rules against intrusions and other invasions of privacy. Other devices are not explicitly a part of Mehinacu culture but are improvised techniques that permit the Mehinacu to limit what their fellows know about them.

The most dramatically defined rule of privacy among the Mehinacu is the sanction against women entering the men's house. The men's house is a small building in the center of the village. This building functions simultaneously as a temple and social club. During most of the day there are a number of men inside, chatting, telling jokes, working on their bows and arrows, or playing a set of sacred flutes stored within. Admission to the men's house, or even setting eyes on the sacred flutes, is absolutely forbidden to the women of the tribe. Should they intrude, the punishment is well defined: gang rape by all the men of the community. The women are genuinely frightened by this threat and avert their eyes from the men's house when passing through the center of the village. The possibility of their willfully intruding is virtually nil, so that the men are thereby provided with a well-defended private area for carrying on masculine activities.

A less dramatic but equally significant rule against intrusions enjoins the Mehinacu against casually entering any residence but their own. Intruding in this way is said to be extremely discourteous, and the Mehinacu speak disparagingly of neighboring tribes who freely invade one another's household privacy. Since the Mehinacu all have close kinsmen in each of the five village houses, the rule against intrusion sometimes make necessary communication awkward. The villagers get around this difficulty by sending messages with their children (who are exempt from the rule) or conversing right through the thatch wall of the dwelling.

Despite the regulation against intruding, the household is generally not a private area. Five or six families may share the same residence, which is usually unpartitioned. They are very much aware of each other's movements, activities, and conversations. To a degree this highly exposed situation is improved by codes of affinal avoidances which all the villagers honor. These codes restrict each Mehinacu from entering those portions of his house which belong to his parents-in-law or children-in-law. Since affinal kinship is widely extended among the Mehinacu, it is not uncommon to find individuals whose movements are limited to their own small section of the house.

Although affinal avoidances only establish symbolic divisions within households, there are certain times when the Mehinacu erect real partitions. These are never permanent but are left in position only when a Mehinacu is in ceremonial seclusion. Ceremonial seclusion[5] is a way of isolating an individual from his society with real and symbolic barriers while he is undergoing a change in status. These periods of isolation vary from a few months to as long as three years, depending on the type of seclusion. A boy who has just had his ears pierced (a ceremony that is a prerequisite for becoming a chief) will be isolated behind a palmwood partition where he must honor numerous food taboos, drink noxious root broths, refrain from speaking in a voice louder than a whisper, avoid any expression of emotional intensity such as anger or sexuality, and, above all, never leave the house during daylight hours. The boy's period of isolation can last as long as two and one-half to three years; from about ages nine to twelve. During this time, he adjusts to a low-keyed life behind the barriers. Although his father will occasionally instruct him in important manual tasks, such as making bows and arrows, feather headdresses, and basket weaving, he is ideally addressing his thoughts toward becoming a strong wrestler and a successful hunter and fisherman. Specifically, he is supposed to imagine himself performing these activities. This mental effort and the restrictions of seclusion are said to be necessary to the boy's social and physical maturation.

There are numerous other opportunities to enter very similar types of isolation, including periods of seclusion at maternity, upon a man's first paternity, at adolescence, upon the death of a spouse, and while learning to become a shaman or curer. The total amount of time spent in seclusion by an individual will vary according to the course of his social career, but in theory it is possible to spend a total of approximately eight years behind seclusion barriers. The average Mehinacu probably spends con-

[5] See Thomas A. Gregor, "Exposure and Seclusion: A Study of Institutionalized Isolation among the Mehinacu Indians of Brazil," *Ethnology*, IX (1970), for a full discussion of seclusion practices.

siderably less time in seclusion, three years in all being a conservative estimate.

Although relatively brief periods of isolation are commonly used in transitions of status throughout the primitive world, the Mehinacu have elaborated the custom far beyond what we might ordinarily expect. In all likelihood the extraordinary duration of Mehinacu seclusion can be accounted for by the exposed setting of the community, since seclusion balances exposure by providing a considerable measure of privacy. It is apparent that seclusion provides privacy for the isolated individual; in living in a small private world, he is so cut off from his fellows that he appears not to exist. In fact, the Mehanicu say that the closer a person comes to appearing not to exist, the more nearly he has met the restrictions of seclusion. To a lesser degree his reduced exposure extends to the rest of the tribe. Often the isolated individual's family lives behind the barrier with him and enjoys the privacy that the partition affords. The remaining residents of the house (and of the village) share in the increased privacy since the seclusion barrier protects them from being observed by the person in isolation.

Seclusion practices and rules against intrusion are the most culturally explicit privacy-maintaining devices the Mehinacu possess. There is another set of noninstitutionalized devices, however, which are probably just as effective in reducing exposure. Among the more important of these are a maze of hidden paths which surround the village, a concealed port and bathing area, and secret cleared areas in the forest. The paths make it possible to go from one house to another without walking across the central plaza. These paths are regularly used by Mehinacu thieves and by lovers who are arranging clandestine affairs. The concealed port and bathing area are also used by villagers who wish to evade surveillance. A Mehinacu who has returned unsuccessfully from a ceremonially important fishing expedition may moor his canoe at the hidden port and return to his house along one of the concealed paths. In this way his failure will not quickly become common knowledge. Similarly, a person who is in a state of shame will bathe in the concealed swimming hole and use the small paths around the village to move about unobserved. In contrast to the hidden paths and port, which are kept clear simply by regular use, the secret cleared areas in the forest are casually maintained by the men of the tribe. These areas are used primarily for clandestine extramarital assignations. Each individual has several such spots scattered around the circumference of the village. Usually a couple will use an area on the side of the village nearest the woman's house so that she will have a good chance of going to and from her rendezvous unseen.

The alternate ports, bathing areas, and paths provide the Mehinacu with a kind of hidden village where they can carry on activities that must be concealed from their fellow tribesmen. These spatial devices would probably be ineffective, however, were it not for a somewhat diffuse set of social rules we can best label as "discretion." Each villager is under an obligation to avoid exposing his fellow's misconduct. A good wife, the men say, is a woman who does not ask where her husband is going when he leaves the house in the late afternoon decorated with red paint and wearing his finest earrings. It is quite possible that he is planning to meet a partner for an extramarital affair, but a good wife will never press the point. Similarly, a courteous kinsman or comrade will not ask questions that might place an individual in an awkward position. These questions include serious inquiries about a man's possessions, his sexual intrigues, his knowledge of village witches, and, somewhat surprisingly, even his plans for the next day. Closely related to discretion as a way of minimizing exposure is the pattern Erving Goffman has labeled "civil inattention."[6] Civil inattention calls for acting as if one were unaware of what was occurring, even though the events themselves are in plain view. Among the Mehinacu civil inattention is properly paid to persons who are forcing themselves to vomit (a common health practice), persons in a state of shame, individuals who are technically in seclusion but who carelessly allow themselves to be seen in a public place, and men who are engaged in a delicate task that requires considerable concentration, such as hafting an arrow point.

Despite seclusion barriers, affinal avoidances, rules against in-

[6] Erving Goffman, *Behavior in Public Places* (New York: Free Press, 1963), p. 84.

trusion, concealed paths, discretion, and civil inattention, Mehinacu social life is highly public in character. All too often socially damaging information about a villager's misconduct and personal failures becomes a matter of public record. At such times there is one last line of defense: falsehood. When pressed, the Mehinacu fabricate information concerning their possessions, sexual intrigues, whereabouts, and activities. Falsehood is used with such regularity in certain situations that the Mehinacu are somewhat skeptical about gossip and often comment that "everyone lies." To a degree, the false tales and rumors that circulate through the community tend to discredit accurate accounts, so that the gossip network is partly compromised as a reliable communications system. Thus, when the truth about a villager's misbehavior becomes common knowledge, there is a possibility that this truth will be dismissed as "just another lie." Mendacity thereby functions as a final device to conceal socially damaging information.

The use of prevarication demonstrates that the methods the Mehinacu have for establishing privacy are not completely effective. Unless an individual strategically manages his movements and social activities, his fellows are likely to gain control of information that would seriously jeopardize their relationships with him. Getting along in a small open community thus demands considerable social and personal ingenuity. The privacy-maintaining devices that emerge from this effort include not only the symbolic restraints against intrusion and surveillance we are familiar with in our own society but also, as we have seen, such institutions as affinal avoidances, seclusion, and the men's house. Privacy as a variable in cross-cultural research may therefore be directly associated with an extremely wide variety of behavior such as kinship and ritual. The study of the Zuni which follows interprets that society's religious system as a privacy- and secrecy-maintaining device vital to the continuity of Zuni culture in the presence of severe stress.

THE ZUNI: DEFENDING THE SAFEHOLD

Unlike the Mehinacu of Brazil, the Zuni Indians of the American Southwest possess a culture which has been exceptionally well described in the ethnographic literature; hence, the general pattern of Zuni privacy is already known. Still, there is one aspect of Zuni privacy which has never been discussed, the way in which privacy figures in Zuni cultural self-management. It will be seen that Zuni patterns of privacy and religious patterns are mutually supportive and that, furthermore, this linkage contributes to the survival of a culture which has been severely threatened for more than four hundred years. The examination of privacy from this point of view once again illustrates the variety in the functions of privacy which exists among the cultures of the world, for this is a system which is quite different from the prevailing American one and also from that of the Mehinacu.

When Coronado captured Hawikuh in July 1540, there were five other Zuni villages, but archaeological evidence indicates that more villages existed at an earlier time. It is probable that the processes of population loss and settlement contraction which were to plague the Zuni for the next three centuries had already begun. By the early nineteenth century there were less than two thousand Zuni, and these were concentrated in a single village. For the next hundred years the Zuni managed to hold their own and even make some gains, but it was only in recent decades that the population began to increase in a substantial way. Throughout this long period of recorded history the Zuni have been subjected to ever-increasing acculturative pressures in all aspects of life. Although it must be admitted that the force of these pressures was reduced in earlier periods by the remoteness and isolation of the Zuni, it is still no small feat to have preserved a distinctive cultural identity for so many centuries under such difficult circumstances.

In 1951, the base year for this particular discussion, the Zuni Indians occupied a reservation in western New Mexico. Their population of approximately three thousand people was mainly concentrated in the central pueblo, although there were four outlying farming villages and occasional outlying houses occupied on an essentially seasonal basis. For all practical purposes, therefore, Zuni culture today is a culture with a single settlement. Furthermore, this settlement encompasses an entire speech community, since the Zuni language is spoken nowhere else in the world. There is not even another language closely related to it. When a Zuni leaves the pueblo and the reservation, he crosses a significant cultural and linguistic frontier.

The village has always been physically distinctive and quite unlike nearby Anglo and Spanish-American settlements. In 1881, the Zuni were known to have lived in a compact pueblo with five terraces of the traditional type. By 1951, however, the sprawling village encompassed an area much larger than that of the old pueblo. Most of the houses were one-story structures of stone or adobe or both, and it was only in the center of the village near the sacred plaza that structures were reminiscent of the old multistoried pueblo. Yet, despite the presence of trading stores, schools, a garage, running water, electricity, graded roads, and other nontraditional features, the village still preserved the flavor of the older physical setting which had existed long before twentieth-century acculturation began.

Indeed, in some respects the modern features of the physical setting were misleading, for the casual visitor could not easily understand that a bilingual Zuni, who spoke to him so easily in English while standing beside his late model truck, was truly integrated into a culture radically different in the areas of domestic life, kinship, social organization, political and legal organization, expressive culture, and, most important of all, religion. Furthermore, this culture was unusually complex and well integrated for such a small society.

The basic patterns of Zuni domestic privacy can be illustrated by considering a single household. Detailed descriptions of daily life in three Zuni households as of 1951 have been published.[7] The largest of the three households exemplified the traditional organization although it was too large to be typical. A total of twenty-three persons were affiliated with the household and were organized around a matrilineage; ideally the Zuni are matrilineal and matrilocal. There was a key nuclear family of a father, mother (the senior member of the matrilineage), son,

[7] John M. Roberts, *Zuni Daily Life,* Monograph 1, Behavior Science Reprints, Human Relations Area Files Press Reprinted Note Book No. 3, Laboratory of Anthropology, The University of Nebraska (Lincoln, Neb., 1956). 137 pp.

and four daughters. Each of the four married daughters had her own nuclear family of husband and children in the household as well. The married son, of course, lived with his wife and children elsewhere, but in accordance with Zuni pattern, he made frequent visits to his maternal household, where he stored some of his most important possessions. The reverse was true of the four husbands of the married daughters, for they frequently visited their own maternal households and kept their most important possessions elsewhere. Finally, on the basis of kinship connections too complicated to be detailed here, there were two additional affiliated males who lived elsewhere but who maintained close ties with this household. In essence, then, the household consisted of five interlocked nuclear families and affiliates, all organized around a single matrilineage. It is worth noting that the visiting males maintained close connections with seven other households scattered throughout the village.

The house itself was a large one-story structure with eight rooms. The members of the household used in common four rooms which can be roughly labeled as kitchen, living room, storeroom, and workroom. Each of the four married daughters had a bedroom-workroom for herself and her family. These rooms were linked by connecting doors and, a feature often to be seen in Zuni houses, by interior windows which frequently permitted visual contacts between rooms. There were some outbuildings as well.

The adult females in the matrilineage managed the house in a cooperative and efficient way. The husbands tended to occupy the common rooms or to stay in their wives' apartments.

A household of this size had frequent visitors. First, of course, the affiliated males provided steady communication with other households. Indeed, when a tally was made with individuals in other households, it was found that adult males usually visited the house occupied by their matrilineage at least once a day whenever they were in a position to do so. Next, close kinsmen often visited the house. Then, since the adults in the household were concerned with religious and secular affairs, there were often visitors who came on business. Here, typically, a visitor would enter the door without knocking, but he tended to stay in the common behavior settings within the house. Finally, there were visits by neighbors and, less frequently, friends. There were also non-Zuni "friends" who visited for the purposes of trade or recreation or both. Finally, of course, the ten children had friends. All in all, there was a great deal of going and coming.

Since the members of the household had an intense interest in the village and its activities, it was a rare moment when some member of the household was not looking out a window, maintaining a casual surveillance of the immediate area. Usually a visitor was noticed while he was still approaching the house and before he entered. In many instances this "warning" permitted the occupants to make appropriate adjustments.

In all the houses the most private of all the settings were to be found in the storage areas within the bedrooms or in the main storeroom, for it was here that objects of religious importance were kept. No visitors would voluntarily poke around in these areas. Indeed, in making household inventories, the greatest resistance occurred when the investigator wished to inventory the contents of the storerooms, areas of little concern to the average American householder.

The settings thus far described existed on a more or less continuous basis. At any time, however, it was possible to convert a room into a setting for a religious ritual or, if an appropriate officer resided in the house, for an informal hearing. In 1951 even the trials before the tribal council were held in ordinary "living rooms." When these special meetings were in session, the ordinary and commonplace behavior settings became quite different. Under these circumstances security was maintained by the privileged persons in the room, by other persons in and outside the house, and by the solid walls of the structure. Looking through the windows from the outside, particularly at night, was not permitted.

Zuni domestic settings might be much more open to penetration from the outside if it were not for the all-important and pervasive Zuni religious organization. In the recent past the Zuni appear to have been a true theocracy, and even in 1951 the religious organization represented the very heart of the culture. Twenty years earlier Bunzel wrote:

> There are households, kinship groups, clans, tribal and special secret societies, and cult groups. A man must belong to several of these groups, and the number to which he may potentially belong is almost unlimited. There is no exclusive membership. He is born into a certain household, and his kinship and clan affiliations are thus fixed, unless altered by adoption. At puberty he is initiated into one of the six dance groups that comprise the male tribal society. He may, through sickness, be conscripted into one of the medicine societies; if he takes a scalp he must join the warriors society; and if connected with a sacerdotal household he may be called upon to join one of the priesthoods.[8]

Again she states:

> Against this background general nonesoteric religious activities have developed a large number of esoteric cults, each devoted to the worship of special supernaturals or groups of supernaturals, and each having a priesthood, a body of secret ritual, permanent possessions of fetishistic power, special places of worship, and a calendrical cycle of ceremonies. I distinguish six major cults of this type which might be named from the supernaturals toward whom their principal ceremonies are directed: I, the cult of the Sun; 2, the cult of the Uwanami; 3, the cult of the katcinas; 4, the cult of the priests of the katcinas (a distinct but closely related cult); 5, the cult of the Gods of War; 6, the cult of the Beast Gods. The functions, activities, and personnel of these groups overlap and interweave in a bewildering intricacy that baffles analysis.[9]

By 1951 the religious system described above had suffered some losses, but the main structure persisted and it was still paramount in Zuni life and thought. Yet the Zuni had been the target of missionary efforts for more than four centuries and the object of much directed social change in many nonreligious spheres. It can be argued that the religious system persisted because it was based in a complex series of private behavior settings which were defended against penetration by foreigners, unauthorized

[8] Ruth L. Bunzel, *Introduction to Zuni Ceremonialism,* Bureau of American Ethnology, 47th Annual Report (Washington, 1932), p. 476.
[9] *Ibid.,* p. 511.

Zunis, and criminals, i.e., witches. This complex can be termed the "safehold."

The archaic word safehold properly refers to a stronghold, but its meaning has been extended here to apply to the complex of behavior settings which exist continually or intermittently in all but the most open of societies as settings for activities deemed vital to the continued survival of the society and which are closed to the unauthorized penetration by others so that the activities may be conducted without interruption or interference and so that information on these activities may not be improperly disseminated to the detriment of the society. In a very simple culture the important behavior setting for a male initiation rite may be denied to strangers, women, and children, and this behavior setting may be considered part of the safehold for that society. In a modern nation-state the safehold may be exceptionally large and complex, particularly in the case of military and political settings, and no ordinary citizen expects to attend cabinet meetings or to participate in the deliberations of the joint chiefs of staff (or an equivalent group). Most societies, then, have security systems of some sort although these clearly vary enormously in importance, size, and complexity.

For at least a century the major ethnographers of Zuni culture have agreed on the salience and importance of the Zuni religion within the total culture. Not only is religion the dominant cultural interest but it is also the very idiom of Zuni cultural identity. There can be no question that the Zuni feel that their religion is necessary and vital to their continued survival as Zuni.

The preservation of the Zuni religion involves many problems, not the least of which is the continued maintenance of religious secrecy. To use a modern metaphor, Zuni religious information is both "classified" and "unclassified." The classified information may be "confidential," "secret," or "top secret." It must be realized that secrecy in Zuni religious life is not a simple matter of form, for the Zuni genuinely feel that their religion would lose its efficacy if the classified, particularly the "top secret," information were to become known to all. Furthermore, the Zuni are convinced that their religious secrets are truly so valuable that knowledge of them is coveted by all kinds of persons, including anthropologists, so that their secrecy must be actively defended. Every effort is made, then, at all levels of the society, to preserve religious secrecy. In general, despite some disappointing failures, the Zuni have been successful in that regard. It is even the case that religious "security" seems to have been tightened as acculturative pressures have mounted, but the total security system must be very old.

In some respects Zuni religious organization has the attributes of a successful underground organization or movement, which it may in fact have been at the time of the most severe domination by the early Spanish. A stranger viewing the beautiful dances in the sacred plaza would not be likely to concur with the statement that Zuni religious settings usually have low visibility, but he would be unaware of the unobtrusive shrines and the important secret activities conducted in ordinary houses dispersed throughout the village. In 1951 the kivas providing the dance groups were no longer open to visitors, but strangers often visited them in the past without realizing, it might be noted, the relatively unimportant place occupied by these organizations in the total religious system. This low visibility was further supported by the circumstance that the Zuni lacked full-time religious practitioners and that all the religious officers and priests serving on a "part-time" basis occupied ordinary secular roles as well. It was even the case not long ago that the powerful theocracy had a "front" in the form of the secular tribal council which was its creature but which often impressed the uninformed as being the veritable source of tribal authority. Even the governor was something of a puppet figure. This general point could be elaborated further, but for purposes of this paper it is enough to say that the Zuni religious organization possessed the following important characteristics: visible but unimportant and even expendable fronts, low general visibility, a strong and powerful central authority, excellent lines of communication, high redundancy throughout the organization, great secrecy in appropriate areas, and very wide dispersal into numerous small groups (priesthoods, cult groups, etc.). All these attributes seem likely to foster the survival of an organization geared to operation in the face of adverse outside pressure.

Since Zuni sacred objects and sacred activities are found widely dispersed among the households of the village, it follows that the patterns of domestic privacy which obtain also serve to preserve "classified" information. This point has been made in summary fashion by Bunzel:

> Objects. All sacred objects are taboo to all people who do not "belong" to them. The strength of this feeling varies according to the power of the fetish. No one would dare to touch one of the priest's fetishes except the chief of the priesthood, and no one will enter the room where it is kept except the chief priest and the female head of the house. This is true also of the permanent masks and society altars. When the people who keep one of the Ca'lako masks moved to a new house they called the head of the kiva whose mask they kept to transfer it, "because they were afraid to touch it." Corn fetishes, prayer sticks, ceremonial garments are all handled with great respect, and no more than necessary.
>
> Places. The rooms where sacred things are kept are taboo to outsiders. All shrines are taboo except when visited officially. There is one War God Shrine (co'uwayällakwi) which may be visited by those who wish to pray for good luck in war or gambling. Otherwise it is not permitted for individuals to visit shrines even for purposes of prayer. Rooms where retreats or ceremonies are being held, unless the ceremony is specifically public, are taboo to those not belonging to the ceremony. If any one crosses the threshold he is "caught" and must be initiated into the group, or where this is impossible (like meetings of the katchna priests), must be ceremonially whipped and make certain payments to his "father." Altars are always erected on the side of the room away from the door, "the valuable place." Strangers are always seated near the door, by the fireplace, and away from the "valuable place." Mourners and warriors who have taken scalps sit "away from the fire."[10]

The foregoing quotation shows the degree to which respect for taboos and ordinary good manners serve to preserve religious secrecy.

There are, however, very severe sanctions against invasions of privacy ranging far beyond infringements of taboos and patterns

[10] Bunzel, *op. cit.*, p. 502.

of etiquette. In the past, and even in the present, persons engaging in antisocial behavior were considered witches. Witches, of course, were considered the largest internal threat to Zuni security and to the preservation of Zuni religion. A single traditional report is quoted below to illustrate the linkage between privacy, witchcraft, and social sanctions. It is quoted at some length because it gives in capsule form a good insight into the total social dynamics involved in the situation.

> Case 12. Witchcraft (ca. 1890), Informant A. An old woman used to go out with her grandson "witching around," and one night at the house of a wealthy family they were caught peeping through the window. The family took them inside, questioned them, and asked why they had been bothering them. After about two hours they confessed that they were jealous of the family because of their wealth, and they had planned to bring sickness and death to them all. "But since you have caught us, we are unlucky, and we shall die instead of you."
>
> The family did not believe this and said: "Maybe you are telling lies. Maybe if we let you go you will come back with stronger power than you have now."
>
> The old woman said: "You have caught us, which proves that we are unlucky and not lying. We came with all our power, but once a witch is caught it is the end of him. You see we are even dressed so as not to be caught." By this they meant that they were wearing the special clothes that witches wear to prevent capture, owl feathers on their heads, and hair tied in "jack-rabbits' ears." The boy wore a small red-painted blanket about his waist, and the grandmother wore a white nightgown.
>
> The family then informed the War chief, who gathered several members of the society, and they questioned both the boy and the old woman. The old woman told them of her jealousy of the family because of their wealth and good fortune.
>
> At daybreak they were taken to the place where witches were hung, and their hands were tied behind them with cowhide straps. They were hung head downward, but when the War chief asked them how many people they had killed, they did not confess, although they were repeatedly clubbed. Finally, however, they stated how many deaths

> they had caused and said they would show the clothing and beads they had taken from the dead, if they were released.
>
> They were then let down and went home but with their hands still tied. There they pointed out mantas, beads and jewelry, and the War chief told the people that whoever wished to do so might reclaim his property. But even though some people recognized their property they refused to take it back. The witches then produced a powder that they had used in painting their bodies, which they said was compounded of human flesh and bones and earth taken from the cemetery.
>
> The two were then hung again and were clubbed some more. Finally they confessed that they had caused the deaths of two members of the family that had caused their arrest. They were then untied but the War chief warned that if they were caught again they would be killed.
>
> The witches went home and that night the boy died, but his family refused to bury him because they said his death had been caused by the War society, which was obliged to bury him. The society then did so.
>
> Since the witches' family was thus "embarrassed," they moved to a corn field three miles away but after a year returned to Zuni. After a short time all had died from some illness.[11]

In 1951, of course, there had been no public executions for witchcraft for many decades, but belief in the existence and malevolence of watches was still strong. Most houses with electricity had outdoor lights which permitted surveillance of dooryards, and even the dogs sometimes provided warning of unusual movement. Since no one wanted to be considered a witch, these beliefs constituted a strong deterrent against invasions of privacy. In 1951, however, many offenses having to do with privacy, such as theft, trespass, slander, etc., were tried by the tribal council.

DISCUSSION

American patterns of privacy are, in the main, the end

[11] Watson Smith and John M. Roberts, *Zuni Law: A Field of Values.* Papers of the Peabody Museum of American Archaeology and Ethnology, Harvard University, Vol. 43, No. 1 (Cambridge, Mass., 1954), pp. 44–45.

products of a long period of cultural development which may have begun at the time when the domestication of large animals, the production of cereal grains, the recognition of high gods, and other traits were worked into large complexes, particularly in the Near East. This of course, is conjecture, but at least it is very clear that our view of privacy as a set of rules against intrusion and surveillance focused on the household occupied by a nuclear family is a conception which is not to be found universally in all societies. Societies stemming from quite different cultural traditions such as the Mehinacu and the Zuni do not lack rules and barriers restricting the flow of information within the community, but the management and the functions of privacy may be quite different. Here institutions such as kinship and religion may have an importance to privacy that is not mirrored in our own society.

Although these findings can at best be considered exploratory, we can say with some certainty that privacy in the broad sense of our initial definition promises to be a variable of considerable cross-cultural significance. It is our hope that its importance will be increasingly recognized by anthropologists in the future.

12

MASKS AND FIG LEAVES

JOHN R. SILBER

Privacy has been discussed from a variety of unphilosophical standpoints, as in the writings of Justices Warren and Brandeis[1] and Dean Prosser.[2] It was a central issue in Vance Packard's nightmarish account of encroaching electronic omnipresence.[3] The invasion of privacy recently provided a belated triumph for pre-electronic techniques when Senator Ribicoff and his lip-readers gave voice and foul utterance to the TV tape of Mayor Daley's remarks at the 1968 Democratic Convention in Chicago. The same sordid breach of privacy is involved in the pictures and broadcasts of Officer Nichols reporting the latest homosexual activities in stalls one and three from his observa-

[1] L. D. Warren and Brandeis, "The Right to Privacy," *Harvard Law Review*, 4 (1890), 193.

[2] W. L. Prosser, *Law of Torts* (St. Paul, Minn.: West Publishing Co., 1964), chap. 22, "Privacy."

[3] Vance Packard, *The Naked Society* (New York: David McKay Co., Inc., 1967).

tion booth atop the men's room of The Emporium department store in Santa Clara.[4]

But I doubt that these approaches provide much more than the context and materials from which a genuinely phenomenological and metaphysical discussion of privacy must develop. Most of the work on privacy, like so many of the commentaries on *Griswold* v. *Connecticut*,[5] suffer, as Hyman Gross has pointed out, from the lack of any understanding of the essential characteristics of privacy.

In an effort to dispel the "pernicious ambiguities" that infect the concept of privacy, Gross suggests that "privacy is the condition of human life in which acquaintance with a person or with affairs of his life which are personal to him is limited."[6] Though methodologically sound, it is scarcely more than a promising first effort to define privacy. Substitute "friendship," "interpersonal knowledge," "acquaintanceship," or "marital love" for privacy and the resulting statement is as sound as the initial definition—and equally baffling. We continue to be haunted by the "pernicious ambiguities." Gross's definition fails to identify the essential characteristics of privacy; those he lists apply equally well to many other concepts. Moreover, he fails to ask whether privacy is compatible with unlimited disclosure. Gross may agree with Bloustein that freedom from certain types of intrusion is essential to the preservation of individuality,[7] but it is not at all clear that either Gross or Bloustein has discerned what types of intrusion, if any, are compatible with individuality, or to what extent the individual is free to set his own limits on self-disclosure.

Some phenomenological and metaphysical issues must be resolved in order to determine the essentials of privacy. The expert

[4] *Britt* vs. *Superior Court of Santa Clara County*, 374 P.2d 817; see also *Bielicki* v. *Superior Court of Los Angeles County*, 371 P.2d 288, and *Smayda* v. *U.S.*, 352 F.2d 251 (1965).

[5] *Griswold* v. *Connecticut*, 381 U.S. 479 (1965). See especially the symposium on privacy in *Law and Contemporary Problems*, 31 (Spring 1966), 251.

[6] Hyman Gross, "The Concept of Privacy," *New York University Law Review*, 42 (March 1967), 35–36.

[7] Edward Bloustein, "Privacy as an Aspect of Human Dignity: An answer to Dean Prosser," *New York University Law Review*, 39 (December 1964), 973.

poker player can read his opponent's hand without actually seeing his cards. He sees the "ace up the sleeve" in an excitement of the eyes or in a slight catch of the breath. By Gross's definition the opponent's hand is still private, since access to it is limited. But although access may be limited by efforts at concealment and deception, concealment, alas, is limited by the practiced eye of the expert, which sees through the effort to deceive or conceal; for the expert, the gestures of concealment are unintentional disclosures. Where is privacy in poker? Poker, of course, would not matter, were it not that its features are characteristic of much of human life.

The strip teaser would seem to forfeit, by virtue of her professional calling, the privacy of her body. She has, it might seem, no private parts, since she has contracted for their public display. But in the blank, dead expression on the face of the dancer one sees the closed door, the wall, behind which she hides in intense, if limited, privacy. She wears her fig leaf on her face. With eyes that disclose nothing—least of all an interest in what she is doing or in those who are watching her—she preserves some part of her individuality from public gaze.[8] Some dancers exhibit such powers of withdrawal that they succeed in totally estranging themselves from the audience. Because she does not value the intimate disclosure of her body, because she makes her body available with such utter indifference, that rare dancer may convey even to a stupid and drunken audience the stark realization that in seeing all they have seen nothing. What is offered publicly to an audience becomes private once again. Other dancers achieve equal distance with vivacity and smiles. Usually the audience exceeds the dancer in self-disclosure: if in wide-open cities like New Orleans arrests were made for indecent exposure, the viewers, not the dancers, would go to jail.

The limits on acquaintance with a person or the personal are not obvious, simple, or even open to calculation by the crude yardsticks of the behavioral psychologists or the average policeman. And, more paradoxical, it is not clear that individual privacy requires any general limitation of access or acquaintance.

[8] I can conceive, of course, of a bored and stupid strip teaser displaying everything or having literally nothing to conceal. Nevertheless, the phenomenon I have described is genuine.

For William Schutz and other advocates of encounter-group programs, privacy itself becomes one of the fundamental barriers to personal fulfillment. These movements extoll the virtues of complete disclosure—the abnegation of all privacy—as the sole means of personal fulfillment.[9] It is their confident assertion that only through sustained efforts at disclosing one's self to others—the conquest of all "guilt, shame, embarrassment, or fear of punishment, failure, success, retribution"—is one capable of full self-realization.[10]

The practices in such groups, however, seem inconsistent with their theory. In many encounter sessions, for example, strangers are brought together under assumed names. Thus the individual's basic privacy is retained while he exposes himself, as a stranger, among strangers. In this limited context exposure costs nothing. The participant may "fail safe" and return home with his defenses intact. In other times, masked balls and festivals like Fasching and Carnival were developed for the purpose of limited and safe disclosure and release; mercifully, these traditions were bequeathed to us without scientific pretensions.

The most alarming aspect of encounter-group therapy is, in my opinion, that it is not grounded in any satisfactory theory of the human person or the human community. The concept of man that is vaguely suggested by the movement is ill-defined and reductionistic. Encounter groups offer pseudo-religious exercises undisturbed and unsupported by a well-defined theology. In a mass culture dominated by science, it is hardly surprising, however, that the culture should appropriate science, not as science but as *scientism,* a quasi-religion offering its own secular salvation. The public has come to expect that science will deliver us from evil and provide solutions to life's greatest perplexities. The public seeks to exploit science for essentially religious purposes, whether scientists like it or not.

If the cultural impact of science includes scientism as a quasi-religious force, must we not also expect that scientism as the "high church" will give rise to more popular "low church" movements? Just as Methodism developed as the popular response to the austere formalism of the Church of England, the

[9] William C. Schutz, *Joy* (New York: Grove Press, 1967), p. 20 and passim.
[10] *Ibid.*

encounter-group movement has developed as a popular expression of scientism. It is the popular religious expression of a scientific approach to human existence. Exciting and lively, it offers in our society what was once provided in religious institutions. We no longer have the Wednesday night prayer meeting. Instead we have the mini-lab in which we bare our souls to one another, confess our sins, and show, finally, that we can accept and be accepted by one another—but without either the protection of human dignity or the clarification of human existence that comes from a well-constructed theology or philosophic anthropology.

But suppose encounter therapy were carried out with rigor, with total revelation. Could it achieve its purposes? If so, the law in its concern to promote the constitutional aims of general welfare and the pursuit of happiness might be well advised to strike down all so-called rights to privacy and zones of privacy, thus truly bringing mankind to new and greater fulfillment through honesty in all things, not just in packaging and merchandising. Truth would be a defense in all cases of libel, and licenses to clothe waitresses would be harder to procure than licenses to operate topless establishments.

But in fact, the greatest dishonesty or self-delusion characterizes these "scientific" assaults on privacy. How does a man rid himself of guilt if he is guilty and of shame if he has something to be ashamed of? What does he gain by looking into the soulful, searching eyes of other nameless persons while bobbing naked in a pool of warm water and revealing his failure and misdeeds? How does one overcome both failure and success by encounter therapy? The aspiring musician manages neither to achieve nor to avoid perfect pitch. The lawyer does not achieve or fail of a philosophical understanding of the nature of good and evil. What are the approved new names of those realities to which the forbidden terms "success" and "failure" once referred? To be sure, we can rid ourselves of cultural fixations that define failure or success in narrowly professional or economic terms. But what of the child who is trying to walk? Does he not either succeed or fail to learn? Is it wrong to expect success of the child in toilet training? Might we not hope for success in learning to talk? (Here we encounter the most important of the paradoxes of privacy. The most intimate secrets of the human heart are voiced, however silently and privately, in a language whose social derivation limits the absolute privacy of the most eccentric of persons.)

I fail to understand the complacency of both the general public and the professional psychologists toward the encounter-group movement with its indiscriminate disclosures. How do we know that self-disclosure of all that is unworthy of one's self can be made within the context of an encounter group without the risk of losing that minimum of self-respect on which the respect and trust of others depends? Might not one tend to retreat into self-isolation as a consequence of such disclosure? I should be surprised if this were not frequently the result of encounter-group disclosures—unless the anonymity of participants is insured and honesty and openness are limited to the safe, contrived context of strangers. If complete disclosure before friends and strangers could be made with impunity and humanely and creatively, we must admit that we do not understand the value of privacy or the human concern to protect it legally and politically. Self-revelation before encounter groups will, in my opinion, ultimately debase the notion of intimacy through realizations which, even if genuine in themselves, become spurious by mere repetition.[11]

I do not question the value of disclosure, openness, honesty. But the context in which disclosure should be made is crucially important. Absolute privacy is impossible and intolerable. Men were not made to live in isolation; they cannot develop apart from others. They must share their lives and their secrets. Solitary confinement is still the most brutal of punishments. For several thousand years men have achieved remarkable heights of fulfillment while confessing—if not proclaiming—the ultimate breach of privacy as an act of faith: "Almighty God, unto whom all hearts are open, all desires known, and from whom no secrets are hid," begins an ancient collect declaring the ultimate community

[11] There are severe limits on the number of initmate relationships a person may have. And the intensity of intimacy decreases rapidly by duplication. It is the strength of monogamy that it offers the greatest potentiality for intimacy; its weakness, however, is that the potentiality is almost never realized and when realized is often, if not usually, destructive.

of the individual and God. It does not matter in the slightest whether one believes in God or not. God as an ideal social Other projected by the imagination of the species suffices as well for this discussion as Jehovah in all his ontological splendor.

The relation of the individual to God in the Judaeo-Christian tradition is one of very subtle complexity that merits consideration. I find it instructive, for example, to observe the different ways in which the Lord's Prayer is expressed in various languages. In the English of the King James Bible, to which we have become accustomed, God is addressed in the second person singular; that is, we address God as a familiar: "Our father who art in Heaven, hallowed be thy name. Thy Kingdom come. . . ." The intimacy of the individual's relation to God is also expressed in the second-person singular in Italian, Spanish, and German.[12] And in all languages the prayer is preceded by Jesus' statement that "Your father knows what you need before you ask him." It is interesting, however, that the French never resorted to the familiar when speaking of God. The Lord's Prayer in French reads: "Notre Père qui *êtes* aux cieux, que *votre* nom soit sanctifié, que *votre* règne arrive, . . ." The French formality[13] becomes identical with the informality of the democratic age when in modern English we say, "Our Father who *are* in Heaven, hallowed be *your* name. *Your* kingdom come, . . ."

The surprise, the excitement, and the miracle of an immanent yet transcendent deity are expressed in those languages that re-reserve for the deity the forms of speech used between a child and its parents, a mode of speech that while assuming familiarity makes no claims of equality.

Complete disclosure, I am trying to say, may be fulfilling, redemptive, and enlarging only when it is disclosure before a person of very special qualities and in an atmosphere of utter trust. We can readily understand the value of disclosure before

[12] Padre nostro che sei nei cieli, sia santificato il Tuo nome, venga il Tuo regno, ... Padre nuestro que estás en los cielos, santificado sea el tu nombre, venga a nos el tu reino, ... Unser Vater in dem Himmel. Dein Name werde geheiliget. Dein Reich komme . . . . The Latin Vulgate also uses the second-person singular, probably without the same force: Pater noster, qui es in caelis, sanctificetur nomen tuum. Adveniat regnum tuum . . . .

[13] The French translation was completed in the reign of Louis XIV.

an all-knowing, all-wise, and all-loving father. In the Judaeo-Christian tradition, in which God is both judge and savior, it is essential to personal salvation to achieve the most complete self-knowledge and to confess that knowledge, no matter how painful. It is the genius of the confession in the Roman Catholic Church and of private prayer in Protestant sects that full disclosure of one's sins, far from being a risk, is the means of salvation. Self-fulfillment is jeopardized by lies and repressions. Here, an ultimate self-confidence, grounded on the esteem of God himself, is possible. And guilt, shame, embarrassment, failure, and success can be overcome in this context because they are overcome in the presence of a being whose goodness is not in doubt and whose love is sufficient to redeem all shortcomings.

Sustained by this encounter, a man may be freed from his concern or anxiety about self-disclosure. Self-confidence sustained by divine acceptance may foster character and personal authenticity rather than concern for "social image." Yet if such a person would live successfully, he cannot attempt complete personal revelation to everyone. His acceptance by the community depends upon his success in hiding the worst of his acts, thoughts, and desires.[14] The world is not value-free even if *Wertfreiheit* and the diremption of fact and value are the prevailing dogmas of social science and of much philosophy.

In a secular age that denies the openness of personal consciousness to a divine presence, the only context in which full personal disclosure is possible is the one provided by a truly intimate friendship. But this exception can provide little comfort for the organizers of encounter groups; even the best of friendships are troubled by the inability of friends to understand each other and their failure to notice their misunderstanding; and friendships are so rare that the number of persons exceeds the number of friendships by a factor not of 2 but of 2^{10}.

In the conviction that God does not hear, that consciousness is ultimately private, that there is no judge, and hence that the individual is not judged or saved except by a social group, our

[14] See *Melvin* v. *Reid,* 112 Cal. App. 285, 297 Pac. 91 (1931). In this action a reformed prostitute sought damages for the loss she suffered in the public disclosure of her past. As long as her secret was hidden from the community, she had been able to live a new and better life.

secular age is obsessed with striking down the barriers of the self and denying privacy. Encounter groups, covens of witches, psychedeliacs, collection agencies with computerized files on all debts and claims against each citizen, employment agencies demanding lie-detector tests as a condition of employment, and private and public police with monitoring devices everywhere—all imperil the individual. The first three groups seek community in communion; the others seek community through the annihilation of whatever differs from the community norm. The former assume the saving role of the lost deity; the latter assume his role as judge. But neither is worthy of his role. The physicians cannot save themselves, and the judges destroy the worth of individual life by gathering data on which to judge it.

The unexamined life, as Socrates said, is not worth living. But neither is the life examined by police and businessmen operating electronic devices and closed-circuit television. And Aristotle was right to say that human life is lived in a polis. But human life is of questionable value when the only sense of community is based on the effects of drugs or the dubious theology of encounter-group therapists.

We cannot breathe new life into a dying religious tradition, however much we may regret its passing. But we can learn from it. The ancient collect, along with the poker player, the striptease dancer, and the encounter-group therapist, reveals important elements of the modalities of privacy. Complete openness and honesty are wholly beneficial only in relation with a wholly benevolent Other. Complete openness is possible only to an omniscient Other. In the absence of an all-knowing and loving God, complete openness is both impossible and dangerous. The person for whom total isolation is impossible and intolerable must remain to some extent hidden. He must limit disclosure before finite persons whose intelligence and goodness are limited. He may risk almost total exposure only with that rare person with whom true friendship seems possible. He will remain reserved to an increasing degree with those about whom he knows less and in whom he has less confidence. He will, likewise, expect and require immunity from the intrusion of others. Privacy to varying degrees will be ineluctable and desirable. He will inevitably reveal more of himself than he may intend, as our poker player; he may also hide more than one would suppose possible, as our dancer. But in every aspect of his life he will require the shelter and protection and encouragement of a legal institution that will guarantee, support, and defend his privacy against unlimited intrusion and scrutiny by limited men. He will also have to be protected by institutionalizing in law the positive right to participate in communities. There the degree of intimacy will vary with his ability to understand and accept, and with his good fortune in finding other human beings who are capable of understanding, accepting, and loving him.

The law has at least two clear functions: It must provide immunities against intrusions destructive of self-respect and preserve as much pretense and hypocrisy as virtue and redemption require. At the same time, it must provide rights of access between individuals—rights that will permit varying degrees of intimacy and association. To perform these tasks the law must also have rights of intrusion and association and immunities from interference. These rights and immunities must be carefully limited if they are not to destroy what they are intended to protect.

We close with a Brechtian paean to scribes and pharisees and even to whited sepulchers: All may be necessary in the community of men from which God is absent and in which privacy must be guaranteed.

13

PERSONALITY AND PRIVACY

JOHN W. CHAPMAN

In the recent past the main sources of danger to privacy, and to the moral attitudes with which it is associated, have been secrecy and science. The threat they pose is that of invasion, and given the will to do so, that threat can be, if not extinguished, at least contained through the law.

Now a new and far more deadly danger has arisen in the shape of the moral psychology of the young. That they intrude and outrage is patent and not the real problem. That problem has to do with their capacity for privacy, to enjoy and to sustain it in all its forms, and whether their form of personality is compatible with it. That such a question should even arise about so fundamental a moral category as privacy is alarming. With the help of the psychohistorians I propose to explore the dynamics of this new form of personality, its origins, and its possible destiny. My argument will be that the new morality is the product of psychic insecurities and represents a condition of disequilibrium. There are, however, powerful equilibrating forces present in our moral economy, and these will work against a permanent change of character. In the end we may find that we have been dealing with only a mood. There are good reasons for thinking that present confrontations between old "Hegelians" and new "Marxians" will be eventually dialectically superseded.

HEGELIANS AND MARXIANS

Most of us, I would suppose, have become and remain instinctively "Hegelian" in our frame of mind. We find psychic security in the thought that Western civilization, despite all the wreckage and the ruin, is fundamentally a rational enterprise, and we think both necessary and desirable the complexity of its institutional articulation. Our feelings and our sentiments flow from and lend support to the commitment to rationality. "Perfectibility" may have so far eluded us, but, unlike Rousseau, we do not really believe that this is because we have sold out. Rather, we were over-confident. But now that we know who we are and how we got to be this way, the obstacles to personal and social integration seem merely historical and institutional, not indefeasible principles of our moral psychology.

Although somewhat shaken, we continue to believe in the power of liberated reason, and we take satisfaction from its achievements. Our mutual respect is founded on our rationality and purposiveness, and like Freud we hold that it is the capacity for love and work that make the man. That we have turned away from individualism in its more Spencerian forms does not mean that we have renounced our concern for individuality. We value privacy and welcome independence and originality. In the liberal philosophy of life there is clearly room for both social morality and individual ideals. We are, or at least we would try to be, romantic rationalists. That is the liberal ideal of personality.

For men who have come to think and feel this way, the sudden and unexpected appearance of what is apparently an instinctively "Marxian" generation cannot be other than disturbing, and for many deeply so. The new people seem to regard the "Hegelians" as the alienated, unable, so to speak, to graduate from the technological absurdities of "Cold War" to the romanticized "humanism" of *Catch-22*. They propose as the alternative to Hegelian rigidities a more fluid and "natural" style of life. They mock the ethic of work, they refuse to compete and to be graded, and they are elaborately casual about their personal relations. To the Hegelians, the easy riders look like a generation gone on leave, or worse still, away without leave. They seem to be toying with life and with death, indifferent to privacies and decencies, both personal and institutional, that took centuries to acquire. For the Marxians an experiment in natural living has been launched; for the Hegelians a terrifying moral misadventure is under way.

It must have sounded very strange to Hegelian ears when one of the new men, Mario Savio at Berkeley, evidently spoke admiringly of Plato and called for "organic democracy."[1] What kind of a psychic need or craving could be implicit in this appeal? Plato stands for love and spiritual union, not spiritual privacy; his ideal of perfect transparency and communion is not the Bloomsbury idealization of personal relations. Can it be that behind the Woodstock mask and manner, that within all the anarchistic mood music about "love," there lurks, as Erikson discerns, "a reciprocal isolation of desperate depth?"[2] If so, then the emotional capacity for love and for privacy has gone, and with it the capacity to take a rational and Hegelian attitude toward life and politics. Savio invoked Plato, but not even Marx replied; instead we heard the voice of that Baroque "Weatherman," Georges Sorel!

IMPATIENCE, IDENTITY, AND VIOLENCE

Stephen Spender observes, "That the students want to relate intimate personal values of living with public values is

[1] Reported by Lewis S. Feuer in his *The Conflict of Generations: The Character and Significance of Student Movements* (New York: Basic Books, 1969), p. 451. Savio wrote that "an important minority of men and women coming to the front today have shown that they will die rather than be standardized, replaceable, and irrelevant" ("An End to History," in Seymour Martin Lipset and Sheldon S. Wolin (eds.), *The Berkeley Student Revolt: Facts and Interpretations* [Garden City, N. Y.: Doubleday, 1965], 216–219, p. 219).

[2] Erik Erikson, "Reflections on the Dissent of Contemporary Youth," *Daedalus: The Embattled University*, 99 (Winter 1970), 154–176, p. 157.

one of the most serious aspects of their movement."[3] This urge toward a fusion of the personal and the political has been widely confirmed. What does it mean? It may be, and certainly is on the part of some, a sign of ethical sensitivity and impatience, as Kenneth Keniston argues; they wish to bring into line more quickly society and our inherited ideals. Moral idealism, unless it constitutes a Sorellian attempt to reduce politics to ethics, offers no threat to privacy. Moreover, the capacity for privacy of the self-assured and morally ambitious is not in doubt. Indeed, their sense of privacy is likely to be intense. And if they do not already, they will surely come to appreciate that "The claim to self-possession, to spiritual privacy, to self-expression, is the most sacred of all."[4] There is no need to worry about the impatient "committed," and I shall not be concerned with them.

This urge toward fusion may be, however, the rationalization of an impulse to violence. It may be the mark of psychic insecurity and ethical immaturity, of a failure to achieve identity and ethical consolidation, to use Erikson's concepts. Persons in this condition are not likely to have a strong sense of privacy, for they lack a firm and well-defined sense of self. Nor are they likely to be respecters of the claims of personality in others. They are not so much fusing as confusing the personal and political dimensions of life. Spiritual privacy cannot matter much to them, if indeed they even understand it. A Hegel would say that these are selves unable to sustain a form of ethical life in which the claims of abstract right and morality are synchronized.

[3] Stephen Spender, *The Year of the Young Rebels* (New York: Random House, 1968), p. 12. "Essentially what they object to are the standards and forms of organization of modern industrial and technological societies" (*ibid.*, p. 155). Kenneth Keniston, a sympathetic observer of the student scene, says, "As these young men and women continually insist, the personal and the political, the social and the historical, are fused" (*Young Radicals: Notes on Committed Youth* [New York: Harcourt, Brace & World, 1968], p. 191).

[4] John Plamenatz' Introduction to his *Readings from Liberal Writers: English and French* (New York: Barnes & Noble, 1965), p. 10. Charles Fried remarks that "To be deprived of this control over what we do and who we are is the ultimate assault on liberty, personality, and self-respect" (*An Anatomy of Values: Problems of Personal and Social Choice* [Cambridge, Mass.: Harvard University Press, 1970], p. 143). And see also R. S. Downie and Elizabeth Telfer, *Respect for Persons* (London: George Allen and Unwin, 1969).

Hobbes would conclude that such people are bound to frighten one another, and the mutually frightened have never been respectful of privacy.

Strictly speaking, the relations of men who lack the capacity to enjoy and sustain privacy can be neither personal nor political; they must rather be said to be politicized. In their personalities, power will occupy the gap left by privacy, and their political manners will degenerate toward violence.

There is a good deal of evidence, both direct and indirect, that ethical and political immaturity is widespread. I refer, of course, primarily to the sudden appearance and continuing presence in the university of a moral climate deeply hostile to privacy and correlative values. There arose a kind of provocative Praetorianism, displayed initially in contempt for civility and decency and then escalated to patent infringements of academic freedom.[5] There have been startling invasions of both personal and official privacy, inflictions of obscenity, and calculated and insulting intimidations. There is a willingness to politicize relations properly personal and moral. Elsewhere other indignities have been committed in the form of public displays of "intimacy," which cannot but imply its absence. To the emotionally isolate and insecure, privacy may appear to be just another conventional hypocrisy that stands between them and the demonstration of moral honesty. The pattern of behavior, however, suggests group dependence, not inner strength.

The significance of these events lies in the fact that privacy performs moral functions of a mediating kind. On the one hand, it is founded on and confirms interest in and respect for personality. Whether it takes the form of politeness or decency, its exhibition indicates the presence of capacities for emotional intuition and appropriateness of response. Maintenance of privacy is a sort of defensive, and yet considerate, recognition of personal integrity and dignity, a dialectical manifestation of the sense of self. Lack of feeling for privacy is not only a symptom of emotional poverty but also a form of moral blindness. On the other hand, privacy provides the moral context or medium

[5] On the pattern of provocation, see Nathan Leites and Charles Wolfe, Jr., *Rebellion and Authority: An Analytic Essay on Insurgent Conflicts* (Chicago: Markham, 1970), pp. 115–116.

in which arise the higher forms of personal relations, the ultimately inviolate and sacred.

A lack of feeling for privacy has institutional consequences as well. The university is fundamentally an intellectual enterprise, in which, however, those moral benefits connected with privacy, such as friendship and trust, may hope to prosper. Here especially any attempt to fuse the personal and the political constitutes an immediate threat to moral independence and spiritual privacy. In this setting politicization of relations amounts to moral violence. Not only are the moral benefits conferred by privacy destroyed, but the very freedom of the mind, for which the university stands, is placed in jeopardy. Only by a sort of courtesy can we continue to refer to some of our institutions as "universities."[6]

A SYNDROME

An examination of the pattern of youthful attitudes tends to reinforce the impression of serious immaturity and retrogression. Not only is there this penchant for the pseudo-natural and the lack of regard for personal integrity. One is tempted to postulate the existence of a syndrome.

We notice that their conception of political obligation appears to be early *Second Treatise;* no one is obliged unless he has given his personal consent. And then some at least respond to the invitation of the later Locke; when obligation is enforced, they get out. More generally, the young sometimes appear unable to appreciate the problem of national security and the cold realities of international politics. They turn to revisionist historians of the Cold War—and appear to be unmoved by the end of the "American century" some thirty years early.

Their attraction to the slogan and practice of "participatory democracy" seems problematical. Is this a sign of political idealism, as some would have us think, or is it political obsolescence, born of a failure to realize that in an advanced society we have to learn to govern more through our attitudes than

[6] "Without a faculty, and its autonomous core position, a university is nothing" (Talcott Parsons, "The Academic System: A Sociologist's View," *The Public Interest,* 13 (Fall 1968), 173–197, p. 187).

by our presence? Or is this attraction something more sinister still, another aspect of the lack of regard for privacy and integrity? Donald G. MacRae remarks on "the contempt of students from Berlin to Berkeley for that great instrument of democracy, that enemy of enforced consensus, the secret ballot."[7]

Still another feature of the youthful syndrome, one which I had also in mind in referring to them as instinctively Marxian, is brought out by Shils: "The very notion of differentiation and specialization in a division of labor among individuals and institutions is repugnant to them."[8] They behave as though abundance were already here and would remain without the effort it took to get it, and without which it would surely slide away. There is a hedonistic, sensate, *"après moi, le déluge"* tone to the New Left aphorism: "If you've booked passage on the Titanic, there's no reason to travel steerage."[9] Here meet and reinforce toward immaturity international insecurities and the exemptions from work afforded by the affluent society.

All in all, the young appear to be in the grip of what Lasswell used to call the "self-reference effect." Strangers and afraid in a world they never made, selves turn inward while simultaneously reaching outward to include the whole of politics; they are apparently expansive but in reality isolate. In their despair, they ask for "relevance" and search for spiritual union, appar-

[7] MacRae, "Between Commitment and Barbarism," in David Martin (ed.), *Anarchy and Culture: The Problem of the Contemporary University* (New York: Columbia University Press, 1969), 185–191, p. 187. In the longer run the outcome of "participatory democracy" may be forms of organization and management that Mary Parker Follett would have approved. According to Ian H. Wilson, "In all types of organizations, the rights and position of the individual, due process and participative forms of management will become the dominant mode" ("How Our Values Are Changing," *The Futurist,* 4 [February 1970], 5–9, p. 7).

[8] Edward Shils, "Plenitude and Scarcity: The Anatomy of an International Cultural Crisis," *Encounter,* 32 (May 1969), 37–57, p. 42. With reference to the university, Talcott Parsons says: "dissident students are highly moralistic, but tend to 'politicize' their value-commitments by making the moral responsibility in question responsibility, not for the implementation of academic values as such, but for a set of more general societal-political values, broadly of a 'radical' character, with which, however, the academic values are linked" (*Politics and Social Structure* [New York: The Free Press, 1969], p. 515).

[9] Reported by Herman Kahn and Anthony J. Wiener, *The Year 2000: A Framework for Speculation on the Next Thirty-Three Years* (New York: Macmillan, 1967), p. 200.

ently unaware that without identity and independence these cannot be had.

Somehow the effort of the young to equate the public and the political with the private and the personal miscarries. Instead of making politics personal, personal relations become politicized.[10] As the sense of privacy becomes weaker, intimacy disappears into ritual. And they are failing to get across what Conrad called the "shadow line" into the world of social and political realities. "Imagination in Power" may be a fine slogan for a psychodrama produced in Paris in May 1968, but to attempt to govern with it would be "to turn a private dream into a public and compulsory manner of living."[11] This is ideological thinking, a product of that state of mind for which even knowledge can be "repressive."

The pattern in the attitudes of these new people points to the presence of an incoherent philosophy of life, a defective version of the liberal ideal of human perfectibility that men can find a form of society in which they can feel at ease because what it has to offer accords with their ambitions and ideals. In any such society the personal and political dimensions of life would be separate, their boundaries marked and kept. For if men are to be free to be themselves and to choose for themselves—to do their own thing—then government, whether it be that of a university or a nation, must stick to the common, to the agreed-upon. To wish to fuse the personal and the political is to ignore the distinction between negative and positive freedom. Not ethical but nuclear fusion is the result.

DIAGNOSES: A SURVEY

How can we account for these developments in thought and feeling, for the emergence of this frame of mind? All ob-

[10] "Today, difficulties that a mere two or three years ago would have passed for private matters—for conflicts between student and teachers, worker and employers, or marital partners, for conflicts between individual persons—now claim political significance and ask to be justified in political concepts" (Jürgen Habermas, "The Priorities of Radical Reform," *Change*, 2 [July-August 1970], 29–34, p. 34).

[11] Michael Oakeshott, "On Being Conservative," in his *Rationalism in Politics: And Other Essays* (London: Methuen, 1962), 168–196, p. 186.

servers of the students in revolt agree that they exhibit paradoxical trends in mood and personality. We seem to face both ethical impatience and immaturity, commitment and alienation, moral earnestness and nihilism, activism and quietism, ideological hunger and suspicion, disconcerting and defensive oscillations between idealism and cynicism, anarchic individualism and communal vitalism, and behavior that is deeply illiberal in its implications and consequences; some would call it a new romanticism of violence, born of a Sorellian contempt for the corrupt and the inauthentic.[12] What can explain these contrasting tempers? Are they merely passing moods, as some contend, or are they indications of something far more serious, of changes in character and ethical orientation?

It will not do to say that this pattern of behavior is the product of their flawed philosophy. We need to get behind them both. Diagnoses and explanations are legion; their very number suggests bewilderment. Here is a catalogue: A novel form of fascism (Trevor-Roper); technological civilization (Schaar and Wolin, and many others); deauthoritization of the older generation and generational conflict (Feuer); the meaninglessness of liberal economy and politics (Hoffmann); in the advanced society, the tension between the desire for equality and the necessity of hierarchy (Aron); in bureaucratized society, the evaporation of authority and responsibility, and hatred of its automaticity (Arendt); romantic revulsion against rationality (Shils); the discontents of "protean man," a new form of personality (Lifton); misplaced religiosity (Frye); hostility to academic aims and values (Trow); emotional starvation of a proceduralized society (Wilson).[13]

[12] "The revulsion from 'hypocrisy' and the resulting quest for 'authenticity' very easily evolve into glorification of instinct and direct action" (J. L. Talmon, "The Legacy of Georges Sorel: Marxism, Violence, Fascism," *Encounter,* 34 [February 1970], 47–60, p. 60).

[13] H. R. Trevor-Roper, "A New Fascism?" *Encounter,* 32 (May 1969), p. 35; John H. Schaar and Sheldon S. Wolin, "Education and the Technological Society," *The New York Review of Books,* 8 (9 October 1969), pp. 3–6; Feuer, *The Conflict of Generations;* Stanley Hoffman, "Participation in Perspective?" *Daedalus,* vol. 99, *The Embattled University* (Winter 1970), pp. 177–221; Raymond Aron, *The Elusive Revolution: Anatomy of a Student Revolt,* trans. Gordon Clough (New York: Praeger, 1969); Hannah Arendt, *On Violence* (New York: Harcourt, Brace & World, 1969); Shils, "Plenitude and Scarcity";

There is a certain, and mutually restrictive, plausibility in all these analyses. They are testimonials to the enormity of the moral crisis in which we find ourselves. But if each were accorded the weight it claims for itself, then our situation would be entirely hopeless; the end of Western civilization would be at hand.

Rather than to try to deal with each of these diagnoses on its own merits, I propose that we return to the insight with which we began, Spender's observation that the new people are attempting a fusion of the personal and the political. This is a theme common to many analysts, and it can be turned around and given a negative formulation. What we face, in the words of Erik Erikson, is "an unprecedented divorce between the culture and the society."[14] We can learn much from the psychohistorians about the nature and significance of the new moral psychology.

REAPPEARANCE OF THE BAROQUE

According to Erikson, the ego-structure of contemporary youth is weak; that is, they suffer from "identity confusion" and hence are prone to more severe retrogressions than usually accompany adolescence. In the outcome, their emotional and moral development is impaired; they do not come into synchronization with society and cannot cope with its demands and requirements. They feel and resent feeling dependent, and yet identify with the dependent around the world. And, as we noted at the outset, they tend to feel emotionally insecure and isolated, or, as I phrased it, they lack the capacity for privacy.

Robert Jay Lifton thinks that the world, and not only the West, is experiencing the emergence of a new type of personality, which he calls "protean man." This new personality is

---

Robert Jay Lifton, "Protean Man," in his *History and Human Survival* (New York: Random House, 1970), pp. 311-331; Northrop Frye, "The University and Personal Life: Student Anarchism and the Educational Contract," in W. R. Niblett (ed.), *Higher Education: Demand and Response* (London: Tavistock, 1969), pp. 35-51; Martin Trow, "Reflections on the Transition from Mass to Universal Higher Education," *Daedalus,* 99 (Winter 1970), pp. 1-42; Bryan Wilson, at pp. 21-33, in Niblett (ed.), *Higher Education.*

[14] Erikson, "Memorandum on Youth," *Daedalus,* vol. 96, *Toward the Year 2000* (Summer 1967), 860-870, p. 863.

the product of "historical dislocation," itself the consequence of the possibility of human extinction and the "flooding of imagery." Protean man lacks a sense of continuity and stability, of inner support for rationality; he has no firmly held beliefs or moral attitudes; his distinctive characteristic is weakness of conscience; and his prototype is visible in Jean-Paul Sartre. Lifton says: "What has actually disappeared—in Sartre and in protean man in general—is the *classical* superego, the internalization of clearly defined criteria of right and wrong transmitted within a particular culture by parents to their children."[15] The young have been existentialized and thrown on their own resources, and not by the writings of Sartre and the existentialists. Rather, their existentialism comes naturally to them from the precariousness of humanity.

Life feels absurd to protean man, pointless. Nothing it has to offer seems quite worth doing; hence, they have a nagging sense of unworthiness combined with destructive energy. They tend to fluctuate between fanaticism and stark skepticism and to remain ideologically hungry. Their capacity for mobilized defiance has been demonstrated. To them, the "Old Hegelians," especially those who used to occupy university presidencies, must look like pitiful, yet corrupt and dangerous, human antiques.

The "New Left" is "protean" to the core. One of its spokesmen wants "organic democracy" (Savio). Another prescribes "anarcho-Maoism" (Rudi Dutschke). One behaves like a clown (Abbie Hoffman), and another is a demonic Leninist (Mark Rudd). One of the leaders of the Sorbonne revolt, Alain Geismar, is reported to have taken to "terrorism" on the Riviera—by marking up boats! Pretending at, I would think, nineteenth-century anarchism, Weathermen take to the "propaganda of the deed." Charles Manson becomes a "culture hero." Can there be any doubt that desperately harmful passions have been unleashed?

If we now make a composite of the personalities described by Erikson and Lifton we discover a contemporary formation of what Zevedei Barbu calls the "Baroque" mind. This is "a man with liberated instincts, with explosive vital energy but without unity of purpose. This lack of unity of purpose is expressed at

[15] Lifton, "Protean Man," pp. 321–322.

the psychological level both by a basically weak ego and an incoherent super-ego."[16]

The Baroque personality appeared in the early modern era, the direct product of the collapse of the medieval super-ego. He is a person whose conscience has gone and who has yet to acquire the ego-structure characteristic of the modern liberal or "bourgeois" personality. He possesses neither the individuality nor the rationality of the men to whom Locke, Rousseau, and Hegel speak. Baroque man is the personality depicted by Hobbes and Shakespeare, restless, anxious, impulsive, sometimes volcanic, sometimes paralyzed. Now he has reappeared in the midst of a rationalized and industrialized society created and occupied by his own direct descendants, the liberal men, those compounds of rationalism and romanticism. Anarchic vitalists stand face to face with romantic rationalists.

The reappearance of the Baroque quite enrages and unhinges the Hegelian liberals, and they bare their teeth. Hence David Martin: "anarchism and vitalism are excellent attitudes for social parasites but are not serious political philosophies."[17] And even more bluntly, Edward Shils: the Baroque men know that "if they do not accept the rules of the regime of scarcity they will go to the wall."[18] The dislike is thoroughly mutual. Sartre has long shown his hatred of the "bourgeois." In 1968 he expressed his admiration for the protean Daniel ("Danny the Red") Cohn-Bendit. And Herbert Marcuse, that "instinctivistic radical," as Erich Fromm once called him, preaches against the "surplus" repressiveness of industrial civilization. The confrontations of the types of personality can be murderously violent, as in the case of Grayson Kirk and David Truman versus Mark Rudd, who said, "This is a stick-up!" and put them up against the wall. Or the conflict may take the form of spectacular psychodrama, as in Paris in the spring of 1968. In this weird struggle it is as though the sons (protean men) are their own grandfathers (Baroque men), who now confront as

[16] Barbu, *Problems of Historical Psychology* (London: Routledge & Kegan Paul, 1960), p. 172.

[17] David Martin, "The Nursery of Revolution," in Martin (ed.), *Anarchy and Culture,* 206–212, p. 212.

[18] Shils, "Plentitude and Scarcity," p. 48.

their fathers (liberal men)—what they had once become. Perhaps one can make out in these ancestral relations a hint of better times to come, but for the time being the tension will be severe.

Lifton calls the new men "proteans," men with morally fluid selves. Shils calls them "romantics," men possessed by expanding and contentless egos. Their psychic structure suggests to me that they are "Baroque," old-fashioned men who find themselves in an advanced industrial society and hence find it convenient to speak "Marxian." In truth, they are ourselves minus the stabilizing counterweight of rationally structured sentiments in their personality. And that is why they cannot feel at home in an Hegelian civilization, nor could they find Rousseau's ideal, with all our scale and technology gone, congenial either. For they cannot keep separate the personal and the political any more than could Hamlet or the men for whom Hobbes wrote the *Leviathan.*

PROSPECTS FOR PRIVACY

I assume that the Baroque personality, characterized by a weak self and conscience, is the result of maturation in a condition of insecurity. This principle of human dynamics appears to be widely accepted. I assume further that the "Marxian" behavior of the modern Baroque man is made possible by our relative affluence; unlike his earlier counterpart, he can evade the stabilizing compulsions of work. He can afford those psychic retrogressions that leave him emotionally and ethically immature and incapacitated for privacy. The divorce which he experiences between his culture and the Hegelian society will not incline this personality to decency.

These reflections suggest that, broadly speaking and in the near future, the prospects for privacy depend on the number of persons who grow up psychically insecure. For these people would tend to become indifferent to privacy, both their own and that of others, and to seek relief in group identification and in symbolic aggression, or worse, in real aggression against the society and those whom they sense to be different. Weak in sense of self and purpose, immediate gratifications would become increasingly important to them as they lose their hold upon those two great freedoms with which privacy is associated, moral freedom and freedom of the mind. Continuing psychic insecurity could conceivably create people who are both emotionally privatized and wanting in a sense of privacy.

Consider the possibility that the kind of pervasive insecurity connected with "historical dislocation" will continue, as it may if Lifton is right in saying that it arises from the very existence of nuclear weaponry. Then persons will continue to grow up with infirm selves and consciences, for these are the characteristics directly related to maturation in conditions of insecurity. Such persons may be expected to experience an additional form of psychic insecurity, that which arises from the formless and relatively uncontrolled nature of their instinctual endowment (unless Marcuse is correct in his peculiar contention that the instincts themselves possess a sort of inner order). Their insecurity would further intensify through their isolation from and fear of one another. They would be trapped in a Hobbesian cycle in which their initial exposure to insecurity generated further forms of it. And Hobbes and Oakeshott to the contrary notwithstanding, our kind of society is not a lake in which these fish could be induced to forget one another.

As we know from the historical record, people exposed to intense insecurity may be pushed in one or the other of two directions. The first of these is toward the emotionality, solidarity, and irrationality that we associate with the dynamic forms of fascism. A widespread movement in this direction would, of course, be catastrophic for privacy and all other liberal values. Equally catastrophic would be the alternative development of flight into the dogmatic rigidity characteristic of the communist personality. In the West it would appear that it is pressure in the first direction that is present. This is the significance of anarchic vitalism. Baroque men are not ripe for communism; to them, as Cohn-Bendit put it, communists are "Stalinist creeps."

This is an unpleasant prospect, to say the least. But then perhaps Lifton's analysis of the source of psychic insecurity that makes for protean men is only speculative. I am not competent to appraise it, but I do notice that well before the coming of the bomb the existentialist frame of mind appeared in the sixteenth century, Kierkegaard was repelled by Hegelian rationality, and Sartre was at work. Again, people may simply become used to the presence of the new weaponry, as they once came to terms with the "Devil." And we may succeed in establishing a state of strategic stability more or less permanently. Clearly the challenge is to prevent the insecurity dynamic from ever beginning, for here lies the real danger to privacy. Once it begins men are swept into their present moral disequilibrium, in which they find no use for privacy and feel an enemy in their only hope for psychic security, rationality.

RESTORATION OF EQUILIBRIUM

In the long run, the prospect for privacy and the values that go with it depends on the restoration of the liberal equilibrium of character. It is encouraging that this type of character historically represents an evolution from the Baroque personality, the reappearance of which is at the root of our present moral crisis. There is, of course, no guarantee that the historical pattern will be repeated. Indeed, it could not be repeated in exactly the same manner. In the rise of liberalism psychic processes of individuation and rationalization advanced together. As the sense of self-reliance grew stronger, men were increasingly able to put their relations on a rational basis and to increase their sense of psychic security by doing so. We are the inheritors of the rational civilization which they managed to create, and it is precisely the arrangements of this civilization that the instinctively "Marxian," our contemporary Baroque, find oppressive and threatening to their personalities. This is why they attempt to escape from its requirements and to shape it in the direction of their personal feelings, with the consequences we have described. The psychological impact of rationality has been reversed. Here is the essential difference between the psychic imperatives of the early modern and our own situation.

These considerations suggest that restoration of the liberal equilibrium requires a strengthening of the sense of self, a deepening of feeling for and of genuine individuality. To some degree this is a process that may be encouraged directly. We could heed Plato and Rousseau on the necessity for emotional supports for rational attitudes and behavior and learn to design our institutions, particularly our educational institutions, so as to improve their emotional climate. We have probably underestimated the emotional deprivations imposed by a proceduralized society.[19] Beyond these measures probably not very much can be done directly except to provide opportunities for moral adventure and accomplishment, no easy thing to do. Fortunately the "committed" among the young will take whatever such opportunities there are and make the most of them. But provided opportunities such as the Peace Corps may be unable to avoid an air of contrivance. Still, by taking thought, more could be done to present outlets for that urge to do important things together, the "commotive impulse," as Hocking called it. What reservoirs of moral energy there are are presently being wasted and debased in get-togethers and confrontations of dubious value for the promotion of a sense of selfhood.

I am inclined to think that return to a liberal form of personality will have to depend far more importantly upon the operation of natural psychic forces. Such a severe degree of moral disequilibrium does not lend itself to deliberate correction. We are not engineers of human souls.

The dynamics of privacy itself may be expected to provide powerful help in the restoration of moral equilibrium. What we see or experience as violations of privacy are only the visible aspects of a moral field in which deeper forces are present. And these will be and are experienced as moral costs in the form of loss of vital personal relations. Moreover, the emotionally deprived and incapacitated know that they are missing something supremely important; their present efforts to reach one another may be sadly misplaced, but the effort expended is remarkable by any standard. No life in which friendship, mutual love, and

[19] "What such angry, rebellious, but idealistic students need is a sense of purpose, direction, discipline, and sympathetic criticism" (Christopher Jencks and David Riesman, *The Academic Revolution* [Garden City, N. Y.: Doubleday, 1969], p. 541).

trust are lacking can be felt as a life worth living. Nor can one with impunity mutilate one's own dignity.[20] A sense of "proper pride" is inherent in being human. The young have a firm hold on Mill's principle of choosing for oneself, and if their substantive choices take them into the realm of the inhuman, they will recoil. And as they discover that moralizing is no substitute for intellectual accomplishment, they should become less careless about freedom of the mind and more willing to make the effort that is required to find satisfaction in work. In the end, it is the human need for these experiences—the sane and central experiences of life, as Bosanquet would call them—that is the ultimate guarantee and guardian of privacy. It may take some time, but anyone who qualifies as human will learn that privacy is essential for these needs, and as his sense of privacy develops or returns so will his sense of self. This could be a self-reinforcing process in which persons help one another.

Notice further that privacy and justice perform somewhat similar functions in our moral economy. Both are intrinsically valuable, but the value of neither is intrinsic only. As a fundamental moral category, each opens the way to higher forms of moral experience. The dependence of these higher forms of experience on justice and privacy works to strengthen our commitment to each of them. These are the great stabilizers in the realm of value, the guarantors of the liberal moral equilibrium. Ordinarily one may expect them to work together. An invasion of privacy, such as entering a man's office and destroying his papers, is also an act of wanton injustice and will be felt as such. It is unfair as well as improper for a corporation to hound a Ralph Nader, to pry into his personal affairs. It is manifestly unjust to subject student leaders to maximum surveillance, not only an assault upon their spiritual privacy.

Or where privacy fails to equilibrate justice may take over. A weakened sense of self may push people toward an excessive equalitarianism. Here respect for the principles of justice may be

[20] "To draw attention to the contrast between personal being and impersonal dehumanized public behavior the Romantic emphasizes everything that is most personal, human, hysterical, and even weak and absurd in himself" (Spender, *Year of the Young Rebels,* p. 161).

expected to operate as the countervailing force.[21] When the sense of justice or the sense of fairness falters, a sense of privacy may be present to restore the balance. So it happened in the years of the torment of secrecy.

In the human moral personality privacy occupies a central position. A person apparently incapacitated for privacy will have both inhuman encounters and losses that cannot but serve to strengthen his self and sense of privacy. Man is sufficiently resilient and stable for that.

Given a strengthening of the sense of self, I would expect that the need and the capacity for rationality would reappear, that the present oppressiveness of technological society would be replaced by a sense of confidence and challenge, and that in its mastery would once again be found both security and adventure. In an important way, history would indeed repeat itself, and the present feeling or mood of incongruity between self and society would pass.

ROMANTIC RATIONALISM

Throughout, my presumption has been that the fate of what we understand by privacy, from simple decencies to the dignities of spiritual integrity, ultimately depends on the viability of the liberal ideal of the balanced personality, romantic rationalism. I wish now to argue that this presumption is sound and is supported by our moral and psychological history. The liberal ideal represents a stable constellation of psychic processes in which reason and feeling, conscience and instinct, intelligence and emotion, are accommodated to one another.

We are not Greeks, and can never be again, natural and at home with nature. Nor are we Stoics, crouching in an inner fortress, freezing our emotions. We are not like the medievals,

[21] "Once meritocratic criteria were eliminated, insiders among the older generation would find it easier to make sure their children stayed in, while outsiders would have less basis for demanding access" (Jencks and Riesman, *Academic Revolution*, p. 141). On justice as the foundation for higher and more personal values, see Nicolai Hartmann, *Ethics*, trans. Stanton Coit, 3 vols. (London: George Allen & Unwin, 1932), vol. 2, chap. 19.

oscillating between the instinctual and the sublime, nor could we stand to remain impulsively Baroque. In the perspective of our psychic history, the romantic rationalist is a sort of Athenian with a conscience who has turned from nature to reason as the prime source of inner equanimity. True, we may have been somewhat compulsive about our rationalism, as when Kant attempted to reduce morality to rationality or when Hegel thought he saw an identical rationality in both society and nature. But these were metaphysical compulsions. Feeling was quickly readmitted, compulsive unification abandoned, the balance restored.

There have also been, of course, deviations in the direction of romanticism, beginning perhaps with Plato's vision of a society based exclusively on love and including Rousseau's sometime craving for total transparency in human relations.[22] More recently, romanticism is implicit in Marx's alternative of the "natural" society in which unspecialized human beings deal with one another wholly on the ground of reciprocity.

Aside from the pathological deviations from the ideal of balance that we have met in fascism and communism, it still remains true that human nature provides the possibility of diverse interpretations as we try our best to accommodate the romantic and the rationalistic aspects of our endowment.

Existentialism is a form of romanticism generated by loss of confidence in the rationality of the human situation. But even Sartre once tried to absorb Kant and now shows a Hegelian concern with history. One senses an inner necessity to come to terms with both feeling and reason.

Another manifestation of the tension inherent in human nature may be seen in the emergence of logical positivism flanked by an emotive theory of ethics, an explosive combination, in which reason and feeling are not so much balanced as divorced. Now the linguistic empiricists seem engaged in a work of human reunification as they show how language itself represents an integration of description and evaluation, an accommodation of the rational and the emotive.

Other signs of psychic tension may be detected in the work

[22] See Jean Starobinski's *Jean-Jacques Rousseau: la transparence et l'obstacle* (Paris: Plon, 1957).

of contemporary Kantians.[23] An attempt to specify the concept of justice rationally and deductively is countered by the claim that our moral life is irreducibly plural and that we cannot avoid the choice of a blend. Others formulate metaethical theories in which principles, the fruit of reason, are tested against our moral attitudes, into which both reason and feeling must enter. Again it would seem that there are indefeasible influences within human nature that work against the suppression of any of its fundamental processes, their dissociation, or the reduction of one to the other.

In the course of our psychic history we have arrived at a condition of balance and equilibrium that resists disruption. Romantic rationalism is a viable ideal of personality, and hence the fate of privacy is secure. It will be even more secure as the new people come to formulate a more romantic, and less compulsively rationalistic, conception of that ideal.

[23] See my "The Moral Foundations of Political Obligation," in Pennock and Chapman (eds.), *Political and Legal Obligation: Nomos XII* (New York: Atherton Press, 1970), 142–176, pp. 161–174.